Total Baby Development

TOTAL BABY DEVELOPMENT

by Dr. Jaroslav Koch

Wyden Books

Library of Congress Cataloging in Publication Data

Koch, Jaroslav, fl. 1959–
    Total baby development.

    Translation of Výchova kojence v rodině.
    Includes index.
    1. Infant psychology. 2. Infants—Care and hygiene.
3. Child development. I. Title.
HQ769.K555513   649'.12'2   76-49943
ISBN 0-671-22408-5

DEDICATION

I take this opportunity to express my deepest gratitude to my friends in the Institute for the Care of Mother and Child in Prague, Czechoslovakia, to the doctors, nurses, and all my other dear colleagues who have helped me in my work. I am especially grateful to my closest collaborator, Nurse Marie Kepertova, who assisted me in the work with the babies, my experiments, assessing the results, and helping with many other tasks. I must also mention our babies, who, with their parents, took part in our experiments; many still come to see us and we stay in friendly contact, even though they will soon be at school.

Contents

FOREWORD BY DR. GRETA G. FEIN ix

1 What's Different About This Book 3
2 Why Timing Is Crucial 9
3 Heredity and Environment: Getting It Straight
at Last 12
4 How to Create Responses in an Infant 21
5 What's Your Baby Ready For? 44
6 How Fun and Games Begin 51
7 Exercises for the Fourth to Sixth Months 109
8 Exercises for the Seventh to Ninth Months 179
9 Exercises for the Tenth to Twelfth Months 248
10 What Is "Normal"? 318

APPENDIX: Results of Experimental Testing 328

INDEX 347

For the Love of Babies

Foreword by Dr. Greta G. Fein

Director of Child Development Research, Merrill-Palmer
Institute

The infant has claimed another admirer. About 25 years
ago, Dr. Jaroslav Koch began to observe infants, to note
fleeting expressions and small gestures. Since then he
has become a devoted baby advocate, a missionary seeking to introduce parents and care-givers to many simple
ways in which adults can enrich their own and their babies' lives.

With affection and persistence, Dr. Koch at the Institute for the Care of Mother and Child in Prague, Czechoslovakia, developed a series of simple, gentle exercises and games that make up an ingenious and varied
program. Dr. Koch's particular concern is not only the
physical fitness of infants but their psychological and
intellectual progress.

Dr. Koch is clear about his mission and we who respond to his work must understand it. The mission is *not*
to accelerate development, if by acceleration we mean
artificially forced skills and performances. Rather, it is to
assure each child ample opportunity to exercise fully
each unfolding capacity in an atmosphere of affectionate
and sensitive caring. And so Dr. Koch recommends the
use of "a strong, warm, human hand, rather than a hard,
cold, metal rod" for early grasping activities. He informs

fathers to participate in exercise sessions and he insists that activities be geared to the baby's current mood and individual temperament.

In Dr. Koch's own words: "The most important message of this book is that the essence of good baby rearing is the sincere love of the parents for their baby. The baby will develop best when the parents recognize that his upbringing is their own primary human objective and one of the main aspects of the 'purpose in life.' "

Whether American parents can share Dr. Koch's commitment and preserve his spirit of playfulness without pressure is a question every parent who reads this book must ponder. It would be easier if in America we had secure institutes for the "care of mother and child" with kindly doctors to help families manage the frustrations and tensions of early child rearing.

In the absence of this ideal, parents will find in this book many fresh ideas for working with their babies at home in ways that will be new and interesting even to readers of our extensive literature for raising children.

Behind Dr. Koch's work, though not elaborated in the text, is an implicit theory of early development. American readers might be puzzled by terms such as "excitation," "differential inhibition" or "delayed inhibition"; some developmental psychologists might argue with Dr. Koch's interpretation of early learning, his use of concepts such as "sensory reward stimuli" or his development of the idea that a baby needs to be taught to react to the spoken word. Fortunately, Dr. Koch has such a keen eye for descriptive detail that these theoretical commentaries do not detract from the appeal of the work.

This is innovative work, and until it is duplicated elsewhere questions will no doubt be raised by educational evaluators regarding Dr. Koch's findings, although most will appreciate the difficulty of designing rigorous evaluations in clinical settings. Dr. Koch does provide a nicely detailed test which, together with his exercises and promising findings, set the foundations for future research efforts.

Meanwhile, there is nothing to keep parents and their babies from enjoying the benefits of his stimulating suggestions.

Total Baby Development

1

What's Different About This Book

Before parents follow the advice in this book, they have a right to know something about its author and how its methods have succeeded in practice.

I have been working with children for almost 50 years, and for the last 25 years I have specialized in the psychological area of research with infants at the Institute for the Care of Mother and Child in Prague, Czechoslovakia.

During my daily observations in the laboratories of the Institute, in numerous nurseries and in my work with many families, it became increasingly clear that an unsuspected and exciting potential for development lies hidden and untapped within infants; that they by no means need to develop as they "normally" do. I recognized that many opportunities for development are lost at a very young age because mothers and fathers don't give them a chance to unfold. Parents may even remove such opportunities from their babies without realizing it!

To be specific: Most readers will think I'm joking when I state flatly that it's easier for infants to climb a ladder than to stand up by themselves. Yet I've witnessed innumerable times how babies of eight to nine months crawled to a barrier with horizontal steps, pulled themselves to a standing position, placed their feet on the first, second, and third step and tried to climb up. For fear of injury, the parents and nursery teachers immediately took the babies down.

I did the opposite. In the laboratory, I made little ladders available to infants. When the little boys and girls were placed on the ladders at the age of 5 months, they held on; at age 8 or 9 months they climbed up *entirely by themselves.* All children to whom we offered this opportunity first learned to crawl along the floor, then to climb the ladder; and only one to two months later did they walk without assistance.

So when infants are given a chance, they easily—even playfully—acquire far more than what parents, pediatricians, and standard guide books consider "normal" capabilities. We were able to document this gratifying fact when we gave 50 infants (20 at our Institute and 30 in their homes) more than the traditional opportunities to move their bodies. Starting with the second or third *week* of life, we in the laboratory and the parents at home stimulated each baby for one to two hours a day with the games and exercises described in this book. The comparison between the development of these children and a control group of 100 children who were raised under normal family conditions was fascinating (for more details see Appendix).

The exercised children doubled their birth weight in the fifth month; the control group in the sixth—and the accelerated weight gain of the exercised group was in muscle, not fat.

Almost invariably, the exercised boys and girls had good appetites and had no difficulties during feeding.

The children in the experimental (exercised) group learned to be active while awake and to sleep quietly at sleeping time. The frequency of half-wakefulness, which is so common shortly after birth (the child's eyes are open but he doesn't move, or else the eyes are closed and he does move), diminished much more rapidly than in the control group.

The generally good mood of the exercised boy and girl babies was particularly pronounced. Visitors to the laboratory were surprised because they almost never heard these babies cry. On the contrary: even the smallest ones smiled frequently and the bigger ones laughed happily, squealed with pleasure, and often made satisfied gurgling sounds.

The relationships between these infants and the adults who played and exercised with them were good. The youngsters often squealed pleasurably even as they were carried into the laboratory and some started to cry when they were prepared for leaving it.

Most notable was the difference in the psychological and motor development of the two groups. In their development of physical movements the exercised children were 3 to 4 weeks ahead of the control group at the age of 6 months; at 1 year the stimulated children were 6 to 8 weeks ahead. At 8 months the exercised children could hold onto furniture and pull themselves to a standing position; at 10 months they took their first steps unattended; after the twelfth month they ran around in the park.

But their excellent psychological growth is best shown by their rapid development of language ability. At one year, the exercised children had an active vocabulary of 20 words and used them in their daily contacts; the control group children used only 5.

And why not? The entire process of physical stimulation makes good anatomical sense: as he becomes motivated to move physically, the exercised infant's brain is supplied with more than the normal amount of blood; the increased blood supply, in turn, makes the child more receptive to stimulation.

And let's remember that intelligence does not emerge without effort. Without activity the brain sleeps and will not develop.

There is a considerable difference between this book and the usual "baby exercise" books. Traditionally, the objective of these books is the strengthening of muscles and the improvement of motor coordination. And usually not even all motor development. The traditional books focus on gross motor skills and ignore the development of the delicate movements of the hands which are particularly important for the entire early development of a child's personality.

In this book I am concerned with much more than physical fitness. I am going to tell you how to unfold the total child: its senses, its playing, thinking, talking, emotions, habits, the collecting of life experience, and more. I will show you how to achieve your infant's potential through physical movement—and not mechanical movement but goal-oriented activity. At the same time I avoid manipulation and passivity. Activity becomes a means for solving a problem, a program of total education for the total child at an earlier time of life than has been tried before, so that the often wasted, precious months of infancy can attain a new and richer meaning for you and your baby.

To dispose of some practical considerations right at the start:

Of course it's neither necessary nor desirable for a mother to exercise her baby for an hour or two at a stretch. For best results, I recommend 6 to 8 exercise periods per day, each lasting 10 to 15 minutes, 7 days per week. In addition, it's a good idea for the father to spend another half hour or more exercising his baby in the evening—longer on weekends whenever possible.

On special, extra-busy weekdays, exercise periods totaling 20 to 30 minutes represent an adequate minimum.

In case of illness or other prolonged problems, there will be no negative effects if the exercises and games have to be neglected for two or three weeks.

What if you want to start working with this book when your baby is already four or 6 or 8 months old? Better late than never! I recommend that such parents start by using exercises designed for children somewhat younger than their own. That is, if your baby is 8 months old, I suggest you begin with the exercises designed for babies aged 6 months and move on from there—always keeping in mind that a baby should never, never be pressured or pushed.

And now let me tell you a bit more about my goals.

Perhaps you often think about the great responsibility of bringing up a small child and ask yourself: am I sufficiently prepared for this difficult task? Quite naturally you may also have doubts about the traditional methods of baby care in these times. You will have found out that many of the old views are wrong. You may have your doubts about the claim that an infant develops by himself during his first year, that certain traits of character appear by themselves without outside impulses, simply as a result of an inner ripening, that interference with the "natural development" of a baby is harmful and that every normal mother "instinctively" knows how to rear a baby.

You undoubtedly realize that advances in science and technology will expose human beings to ever greater demands and will call for greater efforts, especially in the psychological sphere. So it is natural that you should seek ways to improve baby rearing and be willing to apply them.

The purpose of this book is to help you in this demanding, responsible but also highly gratifying work with an infant. It will tell you about the most up-to-date scientific discoveries, about the psychological development of infants and show how these new facts can be applied in the day by day raising of a baby with the help of 333 exercises, games, and small tasks.

Honest, systematic training, based on scientific facts about small babies, is of permanent benefit to your child and a source of joy and true human happiness to you, the parents.

If You're Short of Time

For families where time is at a premium I have developed a mini-program with a drastically reduced number of exercises and games. If you use only these in accordance with the concepts I describe in this book, you and your baby will reap substantial benefits. The following exercise numbers correspond to the numbers given in the following chapters.

For the baby's first month: Exercises 2, 3, 6, 7, 11, 12.

For the second and third months: Exercises 13, 15, 17, 20, 26, 27, 29, 30, 34, 37, 40.

For the fourth to sixth months: Exercises 45, 49, 50, 52, 55, 57, 58, 60, 63, 67, 70, 72, 76, 81, 90, 99, 109, 114.

For the seventh to ninth months: Exercises 118, 124, 130, 139, 144, 151, 156, 161, 163, 170, 173, 181, 187, 192, 193, 200, 203, 209.

For the tenth to twelfth months: Exercises 214, 217, 221, 231, 235, 240, 244, 246, 252, 258, 267, 272, 284, 290, 302, 311, 315, 319, 331.

2

Why Timing Is Crucial

The psychology of human development has coined such new expressions as "early learning" and "early experience" because new research revealed that the learning process in a newborn infant is qualitatively entirely different from learning during later phases of development.

"Early learning" differs from later learning mainly because it is learning without any previous experience. A baby collects his first experiences slowly and with difficulty; he usually acquires further experiences with the aid of previous ones, which makes the learning process easier and quicker. So it follows that learning at a later stage becomes easier and quicker depending on how much experience the baby has already acquired in a given field.

In early learning the infant acquaints himself not only with his environment, but learns about himself and to use his body and sensory organs. He learns to listen, to see, and much more. So early learning is unlike later learning in a new situation, because a "new situation" that arises later can never be all that "new" again. It is bound to consist of known and unknown elements.

Since a particular experience cannot be gained without having previously acquired a more basic one, the first experience is the most vital: this very "early experience" to a certain extent determines what further experience an infant can collect, how he collects it, and how fast. Which is why it is so important to help your baby gain the best possible basic experience from which a system of further experiences can grow.

And the term "experience" does not merely cover experience in the realm of reasoning. Children differ in their interests and attitudes because of the variety of their experiences. Early experiences therefore exercise considerable influence on a child's entire personality: his knowledge, skills, ability, interests, attitudes. Later experiences rarely have so much influence on the child. So the earliest age is a critical period of development.

Recent research not only uncovered the unsuspected capacities of infants but also the fact that this rich potential for development exists in a baby for only a given period and that the optimum stage for its awakening is in early infancy. If the appropriate stimuli are lacking in early infancy then the potential for developing certain skills, abilities, and characteristics gradually disappears.

We learned this from children who spent their infancy in old-style nurseries where good care was taken of their nutrition, hygiene, and other physical needs but less care was devoted to their psychological development. The range of experiences geared to sound emotional development—their exposure to stimuli—was limited. The overall development of these children suffered greatly even though they received a good education when they reached school age.

The richer a child's scope is for collecting new and useful experience, the better he learns and develops his ability to learn more. Even the smallest baby "learns how to learn." And just as important: if he lacks the chance to collect experience "he learns not to learn."

Nonscientists often dislike the idea of drawing on experimental experience with animals for the purpose of investigating human potential. Yet scientific work with animals is often dramatically revealing and helps to accelerate research. Let me mention one such experiment.

A puppy was brought up in a glass cage from which it could observe normal life. It watched other dogs running around the cage, cars passing by outside—the entire range of a normal puppy's experience. When the puppy grew up it was let out into a normal environment. Soon the animal had to be returned to its glass cage because it was unable to adapt to normal life; it could not learn to avoid cars, to defend itself against attacking dogs—in other words it was unable to learn. Lack of opportunity to learn at an early age crippled the animal's ability to learn. It had learned not to learn from experience.

And so the first year is decisive for the further development of a human being and early infancy is a most critical phase of his development. It is in your baby's best interest to make better educational use of the first year than has been made up to now. New methods are needed to ascertain what capacity for development a newborn has brought with him into the world. Even more important are methods to assist a baby to develop, to express, and to apply his true capabilities. This is a very young scientific discipline and is itself still developing. But fortunately, what we have already learned is enough to alter significantly the current methods of bringing up babies.

3

Heredity and Environment: Getting it Straight at Last

Until recently it was thought that an infant's *growth* depends more on hereditary influences and less on environment, while *development* was supposed to depend to a large extent on environment. New discoveries in physiology, however, show that growth, too, depends considerably on outside influences: effective stimulators and inhibitors have been discovered for various organs and organisms which can influence growth positively or negatively. Today we know that although the growth and development of organisms is restricted by hereditary factors, the limits of development and growth are much less restricted than was once assumed. Previously these restrictions were considered so tight because the appropriate environmental stimuli that facilitate the growth and development of organisms were unknown.

So it is impossible to take for granted that a baby will "on his own" develop certain desired traits, skills, abilities and attitudes. To insure these achievements it is necessary, from the very first days of a child's life, to plan his upbringing and take appropriate measures.

Why Children Can't All Be Brought Up the Same Way

Heredity naturally limits development to a degree: it is impossible to turn any child into a Mozart even with the best care and most efficient upbringing. On the other hand, I firmly believe that, with good care and the use of modern methods, many children can be taught to be highly proficient musicians.

Modern society needs good brains in the most diverse fields, and fortunately the capacity to develop is different for each person and is the basis for individual differences between people.

Therefore, all babies can't be brought up the same; each child needs an individualized approach, i.e., he must be reared in a way which will respect his individual personality traits. So we must uncover his individual developmental traits and abilities and develop them intensively. Much is known about the general development of traits common to the majority of children. But our present knowledge of the individual scope of development, which are multiple and varied, is poor precisely because they are so rich and varied. And yet: the parent who is capable of developing the general traits common to all children, is also capable of developing the individual side of his own child's personality, because it is governed by the same laws of development. The task is to be able to recognize an individual and beneficial trait of development—not by relying on some "maternal instinct" but on your own intelligence, judgment, ability to observe, and interest in your baby's development.

You will want to accept your child and not try to force him to develop according to your own wishes and image. Seek what is good and beautiful in him, useful to him and society, what should be accentuated and which disruptive elements can be discouraged.

You can tell what lies hidden in your child—and in other children—just by watching their activities. Each person learns, expresses, and applies himself through activities from birth until death. If you want to find out the developmental traits hidden in your child, you must give him the widest scope for various activities. From what he selects more often, what he understands earlier, in what he succeeds better, from what experiences he learns more quickly, you will be able to tell for what he has the greater or lesser potential for development. Then all you need to determine is whether a "wanted" activity is beneficial to your baby or not.

To enhance development it's not desirable to concentrate only on isolated traits. Individual abilities cannot be cultivated independently; a certain ability can be brought to a high level only when a number of other abilities and traits are at a certain level. The increase of one ability must be in harmony with the development of the entire personality of the baby. This is especially important in early infancy; an infant should develop universally, as an entity. Individual care is not one-sided care.

Earliest Development: How Fast, How Far?

The final aim of baby rearing is not the faster but the fuller development of all the psychological functions of the child, and the proper stimulation of its development scope. We do not want to push a child to learn something sooner than average. Parents who tend to do this often force the child into activities for which he is still too immature, overloading him and often damaging his overall development. Hence my maxim that a child should never be forced into an activity, but stimulated and given opportunity.

Traditionally, a child is taught to reach out for a toy

at about the fifth month. But if you systematically and deliberately give him the suitable opportunity to reach out and grasp interesting objects, he will learn to do so during his third to fourth months. Even very neglected infants finally learn to reach out for objects, because they will always find something to grasp; but they need 6 and more months.

Why does it make any difference whether a baby learns to grasp an object during the fourth or sixth month? A baby who reaches out for objects at 4 months eagerly manipulates them between his fourth and sixth month and learns valuable facts about them—that they are small or large, square or round, rough or smooth, hollow or full and much more. This child gains experience covering the physical, geometrical and other properties of objects at an age when a neglected baby is just learning to reach out for something.

The first child has a lead over the neglected child that will usually increase as he grows older.

So appropriate training will result in a certain rate of an infant's mental development. Lack of stimulation will slow it down. And you cannot expect that a slowly developing child will develop longer and will finally reach the same stage of development as children who develop faster. The development of human beings begins to slow down at a certain age. It even appears that a child who develops slower reaches the limits of his development sooner than a child with a faster rate of development. Since the rate of mental development can be influenced during the infant's first year, this is another reason for intensive care in the upbringing of your child in early infancy.

(Incidentally, it is difficult to determine whether the new method has speeded up the stage of reaching out for an object, to mention one example, or whether it has only removed the brake to development of traditional conditions which have been considered "normal" for many years).

Your Baby's Psychological Needs: the First Year

If a baby should not be forced to develop according to your own wishes, this does not mean, of course, that you should not enhance his development. You cannot plan that your son will be a chemist, but you can set yourself a more general objective—to rear him to be a good person functioning as close as possible to his full potential. This seemingly humble goal will influence your baby's development considerably and favorably.

What are some of the main psychological needs of an infant?

An infant needs to be in good physical and emotional condition—to feel well. After birth the newborn enters a completely new environment to which he must quickly adapt with radical changes of his physiological processes; he must breathe by himself, take in food, control his body temperature, and the like. If he is unable to cope with these needs quickly, then his nervous system especially and thus his further mental development will suffer; good later development also becomes difficult.

An infant needs to establish contact with his environment as soon as possible and gradually become acquainted with it. A newborn is not conscious of the fact that he has arms, legs, sensory organs—or that more than he himself exists. He cannot use his limbs and sensory organs and does not understand the meaning of the signals he receives through his senses. He is equipped with a few neuromuscular mechanism—reflexes—which enable him to defend his life in the first stages of development, but the newborn's nervous system is mostly inactive. If he is to learn to use his body—mainly his motor and sensory organs—and establish contact with the outer world, then he needs gradually and gently to be led out of this state of inhibition and activated.

For instance, show him the milk bottle and then push the nipple into his mouth; after you have repeated this often enough the bottle becomes the signal for subsequent feeding; it acquires the significance of a signal. To acquaint an infant with the world is the same as giving individual phenomena the meaning of signals.

Activate his hands as soon as possible, because hands are his most important tool for the active exploration of the world. When I say that a baby must make contact with the world as soon as possible I mean "contact" literally; the infant must touch the objects and handle them.

It is not enough for an infant to have sufficient random stimuli because overall development depends on the selection of stimuli that ensure versatility. Sometimes, through ignorance or overanxiousness, we give a baby one-sided stimuli which ignore some facets of his development. We may encourage only passive perception (the baby mostly just watches or listens to something), but we give him fewer stimuli-creating active reactions. At other times we support the more general movements (crawling, walking, running, jumping) but pay less attention to the delicate hand movements.

A baby needs to exert an active influence on the world. He has the tendency to be active, because only by activity —experimenting—can he get to know the world. The physiological basis for this is his inborn orientation reflex, which gradually develops into orientation-investigatory behavior. Lack of stimuli at an early age stifles this reflex (later it can be inhibited with a surplus of stimuli).

When awake, the infant should not be generally inactive, and his activities should not lack purpose. The infant tends to be deliberately active and tries to create some interesting change with his activities. These changes are the main motive for his activity and also the source of new experience because they not only excite him, but also draw his attention to the relationship between cause and result. Try giving him opportunity to act on objects and people; cause reactions; discover the relationship between his own activity and the reactions it causes. And useful activities are useful from *his* point of view: because he learns to wave his hand at a certain object, he realizes that he creates a sound; if an adult did the same, he'd be wasting his time.

The infant needs to express himself freely and with minimum restrictions. Even a little infant is more satisfied, happier, and more successful in an activity if he can decide on it independently and do it the way he wants. The subject of authoritative versus nonauthoritative, directive versus nondirective rearing is much discussed. The well-proved principle that extremes are not the best solution is valid here: constant orders as to what is and isn't allowed are undesirable, but so is permission for a baby to be governed only by his immediate impulses.

The middle road is best: give a baby maximum freedom within certain social rules. A baby's freedom and lack of inhibition cannot come at the expense of inconvenience and damage to others. The baby must be gradually led to disciplined freedom. Give him the opportunity for interesting, useful activities and eliminate, so far as possible, opportunities for undesired activities. Interfere with his activity as little as possible. When necessary, act as indirectly, discreetly, tactfully, and calmly as you can.

Often parents restrict a baby's activities without realizing it. They restrict his movements with too much or too heavy clothing, or unnecessary confinement in small spaces—his crib, carriage, or bed. We often prevent him from performing some activities for fear that he will hurt himself or damage something. Proceed reasonably and think whether the activity is important to baby's development and important enough to warrant a certain amount of unpleasantness, danger, or damage.

Baby needs to feel safe, secure and to have his place in the world. He feels safe and secure in conditions to which he is accustomed. In a familiar environment your baby will react positively to new stimuli, but in lesser-known surroundings his reaction to the same stimulus will become negative; at home in his mother's arms he will happily greet an unknown dog, but outside near an unknown person he will be afraid of the same dog. In surroundings where he feels safe and secure the infant will undertake small exploratory excursions. He will gradually acquaint himself with an increasingly wider environment but will venture only to places from which he can quickly return to his island of safety and security. At first this island is a known corner, then the entire room, apartment, house, surroundings of the house, and so on.

Your infant has the need to create a firm bond with a small group of people or at least one person. He needs to feel that he belongs to somebody and that the person belongs to him. Usually he will include several people in this bond (mother, father, brother or sister, grandparents) who form a group which your baby can easily survey. These people contribute most to his feeling of safety and security, and he can take a change of physical or social environment better in their presence.

Your baby forms a strong attachment to the person who gratifies his basic vital needs, usually, of course, his mother. The strongest attachment ties him to whoever gratifies his psychological needs—who plays with him, gives him interesting jobs, shows him the world. The infant clearly realizes that he belongs to somebody who not only lives next to him, but also takes an active part in his activities and shares his joys and worries.

A baby needs to be successful in creative activities and social contacts. For him to continue in his activities, his deeds must be rewarded. One of the main rewarding stimuli for children's activities is success. From successful activities with objects he not only learns; he also controls his ability to overcome difficulties. All this rewards his emerging self-confidence and self-assurance; failure and lack of interest undermine his self-confidence and create feelings of inferiority and deficiency. If you give your baby the opportunity to be successful in creative activities and in dealing with people, you foster in him love of learning and give him self-confidence in dealing with other people.

Your baby needs models. By the end of his first year he will have learned to actively incorporate himself in his social group through imitation. Each person plays some role in society and baby needs to accept roles. At first he identifies with those closest to him, whom he loves, respects, and most important of all, who do interesting things. You'll be surprised at the activities your baby will imitate by the beginning of his second year. Frequent imitation of activities of certain persons creates permanent habits and characteristics of the child. It means that a baby needs good examples from his very first year of life.

4

How to Create Responses in an Infant

Can you communicate with a newborn?

Insufficient knowledge of the psychological develop-ment of infants has been the main cause for the notion that it is impossible to communicate with a newborn and that upbringing can begin only after he acquires some ability to reason.

This is just plain wrong. Research has shown that an infant should be trained from his *very first days* of life and that he becomes more responsive the better he is reared during early infancy—and, of course, later, too.

Because of their obsolete notions, parents did expose their babies to various stimuli but did not expect more in return than passive perception and an occasional smile. Even the authors of many handbooks for parents have not known how to evoke an active reaction from a baby. Proof of this are the various books on gymnastics for the newborn. Mostly they suggest so-called passive exercises such as taking a baby's arms or legs and moving them around. The baby is being moved, but tolerates this movement only passively. Passive exercises amuse healthy children (taking the baby's hands and clapping them), but apart from that their physiological and physiological value is very limited. Badly performed passive exercises can even harm your baby.

How Movement Begins

To raise him to best advantage, you'll do well to stimulate your baby to become active by moving purposefully. There are many ways to persuade even the youngest newborn to perform certain active movements even though he does not yet understand you and does not yet know how to imitate you. But before I describe these movements, let me explain how active muscular motion works.

Various stimuli act on sensory organs in our body (skin, eyes) and inside it (our inner sensory organs which enable us to feel hungry, tired) and create nervous processes which are communicated to the central nervous system (the spinal cord or the brain) and from there transmitted to glands and muscles where they stimulate the excretory activities of the glands or motion of the muscles.

If these nervous processes are transmitted only to the spinal cord or to the lower parts of the brain, which is most common with infants, they react without being aware of the reaction—just as a sleeping adult. Movements which your baby performs consciously and deliberately, which are not seen in a newborn but appear gradually, are caused by nervous processes communicated through the most complicated part of the brain—the cortex. The difference between movement controlled by the cortical and subcortical centers is illustrated by the bowel movements. When an infant soils his diapers in the first half year it is an act of pure reflex controlled by the spinal centers; but when during his second year he asks for his pot and performs the act only after being seated on it, then it is controlled by the cortex. So training a newborn consists partly in changing acts controlled by the spinal cord into acts controlled by the cortex.

In a word, no movements are unstimulated; every movement is a reaction to a stimulus. When you understand the stimuli that cause your baby to react, you'll discover many of the secrets of how to influence his behavior.

Stimuli that Cause Reactions

All stimuli are of two types—internal and external. Reactions which are not caused by external stimuli are called spontaneous reactions. These are mainly caused by internal physiological processes. Although it may appear that they cannot be influenced from outside, there are many ways to deliberately create spontaneous reactions. By making sure that your baby's internal physiological processes function normally—that the baby is healthy, fed, and rested—you will achieve satisfied motions, satisfied murmurs and interest in his surroundings. And good overall care creates sufficient positive internal stimuli to trigger various spontaneous activities that have a beneficial effect.

Exterior inborn stimuli are of two kinds. Inborn specific reactions to specific stimuli are called inborn reflexes. If you touch your baby's open hand he will close his fist. If you touch his heel he will spread his toes. If you touch his foot near the toes he will contract them. If you turn him face down he will lift his head up. If you touch his lips he will begin to suck.

Infant rearing and especially exercises for infants in the first and second quarter-year of life make use of these natural motor reflexes. So the evocation of reflexes in

the first 3 month is one important way to activate your
baby.

A second method of activating him is to set off various
reactions by nonspecific stimuli: stripping him naked,
dipping him into warm water, showing him bright toys,
for example. The baby reacts to such stimuli by moving
various parts of his body or all of it. He kicks his legs and
waves his arms. Every baby reacts differently to these
stimuli and often the same baby reacts differently to the
same stimulus at different times.

You can also use these stimuli to encourage your baby
to make movements. This cluster of vitality can be mobil-
ized by leaning over him, smiling at him and talking
quietly to him, gently stroking his body, or tickling him
slightly. When you use nonspecific stimuli to create vitality, proceed gently and keep a constant lookout for his
reactions to make sure they don't change into expressions of displeasure—irritated shouts, crying, or restlessness.

Acquired stimuli are quite different. An infant does
not react to them at all or he reacts indifferently. Only
after training does he begin to react to them in a definite
way. These stimuli are again internal or external.

So during his first year your baby will progress from
spontaneous, purely reflexive movements to deliberate,
voluntary willpower-controlled movements. Also at this
age your baby will progress from reactions caused by
inborn, unconditioned stimuli, to responses to stimuli
toward which he must first learn to react.

Positive and Negative Reward Stimuli: Reward and Punishment

The smallest infant's reaction should be rewarded
mainly with inborn stimuli. With older infants you can

increase the use of acquired rewarding stimuli which the baby gradually learns to accept as rewards.

For instance, in the first 3 months of life you could teach baby to turn his head to one side at the sound of a bell if you gave him his bottle from that side. In the fourth month you could teach him the same but the turning of his head would have to accompanied by your praise, which carries no rewarding effect during the first 3 months.

Rewarding stimuli, both positive and negative (i.e., reward and punishment) can be physical, material, and social. Physically rewarding stimuli usually work from early infancy—they are inborn. Social stimuli are acquired at later stages; the child must learn to react to them.

Physical rewards create pleasant physical or sensory feelings. Such rewards include tidbits and tasty drinks, immersion into pleasingly warm water, gentle stroking, and rocking. Sensory reward stimuli include mainly optical and acoustic stimuli which create stronger orientation reactions, i.e., the attention of the sensory organs to new, changing, surprising stimuli. After your baby has learned to manipulate a toy he is rewarded by being able to see the toy from various angles; he can alter its shape by pressure and at the same time create certain sounds. If, in the first three months, you teach your baby to lift his head, his efforts to lift it are rewarded by a better view of interesting surroundings than when lying on his back and seeing only the monotonous white ceiling.

Physical punishment can be deliberate or natural. The first includes spanking and various other methods of physical abuse. I assume it is unnecessary to explain that the usefulness of such punishment is not only small, but is an expression of moral cruelty and absolute parental incompetence even with older children. Its use is not only one of the causes of the deprivation of children's rights; it can lead to incarceration for cruelty. Luckily, many parents have brought up beautiful, good people without a single smack. Children are what we make of them. If we see them behave in a way we don't like, then I think this is mostly our fault.

Natural punishments are a result of disrespect for physical and other laws, and these are effective teachers. A child learns that he can wave his hands as vigorously as he likes, but not against hard objects or his own body. A few unpleasant experiences are usually enough to make him stop. Natural punishments usually act on a child all the time. In most cases they do not cause much pain but act as slightly unpleasant stimuli. The infant gains experience with them every day, and so certain objects acquire importance as signals. They influence his behavior: he steps over the threshold so as not to fall; when he walks he moves a little to the side so as not to knock against the table; and he supresses the urge to pick up an object because it once fell out of his hand with a big noise.

How a Baby Learns New Responses to New Stimuli

In the first half year of his life your baby will have to learn a lot of new reactions without your direct participation. Take a baby who is 2 to 4 months old and has an irritating rash.

The baby reacts to the unpleasant feeling with general restlessness: he cries, makes restless movements with his hands, feet, head, and body. These movements express a defensive reflex. Most of them do nothing to alleviate the unpleasant itching, but as soon as the infant touches his itching tummy he feels some relief. The movements of the legs, head, and other parts of the body which do not bring relief slowly disappear, while he will touch his tummy with his hand more often and the touches will slowly change into rubbing motions. If the rash lasts for a while, the hand movement loses its initial spontaneity and he learns to consciously rub the itching skin with his hand.

The inflammation of the skin thus causes a strong irritation process which spreads through the nervous system and is expressed by lively body movements— motor restlessness. Movements which do not bring relief remain unrewarded and therefore disappear. But movements of the hand over the stomach alleviate the unpleasant itch and are thus rewarded. This gradual elimination of ineffective movements and the reinforcement of effective ones creates new motor skills, experience, and knowledge. The baby has learned to react to a new stimulus (irritation) with a new response (rubbing his hand over his tummy) all by himself! The imprecise term for this method of forming new reactions is "trial and error."

Infants and small babies use this method to learn many motor and other skills, gain experiences and knowledge. It looks as if a baby's development under these conditions is spontaneous and cannot be influenced. But let me show you with a baby 4 to 6 months old that even this spontaneous learning can be influenced when the child begins to reach out for objects, and how the number of "trials" and expecially the "errors" can be decreased. At the same time you can prevent the start of spontaneous undesirable "skills."

An infant between 2 and 3 months old becomes very excited on seeing a colored, shining object nearby and will express this excitement with lively movements of his entire body. If, during these movements, his hand chances to touch the object, and if this happens with the open hand, the hand will reflexively close and grasp the object. The more you give your infant this opportunity, the more his touches and grasps will increase. Soon they will lose their spontaneity and the baby will deliberately guide his hand to the visible goal and grasp for it. The ineffective waving of the arms gradually disappears and the hand movements toward the toy become ever more direct.

The development of this hand movement from random waving to the deliberate and sure guiding of the hand toward an object will take longer and often be more complicated the more you leave it to chance. By eliminating chance you can make the process simpler, smoother, and therefore shorter. You will not be accelerating or anticipating future development. You just remove all unnecessary obstacles to the baby's development, hurdles that complicate it and make growing up more difficult.

How can you eliminate unnecessary and random stimuli which make development harder?

If your child is to learn to reach out for an object then he obviously must have it within reach; if all he has at hand are his blanket and the bars of his crib, he lacks opportunity to train this manual skill. The object with which he can train grasping must excite him by its color, brightness, movement, and changes. So don't just hang an object above him and leave it for a week; if he keeps seeing the same thing every day from morning till night, he will lose interest fast. Change the objects at reasonable intervals.

How you give the toy to your baby is also very important. If you just want to place it next to a 2- to 3-month-old baby, you might just as well not give it to him at all. The toy must be properly suspended. If it hangs vertically it will sway away when he touches it with his hand and will be difficult to grasp. Therefore, thread the toy onto a string and attach it across him from right to left about 6 to 8 inches above his chest. If he starts waving his hands there is greater probability that his hand will touch the object and grasp it. Finally, the toy must be of such a size and shape that he can grasp with his small hand and also attract him to grasp it. The quality of the toy is also important; a soft, warm human hand creates a stronger grasp than an equally thick but hard, cold metal rod.

If you do all this and eliminate the factors which make learning more difficult, your baby will start reaching out for toys not in the fifth or sixth month, as most of the literature will tell you, but in his third to fourth months.

Let me show you how a child in his first year learns to handle a simple cube. Once he has learned to grasp it, he learns to transfer it from hand to hand, turn it over in his hand, tap it on the table and later against another cube, then tap two cubes together, throw the cubes into some vessel, place them onto each other, and so on. When your baby learns these types of handling he is not only playing, but also learning various very important movements that increase his overall ability to accomplish tasks.

How Your Baby Learns to Imitate

Your baby is born with an *inborn* ability to imitate. This develops gradually and you can aid its development by knowing the rules that govern it.

Truly voluntary, deliberate imitation is a complicated process and does not occur until the start of the baby's second year; in the first year only a few early stages appear.

First comes self-imitation. In the sixth to seventh month your baby will happen to perform a certain movement—perhaps he'll bang a toy on the table and create a noise. If the noise is not too loud he will be pleased and this becomes a positive reward stimulus. The baby will usually bang onto the table again to create more noise and will then repeat it several times. It is important for him to register his own movement in order to make the connection between the movement and the noise, and for the result to be pleasing and interesting. Only then will the baby repeat the action and imitate himself.

The second stage is imitation by feedback. At around 8 months your baby sits with you at the table and chances to bang on the table. If you don't take much notice, that'll be all. But if you imitate him by banging the table yourself, you'll attract his attention and he will repeat the banging; your baby has imitated what you imitated.

This is how mothers most often develop the mumbling and gabbling of their baby; the child happens to mutter something, his mother repeats the sounds but alters them slightly so they become real language sounds, and the child repeats them after her. If you do not repeat the mutterings and murmuring he may not only be slower to make sounds and pronounce syllables, but might even stop murmuring. (Deaf children start to murmur as normal babies do, but they stop because their action is not rewarded; they cannot hear themselves.)

By the end of the first year true imitation starts: the baby watches activities of adults, animals, and machines, and imitates some part of them. A baby can learn to imitate only whatever he is mature enough to do. He will usually imitate a movement he has already learned, but will alter its form, and perform it in a new connection, in a new combination with another one, or will enrich the movement with a new element. Gradually he will develop his motor abilities by imitation, but he cannot bypass development phases.

After the first 12 months the tendency to imitate becomes expecially strong in children who have many models to imitate and have ample opportunities to do so. So give your baby as many opportunities as you can to observe people performing the most varied tasks and at the same time try to engage him in the activities of adults, consistent with his ability and strength.

How to Verbally Influence Your Infant's Responses

The word (which from the second year of your baby's life is the main stimulus for creating a response in him) exerts only a very slight influence on his behavior during his first 6 months of life. But in the second 6 months it begins to act as a creative and reward stimulus.

Your baby obviously needs to be taught to react to the spoken word. I shall describe this development in more detail later. Briefly, at around his sixth month, your baby can be taught to look at various interesting objects ("Where is the tick-tock?"); in the seventh to eighth months he'll be able to point out several objects named by word. At the same time he can learn to show when asked, "Show how big you are," or "Do bye-bye," how big he is, or wave his hand. Gradually, more complicated responses can be created by words, so that by the end of his first year your baby will understand almost all the simple appeals normally used in bringing up a baby. By the end of the first year the spoken word also acts as a reward stimulus: your baby will gladly repeat some activity when you express your admiration ("You're smart!") or praise ("That's a good baby!").

Excitation Versus Inhibition

An excitable type of baby (or one whom you have temporarily excited) will pick up a toy when told "Pick up your train" but cannot obey when you forbid him to touch it. A baby of the inhibited type, or a baby brought to a temporary state of inhibition (perhaps by an alien environment) will not react to the appeal but will react to the prohibition. Only a baby with a balanced excitation and inhibition process will, most probably, react appropriately to both situations: when told to do so he will pick up the toy and when forbidden, he will not touch it—his nervous system can react to adequate excitement as well as to inhibiting processes.

The aim of upbringing should be to create a person with balanced excitement and inhibition.

Big, exerting movements such as crawling, walking, running, jumping, or climbing barriers, call for the excitation process. In my experience, children who are too often led into such activities have a tendency to become lively, active and mobile, but are also volatile, restless, and they may have trouble concentrating. The more refined, more precise movements (especially of the hands) and activities which call for more calm, concentration, and precision, can be performed only if the nervous system is able to respond to the stronger process of active inhibition. Therefore, normally reacting children should be stimulated more or less equally toward lively movements of the entire body and also precise movements of the hands which have such a great influence on the overall mental development of the baby. If a child has a tendency to excessive liveliness, it is wise to guide him toward tasks calling for concentration and precision. If your baby is too quiet, it needs tasks which call for exertion of the entire body.

When your baby touches some objects and not others, or learns to behave one way in one situation and another way in a different one, you have achieved a so-called differential inhibition. When an older infant learns not to start crying when he sees a bottle, even though he is hungry, you have created a so-called delayed inhibition.

If you develop active inhibition in your child, you teach

him discipline and self-control. Active inhibition is weak at first and gradually increases, depending on upbringing and also to a great degree on the condition of the baby's organism; every weakness of the body is expressed primarily by the weakening of the active inhibition process. When children (and adults, too) are tired, hungry, sleepy, or ill, they lose self-control and the ability to concentrate. A baby's behavior will tell you (sooner than the doctor can) that he is ill, because the first sign of sickness is the weakening of active inhibition; he becomes grumpy, loses self-control, and his reactions become more primitive.

Everything Your Baby Learns Is a Step Toward Further Development

Your baby's first steps are only the start of the walking process; he will take his first steps at around the twelfth month, but it will still take him two more years to learn walking properly, and even after he has grown up he will continue to perfect his walking abilities. After his first steps on a flat surface, he will learn to take more steps under the most varied conditions; he will learn to walk forward, sideways, backward, slow and faster, uphill and downhill. He'll negotiate stairways, walk alone or in the presence of known and unknown people, in known and unknown surroundings. These last conditions are especially important for the healthy development of your child, so the more varied are the conditions under which your baby learns to walk, the better he will perfect his walking capability.

Look at it this way: in your neighborhood there are probably many children who do their homework conscientiously and can show off their knowledge in front of their parents, but in front of the teacher and their fellow pupils at school they suddenly fail to say anything. Your baby should therefore learn early in life to apply his skills not only under certain limited conditions but in the most varied possible situations. I advise you to pay careful attention to this rule while raising your baby.

How Your Baby Responds to Training

You have probably found that your baby reacts to tickling by laughter and then, an hour or two hours later, reacts to the same stimulus with tears. The stimulus was the same but the baby was different. Such changes in all his behavior are rhythmic. The rhythm is subject to the rhythm of physiological processes (natural biorhythms) and the rhythm of some exterior stimuli: because day alternates with night, your baby learns to sleep at night and be awake during the day. This is an acquired biorhythm.

You can observe many physiological biorhythms in your baby; he breathes regularly, his heart beats rythmically, the digestion process proceeds rythmically. Biorhythms are perhaps best described as the repetition of similar phenomena in similar intervals. The study of biorhythms has resulted in many important discoveries applicable to raising babies and I would like to mention some of them.

The younger the infant, the more obvious is the rhythmic aspect of his movement and entire behavior rhythm. A newborn often moves his head and limbs rhythmically. The rhythmical kicking of the legs is usually obvious. His body rhythmically alternates motion and stillness. The movements of his hands alternate rhythmically with the movements of the legs. The first vocal expressions—humming and prattling—also tend to be rhythmic.

You can see more complex rhythms in action when the

child is in the "Jolly Jumper." If you place a 5-month-old baby, who has already mastered the jumping technique, into the seat, he starts to jump immediately. The intensity of the jumping will increase at first, then drop until he stops altogether. After a while he starts again, this time more energetically. Periods of stillness rythmically alternate with the jumping series, and this will increase in intensity. After a while the intensity again weakens until baby stops altogether. Graph No. 1 shows the alteration of the number and intensity of the jumps as time goes on; you can see that the activities in the jumper also form a complex rhythm.

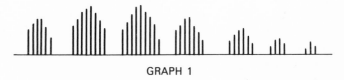

GRAPH 1

The infant in the jumper shows you how to urge a baby to be active. When you perform exercises with him, do about 5 to 6 movements. First increase their intensity, then lower it. Then allow your baby to rest for about the same period or a little longer before encouraging more difficult exercises. Then again allow him to rest or play. This way you will alternate series of movements with pauses while the demands of the activity first rise, then gradually drop, so that you end his tour with easy, undemanding movements.

You can also imitate other rhythmic movements that you observe when your baby plays by himself. You can rhythmically alternate activities during which the baby moves actively with exercises in which he observes something or listens; or alternate games in which you participate with those where he plays by himself; exciting games with quiet ones, and so on.

As your baby grows older, the movements and their

rhythm become more complex. They may even seem to lose rhythm. Arhythmical movements demand more nervous energy than rhythmical. I mean walking along an uneven surface among people, for example, when the foot has to be placed differently with each step so as not to bump into other people. Obviously, this is much more difficult than walking along an unobstructed, flat surface requiring only rhythmical movements. When your baby is tired, sleepy, or sick, he therefore likes to revert to rhythmical rocking, swaying, rhythmical movements with toys, and rhythmic mumbling. This is not only typical for children; when adults want to rest they like to rock rhythmically, relax with rhythmical walks, and go dancing.

If you want to help your baby to learn advanced activities, encourage him to perform them rhythmically. First, enable him to perform steps rhythmically by walking on a flat floor without obstacles. He will train his steps one after the other, in rhythm: one step like the preceding one. Once he has learned to cope with these conditions, let him try a less flat surface where he will have to take one longer or shorter step, make one step to the right, then left, so rhythmic regularity is disrupted and walking is more difficult.

When to Train Your Baby

Mothers often ask me: "At what time of the day should I do the exercises with my baby? When should I train him and play with him?" If the answer is: "From morning till evening and sometimes at night!," some mothers would not take it seriously although they may follow this advice without realizing it.

Take infant training at night. The newborn, as I will discuss later, alternates short periods of wakefulness with short periods of deep sleep and longer semiconsciousness. With training, he learns to sleep at night and alternate wakefulness with sleep during the day. From a certain time on he learns to control his bladder through the whole night. Poor upbringing can teach him to wake up often at night, cry, call for his parents, and learn not to control his bladder.

A baby, you see, can learn to sleep hard at night and be active and awake during the day. Infants in nurseries often do not learn this and spend most of their first year in semiconsciousness, half asleep or awake for very short periods. So you do train a baby day *and* night because you constantly influence his development, directly or indirectly. Of course this doesn't mean that you or somebody else should be in constant contact with the baby. But during his period of wakefulness you can see to it that he performs some beneficial activities.

It is not easy to introduce and guide such activities. Your baby is not trained by people alone; much is due to the environment you create for him. To influence his development indirectly you can adapt his surroundings and create situations which attract (and stimulate) him to certain desired activities and eliminate undesired ones. This requires greater skill than direct guidance.

I would like to convince parents that time not devoted to training their baby is time wasted. Remember: you educate your baby all the time because practically every contact between the baby and adults or objects influences him in some way, positively or negatively. Much, therefore, depends on which stimulus influences him at a given moment.

When is educational activity most effective? I have shown that the state of your baby alters according to certain laws and that the change depends on certain factors. Of these, the main two are the period he has been awake and the state of his digestion.

Experiments with 6-month-old babies who alternated

2-hour periods of wakefulness with 1 1/2 hours of sleep showed that during the first third of the wakeful period —the first 40 minutes after waking—a baby's performance increased and was at its optimum in the first and second parts of the wakeful period. It dropped slightly in the second part and dropped faster in the third. By good "performance" I mean that during this period he was in a good mood; expressed lively interest in his surroundings; was active; quickly and easily acquired new experience, skills, and habits; performed more difficult exercises; reacted faster and better to various stimuli during the experiments.

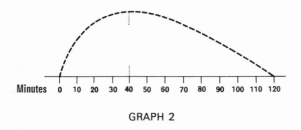

GRAPH 2

So I advise that you plan for the 2-hour period of wakefulness in a 6-month-old baby as follows: during the first quarter of wakefulness (the first 30 minutes) change his diaper, feed him and allow him to play as he likes. Offer him opportunities for activities which he has already performed before. During the second quarter of wakefulness (the thirtieth to sixtieth minute) engage him in more difficult activities from which he can acquire new experience and skills. During this period his activities should yield the best educational results. During the third quarter (sixtieth to ninetieth minute) repeat mostly familiar activities. During the last quarter (ninetieth to one hundred twentieth minute) give the baby the greatest opportunity for free play, independent selection of toys and activities, feed him, and get him ready for bed.

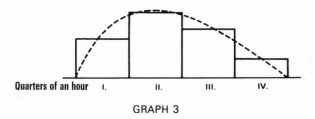

Quarters of an hour   I.   II.   III.   IV.

GRAPH 3

Older children are naturally awake longer and the activity periods will be longer, too. Incidentally the "quarters" of wakefulness are only approximate and for your general guidance. The decisive factor is the baby himself: his state, mood, personality, and other characteristics.

The same applies to the content of the periods of wakefulness. If I have said that during the second quarter your baby should be given more demanding activities I do not mean that you should keep him busy that way during the entire period. Activity should alternate rhythmically during the entire period of wakefulness—more lively games with calmer ones, active tasks with more passive ones (observation, listening). So during the second period you should give your baby things to do which are generally harder, as shown in Graph 4.

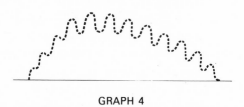

GRAPH 4

The baby's direct and indirect activation should also alternate. Direct activation comes in three varieties, depending on how much time you have.

(a) Educational Minutes. You will usually take a look at your baby every 10 to 20 minutes or so perhaps to change his diaper, correct his position, give him a toy. On these occasions I recommend that you always systematically devote 2 to 5 minutes to a few of the exercises or small tasks listed in this book. You can schedule educational minutes any time, but be careful to adapt them to the baby's state.

(b) Educational Periods. When you're at home with your baby, organize your work so you can devote at least 10 to 20 minutes to him exclusively when he is awake. Use these periods for the more systematic training. This educational period will be most productive during the second or third quarter of wakefulness.

(c) Educational Whole. During one entire period of his wakefulness your baby ought to be in constant contact with his parents. This is a fine opportunity for father, after he returns home from work and has the time, to devote himself to the baby and enhance their relationship. I earnestly hope that the father will not try to make excuses ("no time") because nothing is more important than his baby's upbringing. Besides, raising a small baby is extremely interesting, so fathers would do well to make it their "hobby."

This period is called an educational "whole" because you should keep your baby busy so as to develop all aspects of his entire personality. Again, you should make the most use of the second and third periods of wakefulness.

The second factor which considerably influenced the performance of the babies during our experiments was the digestion period. The babies were fed in intervals of 3 1/2 hours. After feeding, their performance dropped a little and only began to improve at the start of the second hour, reaching its peak at the end of the second hour. Then it gradually decreased as shown on the curve in Graph 5.

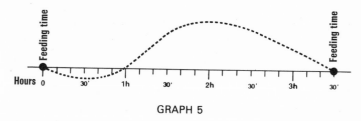

GRAPH 5

Our experiments showed that it's best to feed a baby before he goes to sleep so that he sleeps through the period of lower performance. When the babies woke up, their performance improved not only as a result of the gradient of the wakeful period, but also because their digestion was further along. True, before your baby goes to sleep he is tired not only from being awake but also because he is hungry. A tired baby may be hard to feed and may fall asleep in the process. I also realize that you cannot invariably feed him before he goes to sleep because after spending the whole night without food he must be fed soon after waking up.

N. M. Shchelovanov and N. M. Aksarina, the Soviet experts on nurseries, recommend feeding a baby after he wakes up; they assert that a baby refreshed by sleep feeds happily and is in a good state because he is rested and fed, and therefore easy to work with. Both authors, however, recognize that this method is practical only during the first 9 to 10 months; as soon as the duration of one period of wakefulness and sleep during the day extends to over 4 hours as he grows older, he must be fed twice during his wakeful period, at the beginning and at the end.

I recommend feeding the baby 10 to 30 minutes before you put him to sleep in the first year, or after he has slept, but never in the middle of his period of wakefulness.

What's the Best Cycle?

Graph 6, following, shows when, over a 24-hour period a baby should ideally be awake and asleep; how much of this time should be day wakefulness and sleep; and into how many periods the daytime wakefulness and sleep should be divided. The graph also contains our research data on how many times a day and night an infant should ideally be fed and the best length of the intervals between feeding.

A Day's Schedule

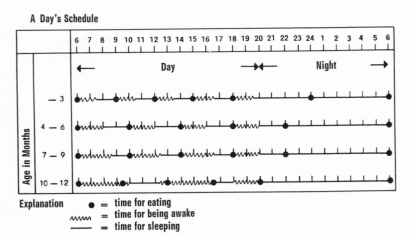

GRAPH 6

These standard figures are drawn from the daily timetables of the children I have worked with. They can only give you some general basis for judgment. If your baby's period of sleep or wakefulness deviates greatly from these standards, discuss this with your doctor.

The Infant's Daily Timetable

During your baby's first year it is especially important not to allow his rhythms to be interrupted by exterior stimuli. In fact, the stimuli which influence his growth and development had best be synchronized with his biorhythms. Your baby's timetable should therefore be regular, using the table as a guide, but mainly according to actual needs of the child. The previous graphs show some timetables for individual age groups.

These timetables are not meant to be binding—only a guide. Do adapt to your baby's needs, your own working and other conditions. It's perfectly all right to move the entire timetable backward or forward by an hour or more.

One school of thought demands that the timetable be strictly adhered to. Another condemns any such timetables and calls for a baby to be fed when he is hungry and put to bed when he is tired. In my view both opinions represent flawed extremes: the first leads to undue imposition on a baby, the second to harmful irregularity. The middle path is best.

Observe when the first signs of tiredness appear; they're a signal that your baby ought to be put to bed. Find out when he wakes up. Record these observations three to four times and work out his average need for sleep. Compare this with the guideline given in the table. Is there any significant difference? In the ensuing days try to put your baby to bed approximately on schedule. Because he is constantly developing, you can put him to bed earlier if he gets tired sooner, or later if he is still fresh. But do not make too great a change without such reason as illness. You will be able to use your timetable only 2 to 3 months at most because during that time your baby's needs will alter and you will have to alter the timetable to accommodate longer periods of wakefulness and shorter ones of sleep.

5

What's Your Baby Ready For?

As with all guides to working with children, the exercises, games and tasks in this book can have varied effects. It would be a poor idea to apply my recommendations mechanically with the misguided confidence that everything I advise is right in all circumstances. No medicine always acts beneficially on a person's health. That is why I want to tell you how to use these methods to improve your baby's development and not to harm him in any way, even unintentionally.

First, you should know your baby's level of development: how far he has progressed in the movements of his entire body and hands, his experience, speech, social relations, and other areas. To help you, I include four tables which show a baby's approximate capabilities for overall movements, the delicate hand movements, speech and social relations, and which habits he can usually acquire during particular months of his first year. If your baby can do more or less than shown in the table you needn't think that his development is too slow or that he is a genius. Only if the differences are very great need you ask your pediatrician to advise you.

Normal development in the first four months can

differ by as much as 1 month plus or minus from the data in the table. In the second and third quarter-year the disparity can be plus or minus 2 months. In the fourth quarter of the first year the difference can be even greater because the limits of normality are about plus or minus 3 months from the data.

Many babies develop unevenly: perhaps your child's movements are more advanced than his speech, in which case you had best adapt his movements training for one age group but his speech training for another.

When you have set your objective, how to help your baby achieve it? One aim of this book is to help you acquire this knowledge.

The most important condition is the appropriate application of the selected method. The correct stimulation of your baby is extremely complicated and calls for considerable theoretical and practical experience, so let me analyze the educational act more closely.

How Feedback Works Between Mother and Child

Observe your baby, his reactions and behavior, and adapt your further activities accordingly. When you adapt your behavior and methods according to how your baby reacts to them, you establish what we call a feedback between your behavior and your baby's reactions; now you are raising your baby sensitively and with understanding and are adapting yourself to him. If this feedback between mother and child is lacking, the child is reared mechanically.

The steps of feedback should include:

1. You perform a certain act,
2. Watch baby's reactions,
3. Deduce what the reaction means,

4. Decide how to react to baby's behavior,
5. Perform the reaction you decided on.

Suppose you're exercising your baby and he is in a good mood. You pick him up under the arms and lift him above your head with his head forward (first phase). You notice that he has stopped laughing and is making a face, although he normally laughs during this exercise (second phase). You assume that you picked him up wrongly and make him uncomfortable (third phase). You decide to support him better with your palms and to release the pressure of your fingers because it is probably unpleasant for the baby (fourth phase). You carry out your decision and correct your grip on the baby (fifth and first phases simultaneously). You see your baby is smiling (second phase). You assume that you are now acting correctly (third phase).

To treat your baby with "feeling," then, requires more than "feeling" alone. Observation, judgment and thought, knowledge and practical experience, fast and sensible decisions are all needed. Indeed, your entire personality and intelligence. So when you play with your baby you should constantly observe him and yourself, assess your own and his reactions, always bearing in mind the educational objective. Good rearing isn't a haphazard piling up of random stimuli to which your baby reacts in an uncontrolled way.

Now, here are some typical baby responses that can tell you whether your action has had positive or negative effect, and whether your baby is in a condition so your action *could* have a positive or negative effect.

Mimicry: Positive: a pleased expression, smile, laughter. Negative: an unsatisfied expression, frown, sobs, starts crying.

Vocal Expressions: Positive: pleased mumbling, prattling, loud laughter, shouting, words. Negative: wailing, whimpering, angry shouts.

Motor Expressions: Positive: lively active movements combined with positive expressions as above, willingness to cooperate. Negative: passiveness, restlessness, lack of cooperation, defensive movements.

Interest and Attention: Positive: wide-open eyes carefully watch all that is going on around him; he moves to be able to watch. Negative: lack of observation; looking passively, resignedly at one spot; refraining from lifting or turning his head.

Expressions of Tiredness: Yawning, rubbing of eyes, red eyes and eyelids, sucking fingers, mechanical nodding of the head or other part of the body, returning to activities typical for a younger age.

Let me also try to show the causes of some of these negative reactions and how to avoid them.

Baby's Physical Condition: He may be tired, sleepy, hungry or overfed, or even ill. Interrupt your activities and do your best to make him comfortable. Many things can be unpleasant for him: he might be too hot or cold, his clothes might be too tight, or some other form of discomfort.

Mental Condition: Various stimuli which create such unpleasant psychological reactions as fear may be acting on the baby. Maybe he is afraid of the person who is trying to stimulate him, or somebody else who is present. He may also be afraid of objects or even the activities to which you are trying to expose him. Try to remove the cause of fear or gradually get him used to it. The baby may also be interested in something else: he may see an interesting object and want to have it. Try to channel your activities toward improving his mood.

Unsuitable Exercise: Your exercise, game, or task may be too difficult for your baby, or may have been repeated to boredom so he rejects it.

Badly Performed Exercise: The exercise, game, or task may be suitable, but you are not good enough at it and the baby does not want to participate.

The scale of reactions is much richer than I have outlined here. Every baby reacts differently to different causes. Rely on your own powers of observation and reasoning, because you know your child best. If you then treat your baby with "feeling" you will both enjoy your games and he will hardly ever cry.

Main Principles for Bringing Up a Baby

The main principles for the rearing of your baby can be summed up from the main psychological needs and the laws of development mentioned above, and can be briefly summarized into 15 points:

1. Education should start from the very first days of your baby's life because this is the time for you to begin shaping his future personality.

2. The objective of education should not be to accelerate development, but to fully utilize all your baby's potential from his earliest age.

3. In his early age the baby learns only through activities: to educate him is to stimulate him to activities from which he can learn something new and useful.

4. Your baby should have maximum opportunity to collect the most varied range of experience.

5. Your baby should be stimulated and encouraged toward activity, but never forced.

6. Your baby needs maximum freedom because the so-called self-developing activities occur mainly when he has enough opportunity to perform them.

7. Always reward new forms of behavior and newly emerging skills.

8. Baby's behavior should be stimulated and guided mainly with positive stimuli, although negative stimuli also have their uses.

9. When your baby is learning something you should help him, but your assistance should be minimum.

10. After your baby has acquired a certain ability under certain conditions, give him the maximum opportunity to apply it under different conditions.

11. Your baby should be in direct contact with people as much as possible.

12. A newborn should be in the most constant possible active contact with a small group of familiar persons, mainly his mother and father.

13. When you are unable to devote yourself personally to your baby, try to keep him occupied indirectly, i.e., create an environment which will contain enough stimuli to keep him active.

14. Try to create and maintain a good mood in your baby to give him a happy and joyful childhood.

15. Babies are not the same and a parent should respect individual characteristics of a baby at any particular time.

One more principle: in bringing up your baby you should of course adhere not only to the principles of good upbringing, but also your own common sense; and in exceptional cases, seek the advice of specialists.

Child specialists frequently advise consistency with children. But complete consistency is not always possible and nature herself demands certain compromises. Also, children who have been brought up too strictly and consistently often lose their good behavior as soon as the educational authority ceases to act. We also know now that children most love those parents who are consistent in principle but also make exceptions. Children love these mothers and fathers more than parents who are strict and coldly consistent, or parents who are completely inconsistent. The point is that children need a certain stability in parents but also love, understanding, and tolerance.

The most important message of this book is that the essence of good baby rearing is the sincere love of the parents for their baby. The baby will develop best when the parents recognize that his upbringing is their own primary human objective and one of the main aspects of the "purpose in life."

6

How Fun and Games Begin

For "early learning" to be possible at all, the newborn must:

Be capable of registering whether his physiological functions are progressing, that he is capable of experiencing feelings of pleasure and discomfort.

Be capable of registering the stimuli of the outer and inner world, their mutual relationship, and their connection with feelings of pleasure or discomfort. So cognitive abilities must therefore be OK.

Have the tendency and ability to avoid signals that are discomforting and to seek and emphasize signals that are pleasurable. We say that the infant is active and in that his motivation is in order.

Your Objective for the First Month

In effect, every mother rears her child from his very first moment because feeding, bathing, changing, and cuddling contain a significant complex of educational stimuli. Much depends on how you feed and bathe your baby and change his diapers because from his earliest days he will relate to these acts; they give him a remarkable array of visual, auditory, and other stimuli.

Your task of upbringing is to help your baby make his first contacts with the outside world. He must learn to respond to some stimuli, to familiarize himself with them. The second task is to activate him mainly by awakening his interest and persuading him to move. Only an active baby can establish contact with his surroundings.

How to Develop the Senses

Although the development of motor and sensory abilities are closely integrated, I have chosen for reasons of simplicity to discuss each one separately. Briefly, your baby should:

Be exposed to enough and sufficiently varied and suitable sensory stimuli;

Acquire some special visual and auditory abilities; you should teach him to fix his eyes on conspicuous objects and follow movement along a short path; you should also teach him to listen to sounds;

Discover that stimuli announce something, draw attention to something, represent and mean something.

To supply him with means giving him sufficient stimuli —visual, auditory sensory, positional, and so forth—you must neither deprive nor oversaturate him. Parents who realize that their baby needs enough stimuli often tend to oversaturate him. So I want to tell you how to stimulate him sufficiently and be able to tell when he is saturated.

Stimulate your baby only when he is awake. He should cooperate and accept the stimuli *actively* and *observe* a visual stimulus (toy, watch, face) for a time and observe it calmly. As soon as he starts to avoid looking or to turn his head away or close his eyes or express his displeasure vocally or even physically, offer him some other object, or cease stimulation and let him rest.

It is more difficult to discern whether a baby is actively listening or not. A change in his behavior could be a sign that he hears you; an infant's spontaneous movement often stops when he hears a sound and an infant who has been lying calmly will react to sounds with some movement.

Which stimuli are most suitable for baby in his first month? They should be obvious, easily discernible from his surroundings, but not too intense. Your baby can easily be persuaded to look at a gay, colorful object, but will turn away from it if it is too brightly lit. Bright light is not only unsuitable for infants; it is harmful. During his first month your baby does not see objects and people; he registers his environment optically as a continuous surface divided into spots of certain colors and sizes, but he has no idea that one group of spots are his mother and another his rattle. So it's wise for you to show the baby the people and objects, as far as possible, against a neutral, single-color background so that the object stands out against it and enables him to see more clearly that these colored spots belong together and form that object.

If he looks at your face against the background of a white ceiling he is better able to separate you from your background than if you stand in front of a colored curtain (of course these decorations can be in his room). If you want to show him his bottle, rattle, or some other object, I suggest that you move it slightly; this, too, enables him to pick it out from the background and discern which colored spots belong together and form a part of one object.

Sounds to stimulate your baby should also be of medium intensity. The most suitable sound is the female voice. A quiet female voice calms a baby more often than a deeper male voice; this also proves that during the first months of life baby is a biological unit with his mother. I would not recommend playing the radio for long periods; this could strain the baby's nervous system. All the sensory stimuli which you offer your baby in the first months should be of medium or weaker intensity: tastes, smells, tactile experiences, and others. An adequate taste sample is contained in your own milk and in artificial baby foods. You can best cater to his sense of smell by keeping the room well aired and keeping him in the fresh air as much as possible (walking him through city streets with heavy motor traffic is the same as giving him 40 cigarettes a day to smoke!). Cuddling baby, rocking him, changing his diapers, and similar parenting provides him with a sufficient supply of tactile, thermal, and cineaesthetic stimuli.

During his first month all the stimuli *must* be presented to your baby gently and slowly. If you show him a toy suddenly you will make him cry, but the slow presentation of the same toy and its slow movements will cause visual fixation. Fast lifting and setting down of the baby, fast diaper changes, and other forms of rough handling cause negative emotional reactions. Newborns especially need gentle, kind, slow, and careful handling and stimulation, and can take faster procedures and acts of basic care only when they are older.

You should devote special care to the development of your baby's hearing and sight. During his first month he should learn to fix an object with his eyes, i.e., to set his eyes onto it for a certain period of time. At first he will be unable to fix both his eyes onto the object. You can tell this by the way he moves his eyes back and forth and looks through the object into the distance, or looks at it with one eye and somewhere else with the other. Teach him to turn both his eyes so that the picture of the object is formed in the retina in his field of clearest vision and develop his eyesight to create a clear, sharp picture on the retina. Here's how:

1. Show him bright objects: colored toys, Christmas decorations, bright vessels, big flowers—but mainly the human face.

2. Bring the object to about 18 inches away from his eyes.

3. The object must be clearly discernible from the background; stand so that the background of the rattle is not formed by your equally bright clothes, but if possible a single-color apron, the white ceiling, cupboard, or drape.

4. At first hold the object where the baby has fixed his eyes—into the center of his field of vision.

5. In the second half of the first month (or toward its end) you can try to show him the object at the edges of his field of vision and so persuade him to turn his eyes toward the object.

6. In either case, move the object gently around in one spot; later move it very gently from place to place, slowly at first and move it closer and further away from his eyes (14 to 22 inches). Later, still slowly, move it from left to right within his field of vision (4 to 8 inches, back and forth).

You can usually teach your baby to follow a moving object with his eyes at the end of his first month. Here's how:

1. A newborn lies on his back with his head turned to one side; turn his head to the center position with his face upward. Show him a colored object. Gently move it from left to right so that the movement goes past his field of vision. The baby will probably move his eyes slowly to

follow the object. As soon as the eye movement stops, move the object to the other side. Gradually increase the object's movement and speed because his ability to follow an object with his eyes will improve.

2. In their first month some infants will follow the movement of an object not only with their eyes but also with their head. If your baby normally lies with his head turned to one side, this is his favorite side. He first learns to turn his head to follow an object from the central position to his favorite side. Later he turns his head from the nonpreferred side to the center position and then on the favorite side; then from the central position to the nonpreferred side; finally he will turn it from the favorite side all the way to the nonpreferred side, which is hardest for him.

3. It is easier for a baby to turn his head when he is in a vertical position. When you seat him in the crook of your arm, rest his chest against yours and let him look over your shoulder. In this position there is no friction when he turns his head. You can encourage him to turn his head either by moving the object in front of his eyes to the left and right, or by fixing his sight onto something interesting and then gently moving with baby from left to right. Finally you can take two or three steps to the left and right of the object which motivates him to turn his head because it keeps the interesting object within his field of vision.

It's best to do these exercises daily with a newborn for about a half to 3 minutes each time he is awake. He probably won't cooperate longer.

If you expose your baby to constant noise in order to teach him to listen, you'll be just as likely to affect his nervous system adversely as if you had surrounded him with permanent silence. Again I want to stress that you should not switch on the television or radio for any length of time. Sound stimuli, like color, must also be easily discernible from the background; the best sound is a pleasant one that's heard for short periods against a background of silence. Again: the most suitable sound stimulus is the human voice, especially the relatively high, gentle voice of the mother talking or singing simple tunes.

It's most important for the stimuli to create expectations within your baby. It's not enough for him merely to learn to follow something with his eyes or to listen. At the same time he can learn to recognize and understand the *relationship* between various stimuli.

It's therefore best not to offer him isolated stimuli. Suppose you often lean over him so that he sees you and hears your voice. Then, during his second month and sometimes earlier, he will look for your face with his eyes when he hears you or he'll quite obviously be waiting for you to speak to him when he sees your face above him. If feeding follows being taken up in your arms or seeing the bottle, the baby will expect to be fed when you pick him up or show him the bottle. He will express this expectation with lively sucking movements which he previously could only make when you inserted a nipple in his mouth.

This is how he can gradually learn how (and which) stimuli are related to each other. He learns that a certain group of colored spots belongs together and represent what he will later call "Mama"; that certain sounds are related to this picture and that this is "Mama's voice"; and that this optical-acoustic entity representing "Mama" is connected to the removal of unpleasant sensations and is the beginning of pleasant sensations.

It is also psychologically important in the very first period of his life for your baby not to be exposed to too many people and objects because this makes it more difficult for him to begin communicating. Only a few people should look after him. His bathing should be rhythmical and regular as possible because the frequent repetition of the same activity will enable him to find his bearings in this world. The main object which should appear within his range of vision during his first month is a human being; and when you stimulate all his sensory organs more or less simultaneously you will become the first object to be separated from the many stimuli that crowd in on him.

How to Start Training Your Baby to Move His Body

Even today many parents think infants should be wrapped up in layers of clothing and that crying is as natural as breathing and feeding. These people look at me with disbelief when I tell them that, given good care, an infant need not cry, much less scream.

Binding infants into tight clothing and shutting them off in cradles is one of the main causes of crying! This is how a newborn protests against being treated like a robber locked up in a small cell. From the first days of his life your baby needs as much movement as possible. Indeed, this is one of his basic physiological and psychological needs. Depriving him of his freedom of movement slows down (and can even damage) his motor and psychological development, especially in his earliest days and weeks.

Your baby should be naked as often as possible. Undressed, he will start making much livelier movements than dressed. Undressing often causes him to stop crying; dressing causes even calm children to protest energetically. Naturally, you'll remember that an infant, especially your newborn, cannot protect himself effectively against the loss of body heat, so be sure that the temperature of the room where your naked baby is playing does not drop below 77 degrees. If the room is colder use an electric heater.

Clothes should not encumber his freedom of movement. Don't think about undressing your baby when it's hot; think of dressing him when he is cold. When you do find it necessary to dress your baby, use as few clothes as possible and pick the kind that won't stifle his freedom of movement. Diapers for normal babies with healthy hip joints should be loose. Lively, natural kicking of legs is effective treatment for slightly underdeveloped hip joints. (Of course if your baby has a serious defect of a hip joint, it is up to an orthopedist to decide what treatment is best.)

Your baby needs plenty of space! The cradle and bed should be places to sleep in, the carriage only a means of transportation; if they become more, they become a prison. The greater an area you give baby while he is awake, the more he will move. So when you change his diapers or bathe him, allow him to remain on the table or on a wide bed for at least a few minutes to give him greater freedom of movement. The time spent on the table, the bed, and later on the clean, warm, soft floor should be gradually extended as he stays awake longer.

These rules do a lot for the development of your baby's movements, because they'll help him move his entire body spontaneously from his very first days. Lively, spontaneous movements enhance his circulation, breathing, digestion, and many other bodily functions. Deliberate movements from head to foot develop from these original reflexive movements, as I've said. So now let me tell you how to persuade your baby to move.

The exercises below are based on the hypothesis that in prehistoric times and in today's primitive cultures a newborn infant was usually carried by his mother in ways that forced him into extremely hard exercise several times a day for considerable periods.

Today's babies also have inborn reflexes that have their use: a newborn holds onto the hair or fingers of an adult with a stronger grip than he holds a rod of the same thickness, and a newborn lying on a warm human body crawls better than when lying on a hard table. Since a baby is equipped with these reflexes, it's only proper to stimulate them and not be afraid of doing something "against nature" or harming him. In fact, I contend that current methods of upbringing which do not use these reflexes are "against nature" because they deprive the baby of movement.

The motion exercises for your baby's first month are systematic, deliberate movements which every mother performs in everyday situations without any specific purpose. Their aim is to give your baby delicate tactile, positional, optical, and acoustic stimuli to help him establish contact with the world and get accustomed to moving. They teach your baby mainly to control the movements of his head. They enable parents to learn how to hold baby and not be afraid of handling him. They contribute to the baby's good mood and the creation of a mutually positive relationship between parents and baby.

Either parent can do these exercises three to five times a day for 3 to 5 minutes at a time—whenever the baby is awake, except just after or before feeding. Your arms should be bare because contact with the soft, smooth, and warm surface of an adult body is pleasant for your baby. Before exercising remember to wash your hands in warm water so you can touch your baby with clean, warm hands. The baby should be naked and lie on the table on a soft blanket (or foam rubber) that has been covered with a clean diaper. Be sure to exercise your baby only when he is calm and in a good mood.

And now some exercises to develop movement:

Exercise 1: Picking him up when he lies on his back. The baby lies on his back. Grasp the naked baby with your naked arms so that he lies on his back with his head in the crook of your right elbow. This is the best way to pick up your baby. Place him onto the table and then pick him up again, but this time so that his head rests in the crook of your left elbow. This laying down and picking up the baby, alternatively with his head right and left, is good exercise for him during his first month. Repeat 3 to 5 times to the left and right.

EXERCISE 2

Exercise 2: Picking him up in your arms when he lies on his side. This exercise is similar to the first, but after being picked up the baby should lie on his side with his face away from you and his back toward you.

EXERCISE 3

Exercise 3: Picking up baby when he lies on his tummy. This is again similar to the first exercise, but the baby should lie in your arms with his face down and his back up. The better the baby holds his head, the higher he should be over your forearm.

Exercises 1 to 3 can be varied as follows:

a. Move baby from the right to the left forearm without replacing him on the table in between;

b. Every time you pick him up take a few steps through the room—the rhythmic movements when you walk act as a stimulus;

c. Each time you pick him up, bend forward, sideways, or turn your body to the left and right several times;

d. You can combine all the above by taking some steps —then, while walking, bend forward, to the sides, and so forth.

Exercise 4: Sitting baby up on your forearm, facing you. Pick up baby and seat him on your bent horizontal forearm so his knees touch you and his chest leans against yours. Now he is lying against you, looking over your shoulder and there is hardly any strain on his spine. Place your left hand against his shoulder blades and gently press him toward you. If his head is unsteady, bring your left hand up higher and support his head with your thumb and forefinger. Put him back onto the table after about 3 to 5 seconds, pick him up again, seat him on your left forearm and hold your right hand against his back. Repeat 3 to 5 times.

EXERCISE 5

Exercise 5: Seat him on your forearm with his back toward you. Pick him up and seat him on your bent right forearm with his back toward you. Baby should be sitting more in the palm of your right hand. Place your left hand onto his chest and press him toward you. You should bend back slightly so he lies against you, rather than sits. After 3 to 5 seconds place him back onto the table, pick him up again and seat him onto your left forearm and hold him with your right hand. Repeat 3 to 5 times.

Exercises 4 and 5 can be varied much like Exercises 1 to 3 (see combinations a–d). Other suitable variations:

e. When baby fixes his eyes onto an obvious object (window, lamp, clock), slowly turn 45 to 60 degrees to the right and left and baby will sometimes actively turn his head to keep an interesting object within his field of vision;

f. You can try various combinations of Exercises 1 to 5 and place him into various positions in your arms in the lying and seated position.

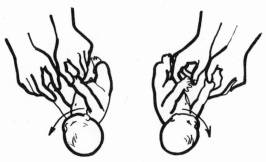

EXERCISE 6

Exercise 6: Turn his body while he is lying down by grasping his hands. Place baby onto his back with his feet toward you. Try to make him grasp both of your forefingers. If he cannot keep hold of you, grasp his hand in your thumb and forefinger and slowly turn his body to the left until his body turns about 45 degrees to the left and his head turns to the left by itself by 90 degrees. Then pull his left hand to the right, turn his trunk a little and his head will turn to the right by 90 degrees. Repeat on both sides 5 to 6 times.

EXERCISE 7

Exercise 7: Lying on the tummy and trying to crawl. Sit in an armchair and bend your body as far backward as you can so you are lying more than sitting. You can assume the same position on the couch, but support yourself with cushions. Then place baby onto your chest and stomach face down so that he presses against your lap. His arms should be bent with his fists below the shoulders, elbows by his sides. He will soon start lifting his head and will push away with his legs as if wanting to crawl. If he holds his head motionlessly to one side, push his face down; he will then lift his head and usually hold it up for a few moments, then lay it down sideways again. Baby will be more active if you place him onto your own warm naked body. Keep him in this position for 1 to 3 minutes.

EXERCISE 8

Exercise 8: Kicking. Lay him down on his back on the table with his legs toward you, touching your stomach. If you bend over him slightly to facilitate contact, baby will soon start moving his legs and alternately touch your stomach. You can persuade him to flex his legs by touching his soles and toes with your thumb. If you press gently he will alternately stretch and bend his legs.

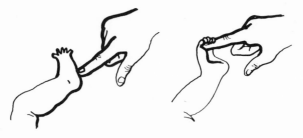

EXERCISE 9

Exercise 9: Spreading and bending his toes. Stroke his sole with your forefinger near the heel; baby will spread his toes. If you touch his soles near the toes he will bend them. If you place a match across the lower part of the spread toes he will grasp it. Spread and bend his toes on each foot 4 to 6 times.

How to Train Hand Movements in the First Month

During his first month your baby usually lies with his arms bent and his hands clenched because the tension of the bending muscles is stronger than that of the stretching muscles. The training of hand movements in the first month is meant to:

  Loosen the fist
  Stimulate movement of the entire arm
  Stimulate the grasping reflex

Exercise 10: Opening the fist. Gently stroke baby's fist on both sides; after a while he will usually open his fist. Your lips and cheeks are a very soft means of stroking; unless you're ill, use these methods—it's pleasant for both you and your baby. The loosening of the fist is important because baby can only grasp with his open hand. Stroking and gentle massage will persuade him to open his fist sooner than if you wait for him to open it himself. Loosening the tension of the bending muscles also stretches the arm.

Exercise 11: Creating the grasping reflex. If you have managed to open his fist by stroking it place your finger into his hand and he will grasp it. The purpose in this case is not for him to hold onto your finger for some time but to alternately open and close his fist; therefore gently release yourself, again stroke him to persuade him to open his fist, and again place your finger into his open hand. Train the opening and closing of the fist with both left and right hands.

Exercise 12: Arm movements. Place baby in front of you and gently stroke his chest, tummy, and arms. He will often lift his arms and start moving them. You can increase the stimulus by softly, gently talking to him and smiling at him.

You should smile and gently talk to him not only during each exercise but during every contact with him. This is the most effective means of establishing social contact with your baby. At the beginning of his second month he will usually show that you have established contact by smiling back at you.

Psychological Development During the Second and Third Month

The tables in this book that show what children should have achieved at a certain stage of development represent only a brief, overall survey and should not be too literally applied to your own baby. But by the end of the third month you'll find that your baby has learned to control some movements and to use his sensory organs better. He smiles to show he can clearly distinguish a person from other objects of the outside world. His first deliberate movement of the hand toward a toy indicates that he wants to acquire the object and get to know it better.

In his second month he will stretch his bent arms and open his fist more frequently. When he sees a bright object nearby he shows his excitement by waving his arms and will sometimes chance to touch the object. If he touches the object with his open hand he will grasp it. If you give him the opportunity to grasp objects frequently by coincidence, then by the end of the third month his arm movements will lose their arbitrary character and his intention of connecting his hand with the observed object will become ever more apparent. At the same time you will notice another interesting phenomenon: your baby will begin to discover his hands, that one hand grasps the other, the hands meet, grasp each other, feel; baby is playing with his hands. This is not only an interesting but also very important step in development, because at this stage the hands become both actors and objects. They are active and passive at the same time. They manipulate and are manipulated. They feel and are felt.

Soon after discovering one hand with his other hand he will discover his hand with his eyes which is just as important as the previous stage. Both discoveries are the first stage of baby's discovery of himself: he finds out that the object and the hand are two completely different things. The object moves when he acts on it with his hands, but his hand moves by itself, whenever he wants it to; therefore he can act directly on his hand but only indirectly on an object by means of his hand.

After your baby has discovered his hand with his eyes at the end of the third or beginning of the fourth month, the development of the hand seems to jump ahead. He quickly learns to guide the hand to an object he sees and to grasp it. Just as the baby learns to reach out for the objects he sees, his strong grasping reflex weakens. By the end of the third month the grasp weakens to such an extent that he cannot hold on even when you pull his hands to the sitting position or turn him around when he is lying down.

Up to the end of his first month an infant usually learns to concentrate his eyes onto an object and follow its movement as long as it is slow and not too great. By the third month a sharp picture is formed on the retina. He also learns to follow an object moving faster in all directions, left and right, up and down.

In the first month the infant learns to concentrate on a sound; in the second month he starts looking for its source with his eyes and turns in all directions; in the third month he can find the source with certainty, because he turns his head with assurance in the direction of the sound's source. He will become calmer or start smiling when he hears familiar voices and he can recognize his mother's voice; from his mimicry you can tell that he likes singing. The first reactions to human speech also appear and he begins to hum reactively (he hums in reply to human speech).

An important source of his information about the world is touch. He begins to discover objects with his hands by happening to touch them. When you do exercises with him he will respond with a smile and cooperate in what is obviously enjoyment of movement and changes in position.

During the second and third months your baby also begins to develop activities which can be considered to be the start of playing. He satisfies his urge to be active and at the same time develops in some way.

Play is an expression of so-called "self-development activities." In the second month it's the observation of various objects, following their movements with the eyes; in the third month it's touching toys with the hand, grasping them, playing with the hands. Baby also plays with his vocal organs and starts to hum in the third month. Even the simple waving of the hands and kicking constitute play, because he learns to use his arms and hands through this self-developing activity.

How many of these activities your baby can do depends to a great extent on the conditions in which he lives. When things happen around him and he is surrounded by objects, he has more opportunity to be active than when only little happens and he has no chance to respond. "Self-development" does not mean a vacuum; he can develop only on something and with something. Your job is to supply him with these things.

How to Train Head Movements

Objective: By the end of the third month your baby is ready to control the movements of his head voluntarily. When lying on his tummy or when vertical he ought to be able to hold it up firmly for some time. In all other positions (on his back or tummy or when held in a sitting position and on the forearm, for example), he ought to be able to turn his head and follow the movements of an object in all directions and at higher speed than before. All exercises previously described for the control of the head movements of newborn infants are also suitable for the second and third month.

A combination of the exercises below are especially suitable.

EXERCISE 13

Exercise 13: Following a toy with the eyes and head. Place your baby on his back with his feet toward you. Show him a bright toy or another attractive object and move it in front of him about 16 inches from the eyes so that he can follow it with his eyes from left to right and vice versa. If he is used to lying with his head on the left, turn his head to the center and then gradually persuade him to turn his head to the right. By the end of the third month your baby ought to be able to turn his head to both sides from any position.

Exercise 14: Maintaining the head position when nursed. Exercises 1 to 5 for newborns can be made more challenging by giving the head less support when nursing him in your arms so he will hold it more independently. When holding baby on his side (or especially on his tummy) make his head overlap your forearm to a greater degree so that by the third month it hangs right over it. In the sitting position hold your supporting hand lower: that is, not under the neck but at halfway toward the shoulder blades. If you bend forward with baby in your arms or if you turn your body to left and right perform these actions to an ever-increasing range and faster, and

despite this baby will keep his head in position during
these motions.

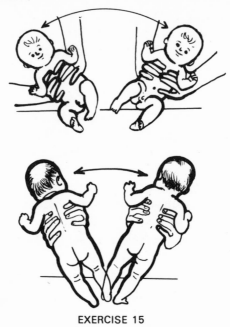

EXERCISE 15

Exercise 15: Bends in the seated and upright positions.
For this exercise you must learn the basic grip properly,
because you will also need it for further exercises. This
means picking up your baby under the armpits. Your
fingers and palms create a wide belt around his chest
which will enable you to grasp him so that the pressure
on the chest is minimum and he can breathe easily. In
this grip your palms meet at the wrist just by the baby's
breastbone. His chest lies against your palms, your
fingers slightly closed aim backward and your thumbs
should point toward his chin. If you grasp your baby like
this and lift him into the horizontal position he will lie in
your palms as in a dish. Now you can open your fingers
around his back without him falling. The father's hands
are most suitable for this grasp. Some mothers' hands

are too small and could not embrace the baby's entire trunk and would have to press his armpits and sides; their thumbs would grip his shoulders and they would have to sink their fingers deep into his back. The child is likely to laugh when doing this exercise with father, but may cry with his mother.

Grip your baby as I've described and almost seat him on the table in front of you (in fact, you are holding the weight of his body in your hands). Tilt him first to the left, then to the right. The tilt should be deep so long as the baby can hold his head like an extention of his trunk. At the end of the second month do the same exercise with the baby held upright. You are holding his weight in your hands. Tilt the entire body to the right and left as far as you can with the baby keeping his head straight. Repeat toward both sides 5 to 6 times.

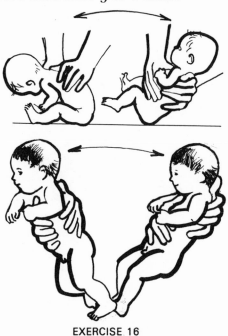

EXERCISE 16

Exercise 16: Bending forward and backward, seated and upright. Again form your hands into a wide belt, but place your left palm against baby's back and your right against his chest. Cross both thumbs under his ⁂ght armpit; the tips of your other fingers should meet under his left armpit. "Seat" the baby almost on the table and bend him a long way forward and (less) backward. At the end of the second month lift baby by the same method till he is upright so that he slightly touches the ground with his feet. Again tilt him a long way forward and less far backward. It is easier for him to hold his head upright when bent forward than backward. Remember to tilt him forward or backward only as far as he can keep his head straight. Repeat this exercise 5 to 6 times backward and forward.

EXERCISE 17

Exercise 17: Lifting the head while lying on the tummy. Lay the baby onto his tummy and arrange his arms so they are bent and pressed against his chest, or slightly under the chest. In their second month babies usually begin to lift their heads slightly. If he lies with his head turned slightly to the side, turn it face down and the baby will lift his head. Let him lie on his tummy for at least 2 to 3 minutes; if he is satisfied he can stay like that even longer. Even if you have to persuade him to lift his head by gently turning his nose toward the floor, repeat this exercise 5 to 6 times. If he does not lift his head even when you turn his nose to the floor, you can help him by:

Placing your hand under his chest (palms against his chest) and lifting his chest by about 2 to 3 inches, so his head cannot touch the ground. He will then lift his head for at least a while.

Placing your baby onto a folded blanket or fairly hard pillow so the upper part of his body is in the air and he cannot place his head on the ground. The folded blanket replaces your hand.

Placing your baby on the edge of a couch so his head reaches over the edge. He will not let his head lie passively over the edge but will lift it with his neck and back muscles. To be safe, hold onto his legs.

Once he lifts his head, place him onto his tummy often, especially when you bathe him.

In all the exercises for activating your baby to lift his head when lying on his tummy, it's best to help him slightly by pressing gently on his bottom with one hand and stroking his back from neck to hips and back.

And finally, remember one very important principle. If your baby is to lift his head, this must have some purpose for him. The baby will not lift his head for nothing. He wants to see something interesting! Entice him with something interesting and let the sight reward his movement.

If he is on his tummy on the table, kneel in front of him so your head is as high as his; then call him to make him look at you.

Always put the baby down so he is looking toward the center of the room where something interesting may happen; if all he sees is a corner or a monotonous wall he will soon lay his head down again. If he is on his tummy remove all obstacles to his vision. If you place a toy in front of him to persuade him to look at it, don't forget that he won't keep looking at one thing for too long.

Exercise 18: Turning the head when lying on the tummy. Place baby onto his tummy as in Exercise 17.

a. From a distance of 18 inches to 1 yard move a toy or your head from left to right fast enough and at such an angle that he can still follow you with his eyes and head.

b. Move the toy or your head up and down so the baby lifts and lowers his head.

c. Turn the toy or your head in a circle, clockwise and counterclockwise, to make him perform more complicated head movements.

Try Exercise 18a first; it's the easiest for the second month. Exercises 18b and 18c are more suitable for the third month.

Exercise 19: Moving the head when baby is carried in various positions. Pick up the baby and hold him upright but with his back up and his head above your forearm. You are holding the baby lying against your stomach and he is able to look around better. Walk through the house, garden, or park with him in this position. He will observe his surroundings with interest, keep his head lifted, and look at interesting sights in all directions. Holding baby in this position activates him; on his back the same position makes him fall asleep!

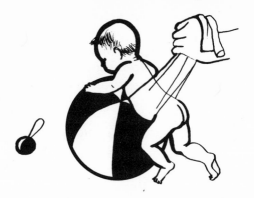

EXERCISE 20

Exercise 20: Lifting the head when lying on a ball. Lift baby under the armpits with his back toward you and place his chest (not tummy) onto a light inflatable ball about 8 to 10 inches in diameter so his legs bear against the floor. The baby will lift his head high and look around. Move him backward and forward on the ball, tilt him to the right and left; he will adapt his body to the changes of position and keep his head lifted. He will kick his legs energetically. This exercise benefits the entire body. The movements are all the more lively if you place a bright toy in front of him. Make sure he lies on his chest. If he lies on the ball with his tummy he might become sick or wet himself.

Movements of the Arms and Hands

The objective: At the beginning of the third month the movements of the arms and hands are still reflexive, but by the end of the third month they begin to become deliberate movements controlled by willpower. By the end of the third month (or beginning of the fourth), your baby starts to clasp his hands and then observe his hands in motion. The clasp gradually weakens, but the strength of his arm support will increase; during the second month baby ought to learn to straighten his arms when lying on his tummy and lean on his elbow, and in the third month to lean on his straightened arms.

How to Train Him to Guide His Hand Toward an Object and Deliberately Grasp It

Show him (and place within his reach) various bright objects to stimulate the so-called excitation complex, which is expressed with lively movements of the entire body, mainly the arms. This leads to the accidental guiding of one or both hands to an object, touching and sometimes even grasping it. The more you stimulate these incidental touches and grasps, the faster these movements lose the character of chance and gradually become deliberate and conscious.

Exercise 21: Grasp when the object is placed in the hand. Enrich the exercise described for the newborn by placing into baby's hand not only your own finger, but other suitable objects: the handle of a rattle, a piece of string, a rubber hose, or a piece of nylon or paper. Place the objects alternately into the right and left hands. Place the objects into baby's hands so they're easy to grasp. Train grasping and releasing, not long holding of objects.

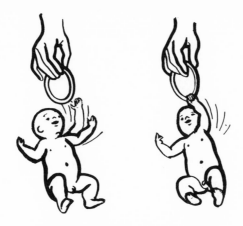

EXERCISE 22

Exercise 22: Placing objects within range of the hand movement. When, in the second month, baby opens his hands more often, or when he unclenches his fist after being touched with some object, do not place the object directly into his hand. Hold it so his spontaneously moving arm "happens" to touch it and after touching grasps it.

Exercise 23: Active grasping and passive arm movements. Offer baby your forefingers. When he grasps them move his arms in various directions: forward, upward, to the sides. During these movements baby should hold you himself.

EXERCISE 24

Exercise 24: Bringing the hand to a large object. Suspend a large, bright, inflatable ball (8 to 10 inches in
diameter) on a string about 4 to 6 inches above his chest.
He should lie on his back. In the second and third
months he will knock against it with his hands, but toward the end of the third month he will bring his open
hand slowly toward the ball and touch it. Other inflatable
toys (e.g., a swimming belt or animal) serve the same
purpose. The advantage of these toys is that the probability of his touching them is greater than when the toys
are smaller.

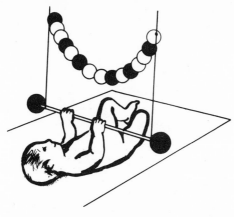

EXERCISE 25

Exercise 25: Incidental touches and grasping of a trapeze. Suspend a rod, about 1/2 inch in diameter and 16 inches long, on two pieces of string about 6 inches above baby's chest, parallel to his shoulders. Cover both ends of the rod with rubber balloons or with cotton wool and cloth. When he moves his arms around he should "happen" to touch the trapeze and will often grasp and hold on to it. He will soon start shoving it around in various ways. If you tie onto the strings holding the trapeze another piece of string with various colored objects the baby will shake the trapeze all the more because this will swing the objects and create a noise.

EXERCISE 26

Exercise 26: Bringing the hand to a smaller object and grasping. Suspend a cord with large balls, rings, cubes, discs, small vessels, rattles, and similar objects about 6 inches crosswise above baby's chest. As he waves his arms he will touch and grasp them, but by the end of the third month he will deliberately begin to reach out for them. The advantage of these horizontally suspended objects is that baby will often touch them and they will not rebound like toys suspended vertically. Give him the opportunity to grasp objects of various types—round and square, hard and soft, full and hollow.

To use grasping as the preparation for suspension, give the baby the opportunity to grasp something and carry a part of his weight. Although the grasp weakens during the second and third months these exercises do have a purpose, because the weakening of the grasp is not the result of weaker muscles but can be accelerated the more his muscles are employed during this period. I want to stress again that the main purpose of this movement training is not the strengthening of muscles, it is only one important means for developing your baby's entire personality.

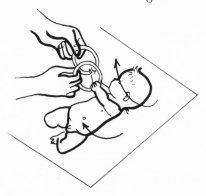

EXERCISE 27

Exercise 27: Turning to the side with the aid of rings. Place baby on his back in front of you. Put a ring (e.g., made of celluloid from an old rattle, a rubber ring, and the like) into his hands. Your forefinger will also do. As soon as he grasps it pull the ring in your right hand so as to turn him onto his left side and then pull the ring in your left hand and turn him to the right. Turn baby onto each side 5 to 6 times.

EXERCISE 28

Exercise 28: Pulling to a sitting position with the aid of rings. Begin the same as in 27: place either a ring or your forefinger into baby's hands. When he has grasped it slowly pull him into a sitting position. Pull the ring with one hand and keep your second behind his head to protect it if he lets go. If he is holding onto your fingers you will feel if the grasp is weakening and you can quickly hold his hands with your thumb and forefinger of one hand. This exercise is suitable for babies at the end of their third month. The baby must exert the strongest grasp at the beginning of the exercise, before reaching a half seated position. You can make it easier for him at the beginning by sitting down with him on the floor and placing him on your bent thighs so he is in a slightly elevated position from which he can easily sit up. The stronger his grasp the less you should lift your knees from the floor, and his position should become gradually more horizontal.

To do strengthening push-ups of the arms, the basic position is on the tummy, and will be described below. If you frequently place baby onto his tummy this stimulates him to do more frequent arm push-ups and straighten them more. By the end of their third month most babies are already "graze horses," i.e., supporting themselves on their arms, and their chest no longer touches the ground. At the end of the third month place some toys in front of baby: he will start to reach out for them with one hand and will have to exert greater strength on the other to hold up the weight of his upper body. The push-ups are easy if he is lying on an inclined surface with his head upward; they're harder if he is lying with his head downward.

Body Exercises

The objective: By the end of the third month your baby should be able to "graze horses" and deliberately turn from the position on his back to his side, i.e., he ought to have learned to control the movements of the upper part of his body.

EXERCISE 29

Exercise 29: Lying on the tummy. The position on the tummy is important, both as a position and an exercise to which baby should get used from his first days of life. Frequent placing him onto his tummy (a) keeps him in an active state—it's an activating position; (b) offers excellent preparation for correct body posture (this position strengthens the back and neck muscles which are weak in humans and every weakening of the body is seen most in the weakening of these muscles: a sick, tired, sad, old person has sagging head and shoulders); (c) is the initial phase of orientation: lying on his tummy the baby sees more interesting things than when he is on his back. You should start as soon as possible to place him onto his tummy and to keep him there as long as you can. He can even sleep in this position. There is less danger of his suffocating than when he lies on his back: vomit can freely run out of his mouth when he is on his tummy; when he lies on his back it can get into his lungs. Some authors say a baby should lie only on his tummy, but this is too extreme; I think he should be on his tummy as often as possible, but a baby likes to change positions, so help him to lie on his back and side, too.

EXERCISE 30

Exercise 30: Lifting from the side. Baby should be on his back with his legs toward you. Place your left hand under his heels and grasp his right foot by the instep with your thumb and forefinger and his left foot with your forefinger and middle finger (your forefinger is between both insteps). Place the fingers of your right hand under his left shoulder blade and turn 90 degrees to the left onto his side. He should end up lying in the palm of your right hand on his left side. Then lift him up to a height of 4 to 8 inches, hold him in the horizontal position for about 2 to 3 seconds and lay him down again. When you lift him he will keep his head in the horizontal position. Then change your hold: hold him by the feet with your right hand, place your left one under his right shoulder blade, turn him 90 degrees onto his right side and again lift him to the horizontal position. This exercise is suitable for children between 2 to 6 months. For a baby 4 months old you can make this exercise more difficult by placing the hand supporting the chest closer to his side; baby must then control a larger part of his body. Repeat this exercise toward both sides 3 to 5 times.

Exercise 31: Lifting from the tummy position. This exercise is similar to Exercise 30. The difference is in that you turn baby over from his back onto his tummy so he lies in your hand with his tummy and face down. When you lift him up into the air in this position he will arch his back and lift his head more as he grows older and the more you exercise him. This is a very effective straightening exercise which strengthens back and neck muscles. Younger babies hold their hands in front of them in this position; older babies lift them up and stretch them out in front. Repeat this exercise 3 to 5 times on each side, by rolling him over onto his right and left side.

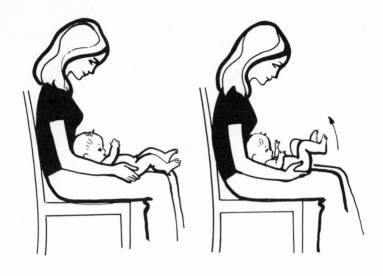

EXERCISE 32

Exercise 32: Lifting the legs. Form your hands into a cup as if for drinking out of a tap. Seat baby onto your hands so his back rests against your arms, his head in your inner elbow. Move your hands to move baby's hips so that he lifts and drops his legs. You feel that baby is taking part in this exercise when he pulls his legs toward his tummy. This exercise strengthens his tummy muscles and should be performed 10 to 15 times. It is suitable for the second to third months.

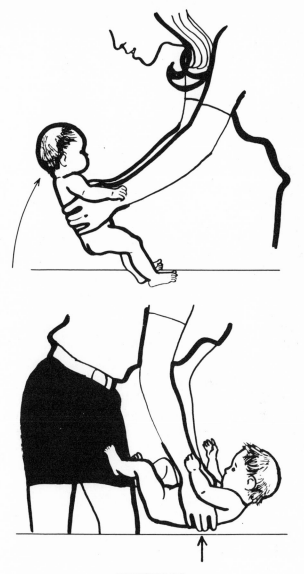

EXERCISE 33

Exercise 33: Lifting to the vertical position and placing on the back. I have stressed that whenever you lift baby up this should be a good exercise for strengthening his trunk muscles. When you lift baby lying on his back by picking him up under the arms and lifting him to the vertical position with his head up you strain his stomach, chest, and neck muscles, which you can see for yourself if you look at his naked stomach, chest, and neck. Because a 2-month-old baby cannot exert the necessary muscular tension in this position, and his head would fall back, his legs would dangle loosely. So you should lift your baby into this position differently in his second, third, and fourth months. In the second month, pick him up under the armpits, lift the upper part of his body 45 degrees while leaving his legs on the ground. You may often have to support the back of his head with your forefingers. This tilted position makes it easier for his stomach, chest, and neck muscles to hold his legs and head, than when horizontal. Then lift him higher until his legs clear the ground and turn him to the vertical position. Place him back to his original position by tilting him in the air 45 degrees, then placing his legs onto the ground and then tilt him the remaining 45 degrees till he is on his back.

Babies 3 to 4 months old can be lifted into the air in the horizontal position. When they are about 4 inches above the floor they should be turned upright. When replacing him onto his back, first tilt him 90 degrees to the horizontal position, then lay him down. Start using this way of lifting and laying him down when baby can keep his head and legs in the horizontal position for at least 1 second as you lift him under the arms after laying on his back. Lift up and lay down 3 to 4 times.

EXERCISE 34

Exercise 34: Turning over to the side and onto the tummy. Place baby onto his back with his legs toward you. Take one leg into each hand. Cross his legs, e.g., right over left, and pull the left leg until baby rolls over onto his left side and onto his tummy. If you cross his legs faster he will turn more easily without any exertion; when you turn him over slower he must strain more and cooperate more. As soon as he can do this exercise, just turn him onto his side and he will complete the roll by himself. When you roll baby back onto his back over his left shoulder, press his stretched left arm to his body and press your right hand onto his right shoulder to turn him over. Be careful not to injure his left arm or shoulder. Roll baby over to the right and left 4 to 6 times.

Leg Exercises

The objective: To stimulate leg stretching, pushing, and kicking. The leg stretch will gradually become weaker but these exercises are the forerunners of deliberate leg movements.

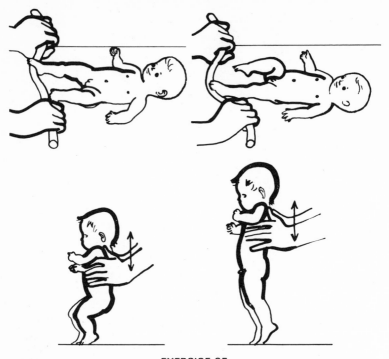

EXERCISE 35

Exercise 35: Leg push-ups. Place the palms of your hands, a cooking ladle, rubber hose, book, or any other similar object against baby's feet while he lies on his back. He will soon begin to rhythmically stretch his legs and bend them again. Press against his feet with sufficient force to make him use medium force to push your hand away. Do this for 20 to 30 seconds. You can also perform this exercise by holding him in the vertical position under the armpits above the ground and let him "hop" in this position. You must carry his weight in your hands and baby's feet should only touch the floor, not stand on it. This way of exercising should not last longer than 10 to 15 seconds.

EXERCISE 36

Exercise 36: Pushing with the legs. Place baby either onto his back or tummy and place the feet of his bent legs into the palm of your hand; when he pushes, do not give way and he will move away from your hand along his back or tummy. The push works when the leg is slightly bent; he will usually not be able to push himself off if his leg is bent too much. Pushing along on the tummy is not suitable too soon after feeding. Try this for 30 to 40 seconds.

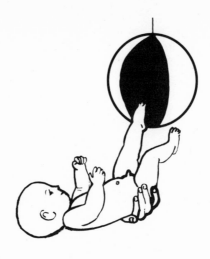

EXERCISE 37

Exercise 37: Kicking a ball. Place baby onto his back. Place the palm of your hand under his bottom and slightly lift his hips so he lifts his legs with his heels off the ground. In your second hand hold a bright inflatable ball (diameter: 8 to 10 inches) on a piece of string. Move the ball so it touches baby's naked lifted legs; this contact will soon stimulate the stretching and bending of the legs —kicking the ball. Kicking the ball is repeated in rhythmical intervals. Do for 1 to 1 1/2 minutes.

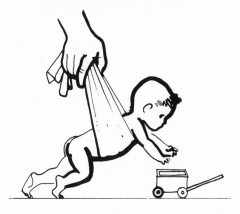

EXERCISE 38

Exercise 38: Push-ups and pushing when suspended. Fold a diaper to make a strip 4 to 5 inches wide. Place baby onto the strip on his tummy with his chest in the center of the strip; join both ends of the strip and hold them in one hand just above baby's back. Lift him about 4 inches above the floor; he will assume a crawling position and will really try and stretch and kick with his legs as if crawling. Try for about 30 to 40 seconds.

Developing Sensory Perception

Eyesight

Objective: By the end of his third month your baby can learn to follow a moving object with his eyes and work out the beginning of coordination between sight and hand movements.

Exercises with which baby at 2 to 3 months learns to follow various moving objects with his eyes have been described earlier in this chapter in the section on head exercises. Here I want to add some instructions which we have found helpful.

You'll best attract his attention with colored, bright, shiny objects which move slightly, differ in various ways, or appear and disappear rhythmically.

Baby is most interested in objects he can influence himself.

Teach baby to follow moving objects with his eyes by increasing the speed of the moving object and the range of the movement. First, baby will turn his head 60 degrees, later 180 degrees. Also, make the head movements more difficult. It's easier to turn the head from side to side than to lift it up and down. It's harder still to use his head to follow movements of an object going round in circles or performing complicated curves.

Teach him to fix and follow objects from various positions: on his back or tummy or upright.

Teach him to fix and follow objects when he himself is in motion—as when you carry him around; If he's in motion it's easier for him to watch stationary objects, harder when they, too, move, especially when they move in an opposite direction, as when you carry him to the right and the object moves to the left.

Try to make sure that the baby always has enough opportunity to watch something interesting. Place interesting objects around the room and place him on his tummy in a position where he can see something. Do not get into his range of vision. Remember: no object is of constant interest.

Eyesight cannot be developed alone, but only in close relationship with other senses, so make sure that baby not only sees, but also hears, feels, tastes, and so on. He should get to know that the rattle he sees gives out a certain sound, that the milk bottle stimulates taste sensations and similar reinforcements.

The most interesting and most important object is the human being. He acts on all the baby's senses. Baby should therefore be in frequent contact with people.

Exercises that create the basis for the coordination of sight and hand movements have been described in the exercises for the development of movement: 21, 22, 23, 24, 25, and 26.

Hearing

Objective: By his third month the baby ought to learn to listen—to calm down when he hears new sounds. Apart from that by the end of the first 3 months he ought to have worked out some coordination of hearing, sight, and movements of the head; he should learn to seek and find the sources of interesting sounds with his sight.

Help your baby to take 3 steps:

1. He must learn the connection between what he sees and hears simultaneously; he must find out that what he sees is also the source of sound. He will learn this in the first and second months.

2. He must learn that when he hears an interesting sound he should also see the object which emits it.

3. He must learn that when he hears an interesting sound, the object that makes the sound is where the sound comes from.

Here's how you can help baby take Steps 2 and 3.

Exercise 39: Turning the head toward a sound which is at the edge of his field of vision. Shake a rattle or other audible toy and hold it so it is at the edge of his field of vision. He will soon start to turn his eyes or even his head and fix the object (second month). Instead of a toy he can just as well seek your face if you call him from the edge of his field of vision. Later you can place the object or your face slightly outside his field of vision and then further away. The main principle is: the object must remain in the spot where the sound originated.

EXERCISE 40

Exercise 40: Hide-and-seek. From teaching the turning of the head toward the source of sound you can also form a simple social reaction. Place your baby onto his back;

call him from the right side and try to attract his attention with movements of your head and hands. At first baby will turn his head here and there. When he finds you, smile at him, talk to him. After a while hide again and call him, this time from the left. By the end of the third month he should turn his head in the right direction at the first call.

Feeling (e.g., Kinesthetic Perception, Taste)

Most of the games mentioned in Exercises 13 to 40 afford rich touching and kinesthetic stimuli. During these exercises you pick up and hold baby in various ways by various parts of his body. Always remember to pick him up gently and sensitively, so as not to cause him unpleasant sensations. When you do these exercises, change his positions often. Remember, you should move him slowly. Fast movements are unpleasant for a 2-month-old, but you can gradually speed up the movements. He will protest if you touch his naked body with cold hands or if you place him naked on a cold nylon or rubber sheet. At the same time you'll want to train him to become hardy by wiping him with a sponge dipped into cooler and then still cooler water after his bath. And his taste and smell senses are developed by sensible feeding and lots of fresh air.

The Development of Play

Objective: During the second month your baby should fix onto objects with his eyes and by the end of the third month also with his hands, thereby laying the foundations for manipulative play. In the third month he will also start playing with his vocal organs—by humming.

Your baby will hum when he is in a good mood. It's a direct sign of a baby's good and satisfied state. This is especially true at the beginning of humming. So the first rule is: if you want him to start humming, see to it that he is in good physical shape and in a good mood. Humming is a sign of activeness. Children who are inactive or exert only little self-development activity hum only a little.

If you want your baby to hum, stimulate him and activate him all round. If you want the humming to develop, it must, like every other activity, be rewarded. So for baby to continue humming and to perfect it, he must hear himself, and the humming must be rewarded by people who either reply with speech or humming.

As I've said, a baby will hum all the more if his humming is rewarded at once by a vocal reply of the parent, and less when his humming and the vocal reaction do not tie into each other. This immediate tie-in of your reaction to his humming leads baby not only to humming more; it becomes social contact. By the end of the third month you can sometimes achieve a direct reply by humming or another vocal reaction. Then you reply again and in this way you can start "talking" to him. This is no longer mere playing with the vocal organs. It's also playing with another person—the beginning of social play.

The Development of Emotions

It used to be assumed that emotions were conditioned by heredity; that loving children was natural; and that the love of children for their parents was natural as well. But observation and research showed that the development of emotions depends more on the environment and that they are just as flexible as other psychological phenomena. Experiments with children show that love, hate, or revulsion are all subject to stimulation and that emotional attitudes are shaped from a baby's earliest days.

My objective: To create a good mood in a baby and maintain that mood during his entire period of wakefulness. Your contact with the baby should involve pleasant stimuli. In the second month these will produce his first smile and in the third month frequent smiles or laughter whenever he is in contact with you or other people.

How to Stimulate and Maintain a Baby's Good Mood

Foremost, naturally, are your baby's basic biological needs. See to it that he is healthy, fed but not overfed, has enough sleep, and that his environment is sufficiently warm and without disturbing stimuli.

As I've said, your baby should not be limited in his freedom of movement and expression. Babies protest by crying when their movements are hampered by unsuitable diapers and clothing, against being too long in one position (constant lying on the back) or staying too long in the same place, such as the crib. Try to eliminate these unnecessary causes of dissatisfaction and see that the baby's room is warm enough so he can spend as much time as possible naked and with plenty of space for free movement.

Your baby needs many stimuli to make him active; don't let him get bored and express his boredom by gazing emptily at one spot or moving his head the same way over and over again. A baby wants to look at something, hear something, do something himself. He needs frequent changes.

Reward his good mood by arranging frequent contacts with an adult who can play with him constructively.

How can you create a good emotional relationship between a baby and situations, things, people? Let me mention a well-known psychological experiment. A 1-year-old baby had a small bunny which it cuddled and stroked. During the experiment a bell rang every time the baby touched the bunny. The noise frightened him. Soon the baby learned to be afraid of the bunny and began to cry even when he saw it. Later, the baby was shown the bunny from a distance. At the same time he got a piece of chocolate. Gradually it was possible to show the bunny to the baby from closer up and he was no longer afraid of it. After a time of systematic rewarding, the baby started stroking the bunny again.

I urge you not to repeat this experiment because it is much too drastic a way to establish an emotional relationship; I only mentioned it to show that a baby's emotional attitudes to objects can be created and altered.

It's important that a baby maintain positive feelings about such acts of basic care as feeding, changing diapers, bathing, or being put to sleep. Parents often cause trouble because they connect care with unpleasant stimuli. The most frequent mistake is to disrupt a baby's relationship to feeding by serving his food too hot or with a nipple that has too large a hole and causes him to choke; or serving food too fast and not allowing him sufficient time to swallow; serving pieces that are too large; holding him too tight when feeding; being nervous yourself; or sudden changes in diet.

The disruption of the baby's relationship to his food can go so far that he may start crying as soon as he sees preparations for feeding. You can create a similar resistance to bathing by using water that is either too hot or too cold, getting soap in his eyes or drying him too roughly.

If you want your baby to accept certain procedures, situations, persons, or objects with a positive emotional attitude, it's wise to combine them with pleasant stimuli.

Good care and love from the mother and father of course create a positive emotional relationship between your baby and other people. By his sixth week your baby will start to react to you with a smile and with gradually increasing expressions of attachment, empathy, and joy. You can also create positive emotional attitudes toward situations by, say, leaving him naked while you change his diapers, or doing some exercises and playing with him. Soon he will start smiling when he senses that he is about to have his diapers changed.

In their second month some infants behave as if they know that they can make their mother cuddle them if they cry; this simple conditioned reflex originated when the mother cuddled the baby every time it cried, thereby rewarding the baby's crying and causing the baby to cry more. Learn to discern when your baby cries for some specific reason or when he only wants you to cuddle him. He'll soon stop crying for cuddling if you don't react to his crying.

How to Cultivate Habits

My objective: In the second and third months you can start to foster a baby's habit to be actively awake during the periods of wakefulness; to sleep calmly; and to take in food as regularly as possible. By the end of the third month your baby should learn to sleep about 9 to 10 hours every night, and four times during the day in intervals of 1 1/2 to 2 hours. In between he should be awake about five times for 1 to 1 1/2 hours. He should be fed five times during the day in 3-hour intervals, and during his second month twice a night, only once a night in his third month. Every baby has his individual need for sleep, wakefulness, and feeding; the standards given in this book are for the "average" child; many children will require adaptations according to individual needs.

Again I'd like to stress that I recommend a *compromise* system: a regular rhythm in the alternation of sleep and wakefulness and feeding, rather than the older methods, which laid down a timetable, insisted it be kept to the minute and ignored and disrupted the individual needs of the baby. The newer self-demand system proposes that the baby determine himself when he wants to eat, sleep, and be awake and that he should live according to his individual rhythm. Proponents of this theory admit that only a few mothers are able to correctly determine their baby's individual rhythm and that this system in the hands of less disciplined mothers often changes into an irregular system of wakefulness, sleep, and feeding.

The compromise system is based on working out the timetable according to the above standards and then adapting it slightly to the individual needs of your baby and keeping to it with occasional adaptations to the needs of the baby. If, for example, he wakes earlier or gets tired sooner than usual you put him to bed earlier than the timetable may advise.

Wakefulness and sleep are also influenced by exterior influences. Here's how:

Your baby will learn to sleep hard if he learns to be actively awake. If you keep him suitably busy when he is awake, he becomes pleasantly tired so when you put him to bed he falls asleep quickly and sleeps well.

But don't get the idea that the more active your baby is when awake, the harder he will sleep; activities which are too intensive before sleep lead to straining the excitation process, which makes the emergence of the sleep inhibition harder. The baby will then have trouble falling asleep, will sleep nervously and usually wake up earlier. The baby should "get it out of his system" in about the second quarter of the wakeful period. After that his activities should gradually be calmed down.

And don't think that your baby will sleep better the longer he is awake. Long periods of wakefulness again stimulate the excitation process and make the sleep inhibition harder to take effect. If the baby's wakeful period is too long he will again sleep badly, nervously, and wake up too soon. You need to be a good observer to tell when you should put your baby to bed. The wakeful period gradually gets longer, but this is a matter of development, so it's not a good idea to extend the wakeful period according to your own needs.

When awake, your baby should not be in the same place where he sleeps. The crib should only be the place for sleeping. From his third month he should spend his periods of wakefulness outside his crib: on the couch, in his playpen, and elsewhere.

Whenever possible, put your baby to bed in the same place (the bedroom at night, the yard during the day) and whenever possible under the same conditions. The sameness becomes a stimulus which facilitates the emergence of the sleep inhibition.

While your baby's sleep should not be unduly disturbed, he should also not get used to sleeping exclusively in total silence or only in the dark. And it's not advisable for him to fall asleep habitually under such special conditions as cuddling, rocking, singing, or in the presence of a particular person.

But, if possible, your baby should get used to sleeping in cool, clean air; this is the best way to induce sleep. Whenever possible, starting with his second month, he is best off sleeping outside during the day, even in winter, in the park or yard, or at least in front of an open window. Many Americans may disagree with me, but this is what my experience suggests.

In the first year of baby's life the daytime periods of wakefulness, sleep and feeding alternate regularly, and some authorities say that feeding should come after sleep; this, it is said, results in a rested and fed baby with all the requirements for active wakefulness and good sleep later. The second school asserts that a depression follows feeding so that it is better for baby to be put to bed after feeding. Our own research has shown that the second rule applies to more children. I therefore recommend what most mothers do: feed the baby and put him to bed, i.e., feed him at the end of the wakeful period.

Furniture and Toys for Babies in their Second and Third Month

A bassinette is best for your baby's stay during the day and night in his first 2 months. It does not take up too much space and you can move it into the kitchen, close to your bed at night, or wherever you are.

In the third and especially the fourth months the bassinette becomes too small for baby and even dangerous if he is very lively, so he needs a normal crib.

Get a sheet of foam rubber about 1 to 1 1/2 inches thick and sufficiently large. Lay it onto the table and cover it with a diaper or a sheet. The foam rubber is soft and warm and you cannot only change the baby on it but also play and exercise him. You can also put the foam-rubber sheet onto the couch and give him more room.

A bright inflatable plastic ball 8 to 10 inches in diameter, serves as a prop for exercise and play.

Make a wooden frame out of three strips and place it above baby so that both vertical strips are to the right and left of his shoulders and the cross strip is parallel to his shoulders, about 2 1/2 feet above him. In the first 2 months you can attach it to his basket; in the third to sixth months, place it where baby can play outside his bed, perhaps on the couch. How you suspend toys depends not only on how your home is furnished, but also on your inventiveness. After the sixth month you should remove this prop altogether; by that time he will be playing with toys lying on the ground. Also, suspending toys over babies who know how to turn over can be dangerous: it's possible for a baby to become dangerously entangled.

Suspend a trapeze from the frame with a bar 12 to 16 inches long. The trapeze should be about 6 inches above baby's chest and both ends of the bar should be covered with rubber balloons or cotton wool covered with a plastic sheet. Tie another piece of string with various toys and rattles onto the strings holding the trapeze about 1 6 inches away from baby's eyes; this will stimulate him to try livelier movements.

Toys for observation should be bright, shiny, reasonably large, and of various shapes. Suspend them about 16 to 30 inches above him or hold them in your hand and move them above the baby. Try a bright red apple, Christmas decorations, a ball of wool, a ball, flags, or flowers. Do not keep the same object above him for too long—the more often you change it, the greater his interest.

Toys for touching and grasping should be similar to those for observation, but they should be smaller so he can grasp them and they should be safe. For babies of

2 to 3 months they should be tied onto a string stretched horizontally about 6 inches above his chest. The items can include colored cubes, balls, cylinders, rings, buttons, ribbons, or a rubber hose.

7

Exercises for the Fourth to Sixth Months

In his second three months your baby will achieve greatest progress in the development of his movements. If you exercise him regularly and are devoted to his needs you'll probably find that the baby is already beginning to be different from other children who get less care and attention; your baby will be more mature in his behavior.

In his fourth month a baby has good control over his head movements: when lying on his back he not only lifts his head but can even lean it back and look upward. He can hold his head up and turn it to all sides in all positions. He can even master the most complicated head movements, i.e., when lying on his back he can lift his head, press his chin onto his chest, and look at his feet.

He also makes great progress with arm and hand movements. The ability to grasp and manipulate is important for the development of play and thought, and I'll describe it in connection with the development of these functions. Here I'm concerned with the general movements of arms and hands and the development of grasping strength of the hand and pushing strength of the arm.

As I've said, the strength of grasping gradually weakens up to the third month. But in the fourth month it again increases so that your baby will grasp hold of your proffered fingers and let himself be pulled into the sitting position. At first his arms will be stretched, but then he will start bending them and pulling his head forward. In the fifth month he will bend the arms a lot so that he will almost sit up by himself. In the sixth month he will pull himself up, not only into the sitting position but also to the standing position. The grasp of trained children in their sixth month is usually strong enough to hold them suspended for a moment or for them to stand on a ladder.

When 3-month-old babies lie on their tummies, they support themselves on their straightened arms, which are at first spread out and later vertical ("grazing horses"). In the fourth month, when the baby learns to reach out toward objects, he also tries it when lying on his tummy; he will bear the weight of his head and chest on one arm and reach out and manipulate with the other. He thereby strengthens his back and neck muscles so by the fifth month he can lie on his tummy and reach out for a toy with both hands and his back muscles will hold up his chest and head. By the end of the sixth month some babies learn to crawl and the main load is performed by the arms. At around this time a baby will also start to draw his knees under the tummy and reach a kneeling position in which the arms must exert a lot of energy.

The muscles of the trunk also become stronger in the second 3 months of your baby's life, and enable him to perform more complex movements. Priority should be given to the development of his back and neck muscles because they are so important for good posture. In the fifth month a baby can usually lie on his tummy, stretch out both arms and legs, lift his head high, and bend his back—play "airplane." This is a very good exercise for strengthening the back and neck muscles, not only for children but also for adults.

Stomach and chest muscles also gradually gain strength so in the fourth or fifth months a baby can catch hold of your fingers, lift his head and legs and almost pull himself into a sitting position. Do not allow your baby to sit too long at this age! Even if he can play airplane his back muscles are not yet strong enough, nor his spine developed enough, to enable him to sit straight.

In the third and fourth months a baby can turn from his back to his sides and onto his tummy, and in the fifth or sixth months he will be able to turn over onto his back by himself.

Babies learn to control leg movements last. There are two types of leg movements—general and delicate. In the fourth month he can probably kick a ball suspended above him (general movement). In the fifth month he will start to touch it gently, feel, and grasp it (delicate). In this period babies often play with a large ball suspended above them by holding it in their hands for some time, then with both legs, then with one hand and leg, and so forth. The strengthening stomach and thigh muscles gradually enable the 4-month-old baby to lift his legs and touch his knees with his hands, and in the fifth month to grasp his foot with his hands and stick it into his mouth.

A 5-month-old baby lying on his tummy can draw one leg under his tummy or at least bend it a lot. At 6 months he can draw both knees upward, usually by putting his head down and lifting his bottom up. If you offer your fingers to your 5- or 6-month-old, he can usually pull himself up into a sitting position or even stand up by pushing himself up with the legs. If you put a 4- to 6-month-old's chest on an inflatable ball he will push off with his legs very powerfully and almost jump forward.

In his fourth month you can place your baby into a jolly jumper, providing, of course, that his hip joints are in good shape. After a few tries (about a week) he will be jumping happily. In the seat he does not stand on his legs but only touches the floor lightly with his feet, enough to "jump" up with a small push. (He will not learn true jumping in the jumper, but will gradually learn to do so during his second year.)

At this age, movement is one of your baby's most basic biological and psychological needs. If you give him opportunity to perform lively movements he will cooperate very actively and will express his joy very obviously and vocally, so when he learns to use the jumper he will probably call out with joy.

The development of sensory perception enables a baby to orient himself better in his surroundings. This is facilitated by closer coordination between his individual senses. As I've mentioned, you can teach your baby to turn his eyes to the source of sound in his third and fourth months.

In the fourth and fifth months a baby will learn to reach out with certainty toward an object and to manipulate it. This develops coordination of sight, touch, and movement and is the basis for the perception of depth, the physical properties of objects, and many other characteristics such as shape, size, surface, or weight.

In his second 3 months the baby will begin to discern faces and their expressions; he will recognize you among other women and adopt a different expression when you smile or frown at him. From his behavior in his sixth month you can tell that he has learned to make subtle sound differentiations because he'll be able to tell your voice and will again have a different expression according to whether you are speaking kindly or scoldingly.

In the second 3 months the number of self-development activities increases and he will start to play more and in more varied ways.

In the third month baby moves his hands spontaneously and will clutch one hand with the other just as much by chance as he will grasp another object. At the beginning of the fourth month the grasping of the hands ceases to be accidental and becomes more deliberate. He will start to play with his hands for long periods—clasp them together, feel his individual fingers, entwine them, for example. By the end of the fourth month he will inspect his hands, clench and unclench them in front of his eyes and clasp them. This teaches him to control his hand movements by sight, which develops visual and motor coordination. He discovers his hands and learns to differentiate them from other objects.

He also begins to discover himself bit by bit, and a month later makes the acquaintance of his lower limbs. As I've said, he begins by touching his knees, then lifting up his legs and grasping them in his hands, feeling them and sticking his foot into his mouth, because at this stage the mouth is just as important an organ of cognition as sight or hearing.

Soon after he has discovered his hands, and his legs, he will carefully start touching objects with both his hands and feet—if they are often kept bare. First he touches them with his fingers, then his palms or foot. Every slowing down of movement at this age is a sign that your baby is beginning to control his movements.

Let's see how a baby at 4 or 5 months behaves when you suspend a toy above him. From the way his hand approaches the object, you can judge not only how he learns to control his movements, but also how he is beginning to understand the object—its shape, position, and distance. In the first phases of approach he moves his hand to the object slightly clenched and will unclench it only after touching it. In the next phase, he will bring his hand toward the object spread out wide. Only later will the spreading of the fingers be subordinated to the size of the object.

After the sixth month he will turn his hand to adapt it

to the position and shape of the object: his hand will be in a different position when reaching out for a vertical or horizontal rod. From the way the baby reaches out for an object you can tell the degree to which he has realized the shape, size, and position of the object and how these sensations affect the position of the approaching hand; these anticipatory adaptive movements indicate not only a baby's developing concept of shape and space, but also his general intelligence.

Even in a small child intelligence can be gauged by the way he takes things into his hands.

At first the baby holds an object with one hand and inspects it, moves his hand, alters the position and distance of the object from his eye, and observes the changes. At the same time he will hold the object firmly and not alter its position in his hand. After a while the object will fall out of his hand because at this stage the baby is still unable to control the release of his grasp. In the fifth and sixth months he starts grasping with both hands at once; after a while one hand will release its grasp, grasp again, and so on. This accidental release and deliberate grasping will soon develop into the purposeful transfer of the object from one hand to the other —an important step in the development of manipulation.

Purposeful transfer from hand to hand begins in the sixth month. But this is only the beginning of the deliberate release of the grasp; the release must be constantly trained because even at 12 months some babies are still unable to drop, say, a cube into a cup; they will hold the cube above the cup but not open the hand.

The transfer of an object from hand to hand also enables the baby to get to know the object better because during the transfer he will turn the object in various positions, clutch it in various ways, and perhaps change its shape.

The ability to manipulate gives your baby all kinds of experiences. While he also acquires them in contact with people, during feeding, bathing, and on other contact occasions, the experience gained during manipulation is especially valuable because your baby acquires it by his own activities, by experimenting. He controls the acquisition of experience himself.

Suppose your baby sees you preparing his food and a little later is fed. If you repeat this several times he will see that the preparation of his food signals feeding time. In this experience the baby has been passive. He had no influence on the preparation of the food or the feeding.

A game involving manipulation is a very different matter. Suppose your baby accidentally presses a squeaky rubber doll and the toy makes a noise. After a few accidental presses he will notice the connection between the pressure and the sound and will soon start pressing the toy on purpose: he will deliberately create the cause (pressure) to obtain the result (sound). When he realizes the connection between cause and result his activity will cease to be mechanical manipulation. It must be accompanied by the beginning of thinking.

So manipulation games and other self-developing activities are a school for thinking. And as these activities are basically movements, I believe that thinking begins with motion.

Your baby signals his physical and psychological state by expressing his feelings. When in the first 3 months he is quiet while awake you can assume he is well cared for; but after that the sign of good care is his good mood and activity. In the second 3 months a healthy, happy baby often smiles, laughs happily and loudly when in contact with a person he knows well. He shouts and murmurs and usually concerns himself with something or observes something with interest. With good care, he may hardly ever cry in the second 3 months. During this period baby begins to establish close contact with his social environment, mainly with his parents. He will discern those closest to him from strangers; he will give both of you a happy welcome but gravely observe an unknown visitor. By the sixth month his relationship to those closest to him becomes so strong that a sudden interruption of this relationship can cause disruptions of his physical and mental equilibrium: hence children react better to being placed in a nursery at the age of 3 months than 6.

During their fourth month babies are still passive in their social contacts, but in the sixth month they begin to establish active contact themselves; they draw attention to themselves by making a sound, they touch their mother and watch to see how the mother reacts to these overtures.

He will also begin to understand some gestures and mimic expressions of those closest to him. By the end of the sixth month some babies begin to react specifically to certain words; they will look at an object named by the mother. This means that understanding between you and him is made easier when only a few people care for him; if there are too many people around and they keep on changing he becomes confused by so many individual expressions and it becomes harder for him to establish deeper emotional relationships.

In the second 3 months many habits are strengthened. He will usually sleep through the whole night and not demand night feeding. He can learn the habit of alternating the periods of sleep and wakefulness at regular intervals during the daytime and to eat at regular intervals. Babies at this age usually sleep about 10 hours at night and during the day sleep about three times for 2 hours each and are fed five times at 4-hour intervals. He will acquire certain regularity in his bowel and bladder movements, which some mothers already make use of. But some bad habits can also be formed at this age, e.g., he may often wake up at night, suck his thumb, start making a big noise for small reasons, eat slowly, sleep under only special conditions, and the like.

Head Movements

Objective: Baby should learn to move his head in all directions in all positions, but mainly to bend it backward when lying on his tummy, and to draw his chin to his chest when on his back.

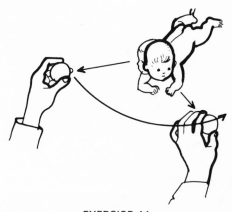

EXERCISE 41

Exercise 41: Watching objects moving in the air when lying on his tummy. Place baby onto his tummy, preferably at the edge of the table so his head is slightly over the edge. Show him some bright object. Move it up from the floor (he will bend his head down) into the air above him so he moves his head back in order to follow it. You can make the exercise harder by moving the object in the air to the right and left so that he moves his head at the same time.

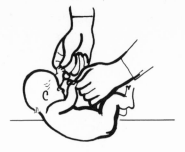

EXERCISE 42

Exercise 42: Lifting the head when on the back. Lay him down onto his back, give him your fingers and when he grasps them, pull slightly; he will lift his head, draw his chin onto his chest and at the same time bend his arms and stretch his legs. You can also show him some favorite object and move it toward his feet; he will again lift his head and draw his chin onto his chest.

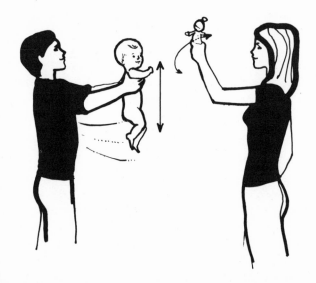

EXERCISE 43

Exercise *43:* Observing a moving object while moving the body. This is in combination with the head exercise mentioned earlier. The baby's father for instance, can do some of the above body exercises while you show him an interesting toy in motion; while watching the object baby also has to move his head and compensate with the movement of his body and the toy.

Arm Movements: Developing Strength of the Grasp and Push-Up

Objective: By his sixth month baby's grasp strength is probably enough for him to hold on when he is pulled upright onto his legs. A baby who exercises regularly will be able to hold on for at least 1 second when hanging onto a ring and held by the legs. His push-up strength should be adequate enough to enable him to crawl with the aid of his arms for at least 2 feet and support himself in the kneeling position (on all fours).

Exercise *44:* Grasping a trapeze when on the back. The trapeze has been described in the exercises for infants of 2 to 3 months and can be offered up to 6 months for more complicated exercises. In the second 3 months baby will grasp it with increasing confidence and will start to pull himself upward; when pulling himself up he will lift his legs vigorously. He will also start to turn onto his side and tummy with the aid of the trapeze. If you place baby so the trapeze is lengthwise above him he will grasp it with his hands and feet and will sometimes pull himself up. If he lies on his tummy and has the trapeze in front of him he will grasp it with one or both hands and at the same time bend his back thoroughly.

EXERCISE 45

Exercise 45: Pulling up into the sitting and standing position. Give your 4-month-old your fingers; when he has grasped them in both hands pull him up into the sitting position. By the fifth and sixth months his grasp will be strong enough for you to offer him a cord, rubber hose, rod, or ring instead of your fingers. Two rules: protect his head from the rear against a possible fall and do not let him sit up right away; lay him down again at once. Once he has learned to keep hold of an object all the way to the sitting position, you can make this more challenging for him by placing him onto his right side, instead of the back, and then pull him into the sitting position from there, then place him onto the left side and repeat (when on the side, baby's legs must be at right angles to his body). By the fifth month many babies not only sit up actively, but even go on to stand up. The exercise will work best if you arrange his legs so they are not crossed and see to it that they do not slide forward. The baby should use his legs himself and stand by himself; do not pull him upright while he passively hangs on with his hands. He is mature enough for this exercise when he can pull himself up and hold himself with his arms upward with the arms at a maximum angle of 45 degrees.

EXERCISE 46

Exercise 46: Suspension with the legs supported on the stomach of an adult. Sit down, if possible on the couch, and sit your baby on your lap facing you and pushing against your stomach with both his legs. Offer him your forefingers. When he grasps them, pull his hands gently. He will press his legs against your stomach, and either draw himself upright and stand with his bottom sticking out or into a standing position with his tummy stuck out. Then sit him down again and again pull him up.

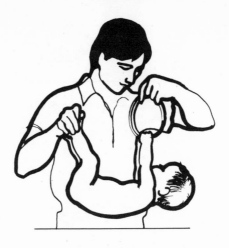

EXERCISE 47

Exercise 47: Combined suspension. When your baby's grasp is strong enough for him to hold safely onto your fingers as you draw him from the sitting to the standing position, try the combined suspension. Lay baby down on his back onto a soft pillow and give him two fingers of one hand. When he grasps them, hold him by the legs with your second hand and lift him about 4 inches above the pillow so that his head and trunk are horizontal. Baby will probably be able to hold half the weight of his body in his own hands; the second half is borne by you holding his legs. In the fifth month this is only a test, so try it about once to twice a week to check his progress. If he can do this without strain in his sixth month, then you can do it more often. You can then make the exercise more challenging by supplementing your fingers with a ring of a rod. It is safer if the father keeps his hand under the baby's head.

EXERCISE 48

Exercise 48: Observation of the surroundings over an obstacle. Your baby will use his arms more if he can observe something over a barrier such as the edge of the baby carriage or the bathtub. So don't keep him on his back in the carriage all the time; lower the hood, place him on his tummy and place a mattress beneath him so that if he grasps the edge of the pram he can observe his surroundings as you walk him.

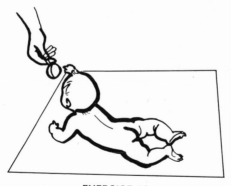

EXERCISE 49

Exercise 49: Reaching out for toys (which are higher up) when lying on the tummy. Place baby onto his tummy and hang a toy about 6 to 8 inches above him. He must push himself up well with one arm in order to reach out for the toy with his second arm and manipulate it in the air. Place baby or the toy so that he alternates with his left and right arms.

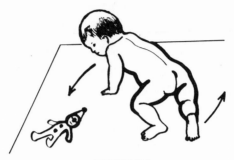

EXERCISE 50

Exercise 50 Pivoting when lying on the tummy. Place baby onto his tummy and place a toy about 8 to 12 inches away from him. By trying to grab the toy, baby will alternately push away with his arms and will thus turn over on his tummy by 90 degrees. He will learn turn clockwise with his hands both right and left and will often change his position and place his legs where his head was. This is preparation for crawling and climbing.

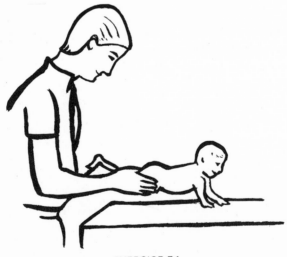

EXERCISE 51

Exercise 51: Horizontal handstand. Sit down comfortably and place baby across your thighs; his body should reach over your thighs far enough for him to be able to support himself on his arms. Encourage him to climb off your thighs in one way or another. By moving his arms, pushing with his legs, and similar motions, he will climb off (this is for babies in the sixth month). You can just as easily lay him down on a rolled mattress or blanket, but his trunk must be well beyond this edge and he must keep upright by leaning on his arms.

Trunk Movements

Objective: The back and neck muscles should become strong enough for baby lying on his tummy to lift his head and chest without supporting himself with the arms (airplane). When lying on his back he should be able to lift his legs high enough to grasp his feet and pull them to his mouth. He should be able to turn over from his back onto his tummy and from his tummy onto his back. When lying on his tummy in his sixth month he should be able to bend one leg and draw his knee to his tummy; some babies can do this with both knees and then push themselves up to the kneeling position (on all fours). He ought to be able to stand while holding onto something in front of him without waving his hips.

Note: Most of the following exercises are quite hard for the parents as well, and so father should do them with baby.

Exercises of the Entire Trunk

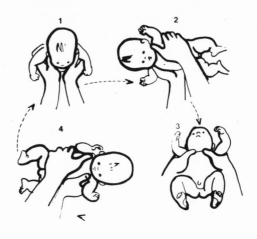

EXERCISE 52

Exercise 52: Circling. Place your baby onto his back, grasp him just above the waist and gently lift him till he is in the air with his tummy downward and his head toward you. Perform a circular movement similar to that of a horizontal clock. First turn him to the left, with his body always horizontal, but with his right side down. His head should be in front of your left shoulder, legs in front of your right shoulder. Then keep on turning, with baby still in the horizontal position, but with his back down and his legs by your head. During the further circular movement baby should still be in the horizontal position, but with his left side downward, his head in the direction of your right shoulder, his legs in that of your left. Finally return to the initial position: baby's head is by your head, his tummy down. Do the entire movement again, but counterclockwise. Do it twice to either side. At first you can make the exercise easier by circling baby not in the horizontal position but at a slope, with the head up and the legs down. This exercise affects all the body muscles.

Back Muscle Exercises

Exercise 53: Lying on the tummy and playing. At this age, too, the tummy position is the main exercise for strengthening the back and neck muscles. During the day baby had best be on his tummy about three times as much as in other positions. After each exercise when the baby sits, stands, or hops, place him onto his tummy and leave him much longer in this position. Again: do try to get him used to lying on his tummy from his earliest days and make this position as pleasant for him in as many ways as you can.

EXERCISE 54

Exercise 54: Airplane. Lay baby onto his tummy and place some interesting toy in front of him but out of reach. He will reach out for it and when he is sufficiently excited he will stretch both his hands and legs, bend his back, lift his head high—and do an airplane. After 20 to 30 seconds, place the toy closer so he can reach it.

EXERCISE 55

Exercise 55: Lifting and lowering in the vertical position holding him under the arms. Place the baby onto his back; grasp him slightly above the waist and lift him high above you in the horizontal position with his tummy down and his face toward you. Baby looks down at you, bends his back, often stretches his legs and spreads his arms (does an airplane) and will usually laugh happily. Bend your arms and lower him toward your face while he is in the same position and lift him again. Repeat lifting and lowering several times. The approach and withdrawal of the face of the father, who talks playfully to him, will make the baby happy and make him enjoy it.

This category of exercises also includes some types of carrying of the baby, with baby cooperating actively when you carry him, not just being passively transported as when you cuddle him. Taking good care of the baby does not always mean giving him the greatest comfort; too much comfort leads to passivity and laziness and spoils him. Our purpose is to make him more active. So it's a good idea for your baby to get used to occasional difficulties and discomfort.

A healthy baby usually enjoys overcoming obstacles and expects to be praised and admired for his success. Do not forget that even at a time of increased technical progress, which gives people the greatest comfort, hardy people will still be needed. The main purpose of sports is to overcome obstacles and fortify health and character. In my view, laziness can lead to moral and physical decay and ultimately to the end of civilization as we know it.

Exercise 56: Carrying on the forearms. Bend your arms in front of you with your palsm upward and your elbows pressed to your sides. Place baby with his tummy downward across your arms with his chest on your right arm and his legs on your left. Your arms form a support and baby lies on them as on a shelf. He will bend his back, lift his head high and look around. Walk around the home for a few minutes or outside so that he has something to look at.

EXERCISE 57

Exercise 57: Carrying baby under the arm in a horizontal position. Imagine you are going to carry a small rolled carpet under the arm. Pick up baby in the same way—under the right arm so he is horizontal with his tummy downward, his head forward, and his legs behind. Again walk around with him in this position; he will not protest against this; in fact, he's almost certain to like this position. You can make this exercise more difficult by placing him onto his side with his tummy resting against you or against your arm, which baby is grasping. If you want to carry him this way but on his back you should do so only for about 5 to 8 seconds because this exercise greatly strains the stomach muscles.

Stomach Muscle Exercises

EXERCISE 58

Exercise 58: Seesaw. Place baby onto his back and lift him by the waist into the horizontal position above your

head with his back up, face toward you. Then slowly
lower your outstretched arms and lower him to your side
again in the horizontal position, but with his back down.
In this position he will bend his legs and tense his stomach muscles. Repeat this up and down exercise about 2
or 3 times. Then place baby onto his back and let him
rest for a longer period and gently stroke his hands to
unclench his fists, which are usually clenched during this
exercise.

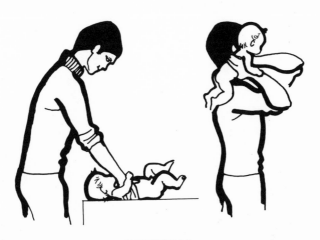

EXERCISE 59

Exercise 59: Back roll. Place baby onto his back with his
head toward you. Grasp him around the waist and lift
him up to your shoulder so that you first turn him from
a horizontal position, with face up, to a vertical position,
head down. Your arms are stretched out and forward.
Then lift and turn your baby into a horizontal position,
face down and forward, his feet close to your right shoulder. Lift your forearms. Finally, place your baby standing
on your shoulder. Now only your upper arms are lifted
forward; the forearms are bent backward. Then perform
a forward roll the same way and place him on his back

in front of you again. Do this 2 to 3 times at most. The father had best do this exercise with baby. With four fingers stretched out over baby's back he will be able to form a larger supporting surface and make the exercise easier and safer.

Exercises for the Side Muscles

EXERCISE 60

Exercise 60: Independent rolling. During the fourth to fifth months baby will usually learn to roll over from his back onto his tummy and later from his tummy onto his back. If baby still cannot turn from his back to his tummy alone, help him by crossing his legs, pushing his bottom, pulling his arms, and so on as described in the exercises for babies age 2 to 3 months. You can make the turning easier if you place him on a slight slope (about 15 to 20 degrees); outdoors you can make use of a natural slope onto which you can place a blanket. At home you can make an incline by lifting one end of a couch and supporting it with a chair. Babies like to roll down a slope. Sometimes the roll-over from back to tummy is so powerful that they will roll over onto the back with inertia but also hit their head on the ground; therefore when your baby is rolling down you must protect his head with your hand. You can motivate baby to roll over by showing him a toy at such a distance that he can reach it only by rolling over onto his tummy. Train this roll toward both sides.

EXERCISE 61

Exercise 61: Side somersault. Place baby onto his side with his back toward you, so his head is on your right side and feet on your left. Place your right hand onto baby's left (upper side) and push your left hand under his right (lower) side. Lift him first to the horizontal position, then turn him clockwise with his feet upward. Continue turning and lay him down again onto his left side with his feet to your right side and his head to your left. Baby's legs have therefore traveled in a semicircle just like the hands of a clock moving from 9 past 12 to 3 o'clock. Then turn the somersault onto the other side, counterclockwise. Do this exerting exercise at most 2 to 3 times a day. After the exercise allow baby to rest and help him to relax with a loosening massage (gently rub his hands and trunk).

Movements of the Lower Limbs

Objective: At this age baby should learn to brace up with his legs and stand up for a short moment while holding onto something (short-term static leg support). He should also be able to bend his knees rhythmically and straighten up (rhythmic dancing). Finally he should learn to grasp larger objects (an inflatable ball) with his legs as well as his hands, and learn the basic movements in preparation for crawling.

To develop short-term leg bracing keep in mind several orthopedic principles. Allow baby to stand with his full weight on his legs for only a short while and only if an orthopedist has checked in the third or fourth months that baby's hip joints are OK. Don't allow baby to stand at all unless he can get up onto his legs by himself. Remember that you are going to teach him to get up, but not stand for any length of time. Lengthy static loading of the lower limbs at this age does nothing to enhance the growth of the skeleton, but gentle, rhythmic loading (jumping in the Jolly Jumper, or kicking a ball in the lying position) help the bones of the lower limbs to develop. Don't let baby stand on a soft mattress even for a short time because the arch of the foot usually collapses; it is better to do this exercise on a hard floor.

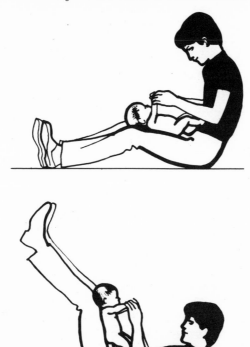

EXERCISE 62

Exercise 62: Cradle. Sit on the floor with your legs stretched out. Lay baby on his back on your legs so his legs bear against your stomach and his head rests on your knees. Then offer him your forefingers. When he grasps them, lie slowly onto your back and lift your legs high into the air. Now baby will stand up on your stomach. Then sit up again so he again rests on your thighs. During this rocking motion (alternately sitting up and lying down) baby alternately finds himself in the lying and standing position. Alternate lying and sitting about 10 times.

Exercise 63: Standing up from the sitting position. Sit baby in front of you with his legs bent and parallel and holding your forefingers. When you lift your arms baby will pull himself up and stand on his legs. Let him stand for about 2 to 3 seconds, then sit him down at once. Make the holding of the trunk in the upright position gradually harder by first holding your forefingers in front of him so his arms are raised at an angle; once he is stable in his standing position, hold your forefingers so his arms are stretched out in front of him. Finally hold your fingers at the level of his hips; he will support himself with his arms almost at his sides. The lower baby holds his arms when standing upright without swaying in the hips, the harder it is. I again stress that baby should not be allowed to stand with his full weight on his legs for more than 2 to 3 seconds. Perform this standing up 5 to 6 times.

Exercise 64: Standing up from the sitting position by grasping a ring or rod. This exercise is the same as Number 63, but instead of your fingers offer baby a rod, ring, or a rubber hose, for example. Hold the aid in one hand and protect baby against falling on his back with the other. Repeat 5 to 6 times.

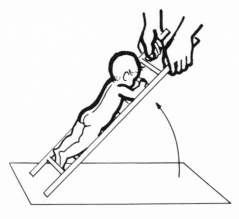

EXERCISE 65

Exercise 65: Transfer from lying on the back to upright suspension. Make yourself a ladder about 5 feet long and 2 feet wide, with the rungs 2 to 3 inches apart and about half an inch thick, or use the walls of a wooden crib. Place baby on the ladder lying on the floor (clothed so the rungs won't hurt him), place his legs onto the first or second rung and let him grasp hold of one of the upper rungs. First lift him by about 30 degrees and lay him down again. If baby does not protest (he will generally like this lifting) lift him up higher. Finally lift the ladder to an angle of 80 to 90 degrees, so that baby moves to suspension while standing on the ladder. Lift the ladder with one hand and hold and protect baby with the other. This exercise is suitable for babies age 5 to 6 months.

EXERCISE 66

Exercise 66: Suspension in the upright position. After baby has fully mastered all the above exercises, stand him on his feet next to the wall of his crib for about 3 to 5 seconds. Baby will usually hold onto anything (such as the ladder) if he can easily brace himself with his legs and hold on with his hands. For babies age 5 to 6 months this

exercise should only be a practice of sturdiness to see
how they are getting on, and should be done only about
2 to 3 times a month. It should become a regular daily
exercise only during the seventh month when baby can
stand up next to the wall of the crib by himself.

Development of Rhythmical Jumping

Exercise 67: Rhythmic jumping while held under the
arms. Pick baby up under the arms and hold him upright
above the table or your lap. Let him down into a crouching position and help him up again with a gentle lift.
Alternate the bend-downs and straighten-ups until baby
starts jumping almost by himself. You should bear as
much weight as possible to enable him to lift himself up
with minimum exertion.

EXERCISE 68

Exercise 68: Jumping in a jolly jumper. During his fourth
month you can put baby into a jumping seat, described

under "Toys and Furniture." Place one to two diapers between his legs to spread them. Baby should be suspended in the seat high enough to be able to touch the floor only lightly with his legs (the seat has a chain to regulate its height from the floor). Baby is ready for the seat when he can sit in it for about 10 minutes with his head up and his back straight. While jumping the baby should be barefoot to feel the floor and also to help him place his foot on the floor properly. Put a folded blanket on the floor under his feet. At first do not leave him in the jumper for more than 3 to 5 minutes once or twice a day. Once he has learned to jump you can extend the exercise to 5 to 10 minutes and in the sixth month to 10 to 15 minutes.

At first your baby will be inhibited and will probably hang without moving and look around curiously. After all, he has been lying down most of the time till now and suddenly finds himself upright without anybody holding him. Also, he can now suddenly see his surroundings from below, from the floor. After 1 to 3 days the inhibition will probably pass. He will get used to the novelty and start actively trying to see what he can do in these new circumstances—first by feeling the floor with his feet.

After 3 to 5 days he will start pushing himself up, first with one foot then with both. At first he will come down onto his straightened leg thus cushioning the jump. In 6 to 8 days he will learn to come down on his bent leg and to tie the next hop upward into this landing. Now the jumping will really begin. After about 10 to 15 days he will jump so well that after jumping up he will turn by 180 degrees to see anybody who is calling him. The better he hops the happier he will be. He will laugh loudly, shout, even scream. His joy stems from the fact that with minimum energy he achieves extremely strenuous movements. He can also orient himself in his surroundings with little exertion because he can turn to all sides. Finally, the rhythm itself, the alternate gentle muscular stress and release, is a further source of pleasant sensations. As soon as he learns to crawl, his interest in the seat will wane because crawling is a much richer source of orientation: he can crawl to interesting things, inspect and feel them from all sides and more.

Parents sometimes act against the healthy development of their baby by placing him in the jumper for longer periods of time to be rid of him for a while; there have even been cases of babies falling asleep in their seats. Perhaps your baby would like to stay in his seat longer than I recommend. But an extended stay in the seat taxes his strength and can affect his development of good posture, because there is too great a load on his weak spine and comparatively weak neck and back muscles. So you should keep to the recommended time and after every hopping session you should allow your baby to lie on his tummy for at least 2 to 3 times the length of the jumping period.

Development of Leg Games

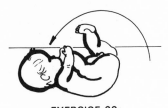

EXERCISE 69

Exercise 69: Catching hold of the legs. If baby is often naked, he will, when lying on his back by the third month, start lifting his legs. In the fourth month he will touch his knees with his hands and in the fifth he will grasp his toes in his hands and pull them up to his mouth.

If your baby does not lift his legs spontaneously and lets them lie passively, place a folded blanket under his backside and lift his legs so his heels do not touch the blanket; he will then actively lift his legs and will gradually lift them higher even when the blanket is no longer under him. You can achieve the same effect if you place him onto a couch so his heels and shins are over the edge. When the heels lose their support he will lift his legs and pull them up to his tummy.

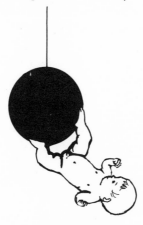

EXERCISE 70

Exercise 70: Catching a ball with the legs. Hold or suspend a large inflatable ball above baby's knees. During his second to third months he kicks it; in the fourth month he touches and feels it with his legs; in the fifth to sixth months he catches and drops it, pulls the ball up to his hand with his legs, and alternately holds it with his hands and feet, but most often with all four. You can also use a lifebelt instead of the ball, or various inflatable toys, cardboard boxes, and the like.

EXERCISE 71

Exercise 71: Feeling objects with the feet. If you leave baby's feet bare often, he will start using them to feel, perhaps the bars of his crib. To facilitate feeling with the feet, which is important to strengthen the muscles which form the correct arch of the foot, give the feet the same opportunity that you gave the hands. Stick various strips and objects (balls) onto a plank which he can easily feel with his feet. Place the plank at the edge of the bed and lay baby down so he can feel objects on the plank with his leg slightly bent. A frame (ladder) with horizontal bars about 1/2 inch in diameter is best. Baby will feel the rungs and you will be able to see how he forms the correct foot arch by bending his toes.

Development of Sensory Perception

Objective: Your baby should be able to discern the source not only of intensive but weak sounds, too. He should learn to recognize voices of people close to him and make out the various tones of the voices so he can react differently to kind and strict voices. By the sixth month he should also start learning to recognize words, to look for one or two objects with his eyes when he hears the names of the objects. By the sixth month he should have learned to assess visually the position and distance of nearby objects and express this ability by sure movements of his hands to the object. He should also be able to discern visually similar objects by their details—recognizing people by their faces and objects by various small characteristics.

EXERCISE 72

Exercise 72: Seeking the source of sound. This exercise can be combined with various games and handling. For example, you can play hide and seek. Place baby onto your lap and father can slowly hide behind a table, cupboard, or door and call him. When baby looks in the right direction, mother should praise him as father appears and smiles at him. Father can also ring a bell at baby from various hiding places. He can alter the intensity of the sound and try to achieve a reaction from baby to a low call or clapping.

EXERCISE 73

Exercise 73: Distinguishing between sounds according to whether or not they act as signals (announcing or not announcing something). Place baby in your arms. Let father hide behind a table which baby cannot see. Father should then knock against a glass and when baby turns around he should stick out his hand with some interesting toy, move it, and perhaps make sounds with it. After 8 to 10 seconds let the toy disappear. About 15 to 20 seconds later father should knock against a plank. When baby looks toward the table he will see nothing. After a further 15 to 20 seconds knock a glass again and show baby another toy over the edge of the table. Repeat both sounds about 10 to 15 times a day. After 3 to 5 days your baby will turn toward the table only when he hears the tinkle of the glass. He will not turn when you knock the plank. Since the turning of his head toward the table at the sound of the wood has not been rewarded, he has formed a so-called differential inhibition toward it; he has learned to distinguish between a sound that acts as a signal and another that does not. Success in this exercise depends on conditions remaining unchanged: the baby sits in his mother's lap, the table remains where it is, and so on.

EXERCISE 74

Exercise 74: Differentiating between a kind and strict tone of voice. I suggest you use all everyday situations so your baby can distinguish between kind and strict voices and facial expressions. You'll of course speak to him normally in a kind voice and smile at him, but when he does something that he should not (tries to knock away the spoon you feed him with or pulls the tablecloth) you'll alter the tone of your voice to a stricter one and also change facial expression. But some artificial situations are also educational. For instance, you can place a spoon and a knife in front of your baby. When he reaches for the spoon, encourage him with kind words. When he reaches for the knife, you can say in a strict voice, "You mustn't," frown and move the knife out of his reach.

Exercise 75: Rhymes and songs with rhythmic movements. From his early days it's a good idea to sing simple folk and children's songs to your baby and from the fourth to fifth months recite simple rhythmic verses. Your child likes the rhythm and intonation, even though he does not understand the words. You can stress the rhythm by performing rhythmic movements with him at the same time: rhythmically nurse him in your arms, move his hands in rhythm, his feet, his limbs. You can also teach him to discern the kind of song you are singing: when it's a merry one, smile at him, sing louder, and perform livelier movements. You'll want to sing a lullaby more softly and make slow, gentle, movements. Give him the opportunity to hear the songs and verses from close by as well as from a distance. Baby should hear the same song from you, his father, grandmother, and others close to him so he gets used to different voices. These exercises will make it easier for him to understand human speech.

I'll discuss ways to teach him to understand words when I go into the development of speech.

Before I describe an exercise to develop your baby's sight, I must stress an important principle which is also valid for other senses: a baby's sight cannot be developed by viewing alone, but only in connection with his other senses, mainly tactile. It is not enough to see in order to be able to tell a ball from a ring; it is also necessary to think and to have certain experience.

An adult knows from experience that a metal ring shines uniformly while a ball may be lighter in some places than others. He also knows that a ball looks like a circle from all sides; a ring can look like an elipse. The adult therefore distinguishes the ball from the ring not only by sight but experience and thought. So from the fourth month, when your baby learns purposefully to grasp objects, you can develop his sight by enabling him to confront visual stimuli against tactile kinestetic, taste, and smell sensations. One of the basic conditions for the development of sight in the second quarter year of life is therefore the manipulation of objects.

Exercise 76: Manipulating objects of various geometrical shapes. Give baby objects of various shapes, colors, and sizes to play with. The most suitable are various round, cylindrical rattles or chains with square and cylindrical boxes. Suspend these toys above him during the fourth and fifth months. He will observe them, grasp, move, feel, and turn them over in his hands, see what he can do with them and observe how they change color, brightness, shade, and shapes when he manipulates them. In the fifth and sixth months place them in front of him when he lies on his tummy, place them close and then further away and in various positions so he can see how they look in various positions and distances and by grasping for them learn how to judge visually various distances. At first your baby will judge by direct contact and manipulation and gain much experience which will enable him to later see at a distance whether an object is flat or not. If the objects which baby manipulates are square, cylindrical, triangular, or spheroid, he will gain further valuable experience: he will develop his sense of basic geometrical shapes and get used to basic optical concepts because he will gain intensive experience with vertical and horizontal directions, right angles, flat, cylindrical and round surfaces. He will constantly encounter objects in his environment which are also composed of the basic geometrical shapes. "Feeling" for shapes can develop very early and the sooner the better, because baby will do better later in school and in technical skills.

Exercise 77: The differentiation of objects according to their appearance. If your child has an old rubber duck which no longer makes any noise buy a similar one which does. Offer both to baby. During his fifth and sixth months he will learn to differentiate between objects by mere sight, according to various small differences in color and design, and will more often reach out for the new toy because it gives him greater pleasure. This exercise has variations. You can, for example, play the following game with your 6-month-old baby: place two small boxes (which differ only slightly) in front of him. Always place something interesting beneath one of them, and always keep the other empty. After several trials the baby will more often reach out for the first to see what is hidden in it. Think up other versions: the principle lies in offering your baby two almost similar objects but one offers him a reward while the second does not. Baby can learn to tell them both apart by sight.

As he learns to discern various objects by small optical characteristics, he can also learn to tell objects by size or other criteria. So try to hide an interesting toy in a larger and in a more distant box.

How Games Develop Experience and Thinking

Objective: During his fourth to sixth months you can help your baby to:

1. Grasp various objects
2. Play with his hands
3. Reach out for objects in more diverse ways
4. Grasp objects in more complex ways
5. Manipulate objects in various ways
6. Recognize a table and manipulate an object on the table
7. Act with an object on another object
8. Process various materials

Teaching Baby to Grasp Objects

In Exercise 76 (manipulating variously shaped objects) I described how manipulation of objects enhances the development of visual perception. To realize why you must train this grasping movement, let me show you how it develops during the first year. In the third month your baby brings his clenched fist to an object and, after touching it, unclenches and grasps the object. In the fourth and fifth months the baby approaches the object with his hand open, prepared to grasp. At this age he grasps toys with all his fingers bunched together, his thumb parallel with his forefinger. In the fifth and sixth months he begins to place his thumb counterwise to his other fingers.

The development of the grasping motion gradually develops so an object is first grasped by the entire hand, later only by the fingers. Gradually, it moves from the palm of the hand to the fingertips. In the sixth and seventh months babies grasp smaller objects with their fingers alone—bent at first, but stretched out later. In the eighth and ninth months the little finger and the ring finger cease to participate in the grasping movement, and by the ninth month the baby grasps objects only with his thumb and forefinger. In the tenth to twelfth months babies become greatly interested in small crumbs and threads and grasp them with a tweezer touch.

Exercise 78: Grasping various objects. In Exercise 76 the object was to develop a "feeling for geometric bodies," but the object of this exercise is to teach your baby to grasp various objects which differ not only in shape but also physically. Give him the opportunity to grasp:

Hard, long objects (rattles, spoons, ladles)
Hard flat objects (plates, lids, discs)

Hard full and empty objects (cubes, balls, cups, boxes, bowls)

Flexible objects (rubber toys, foam rubber, rubber tubes)

Bendable objects (diapers, paper, plastic)

The objects should be easy to clean, not brittle, without sharp edges or ends. Do wrap the end of the ladle with some rubber or clean cloth for safety. The principle of the exercise is that the baby has to grasp a rod differently from a plate or a diaper and that the object behaves differently after being grasped, i.e., paper is different from a cube. The mere grasping of objects gives him experience with various materials.

Teaching Baby to Play with His Hands

When your baby finds out that the movement of his hand can be influenced directly and that a rattle can be put into motion by means of the hand, he will deliberately reach out for objects and grasp them. So it's a good idea for you to help your baby discover his own hands as soon as possible.

EXERCISE 79

Exercise 79: Grasping one hand in the other. Gently grasp baby by the wrists and move both hands toward each other and make them touch. If you make washing movements with his hands, one hand will soon grasp the finger of the other. Start this exercise at the end of the third month and by the fourth month baby will usually grasp his hands himself, though without visual control. This is a very important game for your baby's development, but he'll learn it only slowly if his sleeves are too long and if he has too much cloth around his chest which prevents his short arms from coming closer to each other.

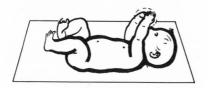

EXERCISE 80

Exercise 80: Playing with the hands in front of the eyes. When baby plays with his hands in his fourth month without visual control, lift his clasped hands so he can see them; now you are helping him to discover his hands with his eyes. During the fifth month this play with the hands usually wanes.

Reaching for Objects in a More Complex Way

Exercise 81: Reaching out for objects handed to baby from different directions. First offer baby interesting objects from the front. Later, gradually, offer them more from either left or right, above and below, at angles, and so forth. First offer them from close up, then from further away so baby reaches out for them with his arm crooked as well as completely stretched out. Also offer the objects so that baby reaches out for them with the right as well as left hand.

Exercise 82: Reaching out for moving objects. Move an interesting object slowly in front of baby so it is always within reach of his hands. He will follow the movement not only with the movement of his eyes and head but also with his arms. You must not overtax baby's patience. It's enough to let him follow an object with his arms for 1 to 2 seconds and then allow him to grasp it.

Exercise 83: Reaching for a stationary object when baby is in motion. Sit down at a table with baby and place an interesting toy on the desk. In the sitting position gradually turn with baby to the right and to the left; in order to grasp the object, baby will have to compensate with his hand the movement you're performing with him.

Exercise 84: Reaching out for various objects in various positions. Offer baby interesting toys when he is in various positions—not only on his back, but also on his side or tummy or while sitting in your lap. You can make this more challenging for him, for example, by having father lift him up into the air into the horizontal or vertical position and yourself offering him the object in this unusual position.

Exercise 85: Reaching out for objects in combination with other movements of the body. In the sixth month offer your baby toys so he has to incorporate other movements into the reaching movement, such as having to turn over onto his side from his back, or onto his tummy, or to turn more to the right or left on his tummy. He will thus learn to combine reaching out for objects with various other movements, such as turning, bending, or stretching. This is important training toward the sixth to twelfth months when he will have to learn to combine partial movements into larger complex movements.

EXERCISE 86

Exercise 86: Reaching out for objects over obstacles. In the sixth month, when your baby has fully mastered the guiding of his hand directly to a seen object, teach him to reach out indirectly, that is, to avoid obstacles. Place an interesting toy into a drawer or into a less interesting box so that the box does not become an attraction of itself. If he wants to touch the toy he cannot do so directly, but must get past the wall of the box and use his hand appropriately. You can place the box so that baby reaches into it from above, or to his right or left. If baby deals with the situation by hand movements this is proof that he is beginning to understand spatial relationships.

Complex Grasping

EXERCISE 87

Exercise 87: Grasping large objects with both hands. Hand baby a large inflatable ball or something similar. In the first three months he will start banging it, then gently touch it. By the fifth month he starts learning to grasp it by pressing both palms together. Hand him the ball several times. The objective is achieved when he reaches out for it with both arms and spreads his fingers. This shows that he has defined the ball as a large object which cannot be grasped with one hand.

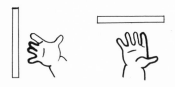

EXERCISE 88

Exercise 88: Grasping an elongated object in various positions. Offer baby an elongated object (a ladle) from the vertical position, then horizontal, then inclined. In his fifth month he will reach out for the object with his hand spread out. Only when the hand is close to the object will he turn it to grasp. In his sixth month he adapts the position of his hand while performing the reaching movement. By the movement of his hand baby indicates that he understood the position of the ladle before he grasped and is adapting the position of his hand in advance. You can also offer baby a string, rubber hose, plate, or other object to teach him to understand its position and grasp it in various ways.

EXERCISE 89

Exercise 89: Asymmetrical grasp with both hands. Hand an empty tin or plastic cup to baby so his left hand grasps the handle and presses his right hand against the side of the cup. Then hand it to him the other way around so his right hand grasps the handle and his left the side. This teaches him simultaneously to grasp something differently with each hand—a comparatively difficult task for a 6-month-old.

EXERCISE 90

Exercise 90: Grasping lying objects. It is harder for baby to grasp a lying object than to grasp one that has been placed or offered to his hand. Sit down with baby at the table and place various objects in front of him, tall ones at first (rubber animals, cubes) and later smaller and flatter ones (spoons, lids, a ladle, plate). In the fifth and sixth month baby will grasp an object on the table by placing his entire hand onto it and grasping it with all his fingers, which is why he cannot pick up coins and similar small flat objects from the table.

Simple Manipulation with Objects

Exercise 91: Feeling objects with both hands. Give baby a celluloid ring, a bunch of rings, a small pot and similar objects which are easy to grasp with both hands. Baby will grasp an object with both hands but occasionally loosen the grip of his right or left hand and grasp the object in a different place and in a different way. At the same time he will observe his hands and the objects visually; now he is investigating objects with both his hand and eyes.

EXERCISE 92

Exercise 92: Transferring objects from one hand to the other. Give baby objects similar to those in Exercise 91. In that exercise the baby let go of the object with one hand for a moment and then grasped it again, but the act was purely reflexive. Gradually, however, baby can let go of the object with one hand with obvious purpose and again grasp it and at the same time let go with his other hand. Now he is purposefully transferring the object from one hand to the other.

Exercise 93: Turning and inspecting an object in the hand. Give baby a cube covered with simple pictures or another object which looks different from each side. He will hold it in his hand, turn it around and watch the change of pictures or colors. He will often shift it from hand to hand, but before putting it into his other hand he will turn it so that the other hand grasps the object in a different position.

Exercise 94: Moving objects in vessels. Take a transparent tube, place one or two colored balls into it and close the tube. Baby will turn the tube around to make the balls roll from one end to the other, and he'll move it around to make them roll backward and forward. You can produce the same effect with a transparent box with a lid: baby will again observe the box and move it so the colored balls roll backward and forward. For baby to be able to observe the movements he must learn to move the box slowly and gently.

Getting to Know a Table and Manipulating Objects on It

In his second three months baby should become acquainted with a table, because games at a table are considerably different from those played on the back or tummy.

EXERCISE 95

Exercise 95: Feeling the edge of the table. The first time you sit with baby at a table (without table cloth) he will be most interested in its edge. Feel the edge of the table with him and he will soon become interested.

EXERCISE 96

Exercise 96: Banging the table and sliding. After baby has become acquainted with the edge of the table he will start investigating the rest. He feels it, slaps it with his hands and wipes around it with his arms as if wanting to brush something off the table top. You can help baby by banging the table and performing swiping movements so he can imitate you.

Exercise 97: Slapping the table with the right and left hand alternately. At first baby slaps the tabletop with both his hands at once. Sit down with him at the table, take both his hands in yours, and slap the table alternately with his left and right. Babies usually learn this during their seventh month, but some can do this at 6.

Teaching Baby to Make Object Act on Object

Exercise 98: Banging a small object into a larger one. After baby has become acquainted with the table and is slapping it with his hand, give him a cube or some other toy. He will pick it up and start banging the table with it; the greater the noise, the more he will bang. Now you should teach him that he can bang on the kitchen table, but not on the table in the living room.

EXERCISE 99

Exercise 99: Banging an object with aim. In the previous exercise baby banged onto the large surface of the table, without aiming; now you can teach him to aim. Hand him a smaller cube and place a larger one in front of him. Pick up a small cube yourself and knock it against the cube lying in front of baby. He will soon imitate you. Help him by grasping his hand with the cube and knock it against the larger cube. This teaches him to aim a blow in a particular direction. Gradually replace the cubes with other objects and baby will bang them on a box.

Exercise 100: Shifting objects across the table. Show baby how he can move around objects that lie on the table. Baby will imitate you and slide objects across the table. Take his hand and let him do the sliding movement passively at first. Baby will soon understand and do it himself with various objects such as a ladle. This is preparation for an exercise that teaches the baby to move a cube with an object like a ladle and thus use the ladle as a tool.

Teaching Baby to Process Materials

Exercise 101: Pressing rubber toys. Give baby some squeaky rubber toys. He will soon find out that by squeezing them he can make various noises. Soft rubber toys are best because by pressing them he can also change their shape.

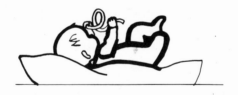

EXERCISE 102

Exercise 102: Playing with a rubber hose. If baby picks up a rubber hose about 2 feet in length and moves it around he can create various loops and bends; he will watch these changes of shape with interest.

Exercise 103: Playing with a diaper. If you give baby a diaper, towel, or cloth, he will start pressing it, pulling it apart and find other ways to amuse himself.

EXERCISE 104

Exercise 104: Playing with a plastic bag. Place various objects into a plastic bag (e.g., nuts and cubes) and tie it up. Baby will press the bag, pick up the various objects inside it and change their positions. The changes in the shape of the bag, the movements of the objects inside, and the noise of the plastic excite him and trigger lively manipulation.

Exercise 105: Squeezing and tearing paper. If you give baby a sheet of clean paper he will soon start squeezing and tearing and will keep this up for quite some time.

Note: Baby can play some of these games in your absence. But of course you'll be careful not to give him objects he could swallow, breathe in, or use to strangle himself.

Development of Thinking

Objective: In his fifth and sixth months baby begins to react to relationships—to action and its effect—and he can slowly be prepared for abstract thinking: to react differently to certain characteristics of objects, depending on, for example, whether they are large or small or round or square.

Exercise 106: Reacting to the relationship between action and its effect. During baby's fifth and sixth months I recommend that you start creating situations where his own activity causes an immediate result. Use toys that make sounds. At first baby will accidentally press a toy and it will squeak; after several such chance successes he will be attracted by the connection between his own action and the reaction. He will start pressing the toy on purpose in order to make it squeak.

When your 5- to 6-month-old plays with the trapeze that I've described, you will see that he is beginning to experiment by purposely altering his activities; he will probably move the trapeze gently, then vigorously and observe the difference in results. Toys which facilitate a variety of activities and create observable results therefore have a greater educational value than those which permit only one activity and always with the same result.

If the plastic bag containing various objects is hung up above your baby he will manipulate it for a long time, because he can grasp it in various ways, press and rub it, shift the objects inside it, and so on. This yields a remarkable variety of results because the bag rattles and alters its shape. On the other hand, your child will soon get bored playing with a ball suspended above him, because there is not much he can do with it.

Babies love games that let them set off the causes of results quite on their own. Such games are also best for keeping him active and launching fundamental mental processes. It is important for the baby's action to create an immediate result and for the relationship between cause and effect to be obvious. Only toward the end of his first year is a baby able to discern the relationship between action and reaction when the reaction is a bit delayed.

Exercise 107: Preparation for primitive abstract reasoning: playing with objects which differ only in one characteristic. Experiments have shown that a 6-month-old is capable of actions which in adults call for the ability to deal with abstractions. The following game prepares the ground for the development of this ability. On various occasions give baby several similar objects which differ only in one respect, perhaps two or three large spoons and two or three small spoons of the same shape. Baby will notice the difference between them and his attention will be drawn to the large ones. Give him some small plastic containers which have the same shape and size, but differ in color; baby will be attracted by the difference in color. Use other objects to draw his attention to the difference between long and short, thick and thin, and such other characteristics. By attracting his attention to these you create the foundations for coping with the abstract. The ability of 6-month-olds to abstract and generalize is closely connected with the development of speech.

Development of Speech, Social Relationships, and Emotions

Objective: The development of speech, social relationships, and emotions during the second 3 months (and later) are so closely related that they cannot be cultivated separately. By the sixth month your baby will probably learn to pronounce all the vowels, some consonants and even a few simple syllables. He'll also learn to seek out visually a particular object you have named. He begins to create a close relationship to persons near to him and to differentiate between them and other people with his behavior. He will begin to establish actively a relationship with his social environment. He will seldom cry and when he is in contact with persons close to him he will often laugh aloud.

Humming and Mumbling in the Second Three Months

I've mentioned that the development of humming and later mumbling depends on how babies are stimulated to be active; a further condition is the gratification of their basic biological needs. When baby is rested, fed, and healthy, and when he can observe and hear something interesting, he will happily move his entire body, including his vocal chords, and will mumble with pleasure. The following exercises should stimulate your baby to mumble.

Exercise 108: Stimulation of mumbling by simple social contact. When baby is in a good mood, fed, and rested, place him before you, bend over him, smile at him, touch his chin, cheeks, and neck gently with your fingers and mumble at him in a gentle voice. A female voice is most effective because it is higher than the male's. By the end of the second month he is likely to emit some sort of occasional mumbling sound. By the fourth month you will be able to encourage him to make such a sound almost every time you try. Alternate about 5 seconds of mumbling with 5 seconds of silence. Baby will often mumble during the period of silence: reward him by laughing and stroking.

To make baby mumble frequently and teach himself to create syllables, it's best that you react as often as possible to his spontaneous mumbling. Let him see you, smile at him, and imitate his sounds with your own voice.

Exercise 109: "Conversation." When baby starts to mumble often you can begin to "talk" to him. As in Exercise 108, persuade him to make sounds. When he does, imitate them and then be silent. When he mumbles again, reply again. Converse with him like this often, but be careful not to bore him with this game.

Exercise 110: "Shouting." After baby is used to "talking" to you when you're close by, try the same thing (during the fifth to sixth months) from a greater distance. For the baby to hear you, you must shout. Now baby learns to shout by alternately shouting with you.

Babies whose mothers respond most often to mumbling mumble more than babies whose mothers have less time for them, or children brought up in institutions where the nurses do not have the time to react frequently to each baby.

During his fourth to sixth months a baby learns to create various syllables. Some are similar to the noises of animals; others resemble any number of languages. Around the fifth month a baby learns to grunt, squeal, growl, purr, smack his lips, blow "rasperberries," and so on. He sings melodiously and articulates various vowels and such combinations of them as "a-o-a-o" and the like.

Around his sixth month your baby will probably begin to form some consonants; the most frequent are b, p, m, d, t, v. At this age some babies begin to combine some vowels with consonants into a syllable; they babble.

As I've said, up to the fourth month it's a good idea to repeat all the baby's vocal expressions, but from the fifth month you should begin to differentiate. Sounds that resemble sounds of your mother tongue should be repeated after the baby, but do pronounce them correctly. Sounds which are foreign to your mother tongue (e.g., grunts, squeals, purrs, smacking the lips, spitting) should yield lesser rewards. Smile at him in order not to inhibit his pleasure in producing sounds, but do not repeat those sounds; gradually cease to reward them even with a smile. This is what almost all mothers do— most of them unconsciously—which is why nearly all children in the world make the same sounds during the first six months of their lives. By the end of the ninth month differences begin to appear in the babbling of children of various nationalities. If, starting with the fifth month, you begin to differentiate some of your baby's sounds and syllables and reward some and not others, then his repertoire of sounds will begin to contain some more often and others will gradually disappear. The baby thus starts to imitate the sounds of his mother tongue providing, of course, that he has already spontaneously pronounced some that are similar. This modeling stage precedes true imitation which usually develops at the end of his ninth month.

Here's how to teach your child to use vocal expressions as a means of establishing social contact. During his fifth month he begins to mumble and deliberately tries to create responses in his environment—which he'll soon discover to be of two kinds. His mumbling creates no reaction in the world at large, but it can set off a considerable effect on the people around him. This experience is the condition for a baby to begin using his vocal expressions as a means of establishing social contact. Till now the baby reacted passively in contacts with people; e.g., he turned his head in the direction from which you called him. But in this sixth month he is likely to start using his voice as a means of establishing direct contact with you. When you take no notice of him, he'll try to attract your attention by making sounds. This is an important stage in the process of socializing, but it's not yet a specific human sign, because many animals also draw attention to themselves purposefully. The mumbling which is meant to attract your attention has the same purpose as primitive crying, but differs because it is deliberate, not reflexive, and is aimed at a specific person, not just anybody.

The following games for 5- to 6-month-olds are designed to teach a baby to use his voice to achieve social goals.

EXERCISE III

Exercise 111: Calling mother. When baby is in the mood to mumble, cover your face in front of him with a diaper. When baby mumbles, pull it off your face, let him see you, smile at him, mumble back at him. After a while cover your face again. Baby will soon understand the principle of the game and will begin to call on you to show yourself.

Exercise 112: Handing over toys. When baby mumbles, give him some interesting toy, let him play with it for a while and then take it away. When he mumbles again give him some other toy. Hand over toys after mumbling 5 or 6 times, 2 to 3 times a day.

Exercise 113: Lifting baby after he mumbles. When baby mumbles pick him up under the arms and lift him high up into the air, smile at him and lay him down. Repeat when he mumbles again. Repeat about 5 to 6 times. Instead of lifting him you can do something else baby likes.

Understanding Words (Passive Speech)

Before your baby utters his first intelligible word (active speech) he will learn to *understand* many words (passive speech). He must form an inventory of passive words before he starts to use one of them actively. Adults also maintain a store of passive words which we understand when we read them or hear them, but do not use in active speech, and the store of these words is greater than our store of active words.

If you call your 4- to 5-month-old by his name and he turns his head, he is not responding to the word; he would have turned his head at the sound of any other name or word. He is reacting to sound alone. The true response to a "word" appears at around the sixth month, assuming that your child has had the right education. To convey the meaning of the following exercises, let me show how your baby's first reaction to a "word" (not a sound) arises. If, during his fifth and sixth months he watches the pendulum of a clock with interest, I recommend that you accompany his observation with the words: "Clock, tick-tock!" In the sixth to seventh months, say the same words in the same place and the same way, but at a time when baby is *not* paying attention to the clock. When the baby turns his head and eyes to the named object you can consider this proof that he has formed an association between the word and the object and that he understands the meaning of the words.

Exercise 114: Turning the head toward an object named under the same conditions. Select an object which interests baby a lot: a clock, lamp, picture, statuette, window. It should be attractive in size, color, brightness, changes (it ticks, lights up, turns off). It should always be in the same place. Stand with the baby in a certain place near the object. Hold him in a particular way of your choice. Concentrate his vision onto the object. Then name it clearly and produce some action. For example, say "lamp" and at the same time switch the lamp on and off. Repeat this several times under the same conditions: same person, same voice, same words, same holding of the baby.

Then sometimes ask, "Where's the lamp?" at a moment when the baby is not looking at the object. At first if the baby turns his head toward the object this will be more or less accidental. But gradually it will become a deliberate reaction to the word "lamp."

Exercise 115: Turning the head toward a named object under various conditions. The response in Exercise 114 occurs fastest if you keep the conditions stable. But as soon as anything is altered, the baby's reaction becomes unsure. The baby probably will not react if, instead of you, his grandmother poses the same question. The present exercise is to teach baby to react even when the situations are altered. Begin by standing in a different spot in relation to the object; the baby must then turn his head differently. Hold him differently—not in your arms, but perhaps sitting in your lap. Later, you can alter your voice. Finally give him to father, grandmother or somebody else. Only the *object,* the lamp, remains the same. This creates an association between the two fundamental phenomena—the word and the lamp. The other ones gradually lose their significence. You can see that this exercise also exercises the baby's ability to abstract.

Exercise 116: Distinguishing between verbally named objects. This exercise should not be tried before baby has mastered Exercise 114 and 115; you should usually be able to begin during the seventh month. It serves to reward and perfect the responses learned in the two preceding exercises. Place two or three objects which baby knows onto the table or somewhere else in such a way that baby has these objects in his field of vision. Place baby onto your lap and ask him: "Where is the teddy?" After he has looked at the teddy, praise him and then ask "Where is the lamp?" Ask the questions alternately, and after 1 to 2 minutes, move the objects around and ask him again. Praise and stroke baby for every correct response. When he makes a mistake, correct him gently by saying "That's not the lamp, that's teddy!"

Developing Relationships with People

All activities that I've described encourage closer and firmer emotional relationships between a baby and his parents. By his fifth month he will be able to demonstrate the difference between his relationship to his parents and others who are close to him, on the one hand, and outsiders on the other. He will give his parents precedence over other people, seek *their* protection and help. But it would obviously not be good for your child to reject other people or be afraid of them. If you tie your baby to yourself too much you can make life more difficult for him later on.

Exercise 117: Getting used to contacts with other people. From his fifth to sixth months, begin to get baby used to visits of your friends, relatives, and neighbors and ask them to play with him for 2 or 3 minutes: to hold him in their arms, walk around the house with him, talk to him, show him toys and other objects, or perform some simple exercise, to get him used to unknown persons, cease to be afraid of them and establish contact with them. Naturally, you should be present so he gets used to establishing contact with visitors only in your presence. Babies who make contact with people outside the immediate family will not be afraid of strangers later in life or shy about greeting people and speaking to them. Many adults are less successful than they might be because they are handicapped by inhibitions in social contacts. If you begin to get your child used to people starting around his fifth month, he will socialize quite easily. It is important for him to get used not only to passive contact with people (so he won't protest against the mere presence of an unknown person), but for the outsider quite actively to do something with the child and have the child react without inhibitions.

Creating Happy, Pleased Moods

A person's general mood is determined not only by hereditary factors but also by factors of environment which are perhaps even more important. Human beings are most receptive in this respect during their earliest days. Therefore, the taste for life, the urge to be active and optimistic depend to a great extent on the educational environment at the start of life. Let me summarize once more how to make your baby happy and satisfied.

A good mood assumes the gratification of baby's biological and psychological needs. Of these I should stress the baby's activity. He should have space, time, and means to play or be busy with small tasks so he can do or observe something on his own. An inactive baby has nothing to make him happy and neither does a lonely one. Your child is most likely to laugh happily when he is playing with you or people close to him.

Cultivating Habits

The Development of Waking and Sleeping Patterns

Objective: Up to his sixth month your baby probably sleeps about 16 to 17 hours a day. Ten to 11 hours are during the night, the rest are four periods of sleep of 1 1/2 to 2 hours. Baby will be awake five times during the day for periods of 1 1/2 to 2 hours. After the third month the periods of daylight wakefulness become longer.

Even at this age wakefulness and sleep undergo changes and can be influenced by external influences for better or for worse. If you keep your baby busy during his wakeful periods in ways I've described in this chapter you will find he will really be actively awake, and sleep calmly. Large individual differences exist between the sleep needs of children, so the standards for wakefulness and sleep mentioned earlier in this book are only averages; many children have greater or lesser needs.

I recommend that you observe your child continually and put him to bed as soon as he shows the first signs of fatigue. If you put him to bed at the right time he is almost certain to fall asleep easily and sleep calmly; but if you extend his period of wakefulness he will fall asleep with difficulty, wake up early and will be irritable and nervous during his next period of wakefulness. If you continue to extend his normal period of wakefulness, your child will get used to it but his nervous system could become strained which may create conditions for the onset of neuroses.

How Can You Tell When Baby Is Tired? Not all babies show tiredness the same way. Parents naturally look for yawning, rubbing of eyes, loss of mobility, not wanting to play, and similar signs. But there is a type of child— the excitable ones—who express their tiredness by becoming *more* active. An experienced parent can learn to tell that these activities are relatively primitive and therefore not an expression of freshness and strength but evidence of weakening active inhibition; the baby cannot control himself and acts more primitively.

When baby is tired:

He begins to behave as he did a month or two ago, and his recently acquired abilities cannot be stimulated.

His mood becomes less stable, his temper gets worse even after a mildly unpleasant stimulus, which he would hardly notice when fresh.

His activities become rhythmical; he rhythmically moves his head or arms or body. His movements become less varied and he repeats only certain primitive ones. Older babies, when fresh, mumble various syllables; when they are tired they begin to hum rhythmically and keep repeating the same sound.

Primitive reflexes appear; more complex responses are difficult to stimulate; the baby reverts to primitive activities such as sucking his fingers.

Movements and posture of the body change. A baby lying on his tummy lifts his head only a little and often lays it down. He may hold a toy and do nothing with it.

A fresh baby cooperates during exercises; a tired baby is passive, weak, and shows little or no interest.

Baby has red eyelids; he rubs his eyes and yawns.

He may also, as I've said, become restless, aimlessly move his entire body, perform lots of movements with no visible purpose. Parents often think that these excited children just don't want to sleep yet. If such children are put to bed before restlessness appears they usually fall asleep easily and sleep calmly. But if restlessness overcomes them, they fall asleep with difficulty, their sleep is restless and they wake too soon.

If you observe your child carefully you will find other signs by which he exhibits tiredness. When you spot these signs, stop all activities and put him to bed. You should not wait for him to show he is tired by crying, shouting, or protesting. This would lead to an unhealthy strain.

Why Feeding Is Educational

Feeding your baby is far more than transporting food into him; it's an important educational act beginning with the very first days of life. The first conditioned reflexes are born from feeding, the basic relationship between mother and child is formed, and it is also the basis for skills, attitudes, and habits.

So feed him when he is hungry, calm, and healthy; give him as much independence as possible and do not combine feeding with unpleasant situations and stimuli: scoldings, anger, hurry, force-feeding, or punishment. Respect the state of your baby; allow a tired and sleepy baby to rest first—or, better still, do not allow him to become too sleepy and tired! And feed a sick baby with maximum consideration.

You can stimulate baby to be active during feeding by showing him the bottle and then handing it to him so he can bring his head toward it and grasp the nipple himself. Some babies meet the bottle with their hands. During the fourth month, sometimes earlier, you can teach him to eat from a spoon. If you pass him the spoon while he still has his mouth full, he will cease to open his mouth when he sees the spoon and grasp it. Never open his mouth with the spoon. In the sixth month you can put a piece of roll or apple into his hand to teach him to take food to his mouth. At first he will suck the food, later bite it.

You can teach him neat eating habits from his earliest age. If you spoon feed him, give him a bib, wipe his dirty face, keep the table clean, and get across the idea that you find a dirty face and table unattractive, you are creating resistance to dirt.

The Role of Furniture and Toys

The Ideal Playpen. At 4 to 5 months I believe a baby should be placed on a clean, warm floor atop a foam rubber sheet about 3 by 6 feet and 2 inches thick, covered with a sheet or blanket. Ideally, his playpen should be made of wood, about 2 feet high and spacious (3 feet by 3 to 6 feet). A father or grandfather who is skilled with tools can make one himself; the best ones can be taken apart to make four ladders. These parts can also be used as bridges, fireguards, barriers in the doorway, and for learning to walk (baby holds on to the fence and walks around it). You can attach pieces of rubber hose to the bars of one side. Such a rubber runged ladder is very useful to teach your baby how to climb in the third quarter-year. The rungs of the ladder should be no more than 2 inches apart.

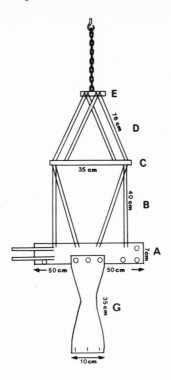

"Jolly Jumper": The chair is suspended from rubber or steel springs and enables baby to bounce up and down with only slight impulses from his legs.

Inclined Surface, a Gymnastic Plank: You can easily create an inclined surface by placing one end of a couch on one or two chairs. Or you can use a wooden desk top about 2 to 3 feet wide and 5 to 6 feet long, with cotton wool or foam rubber covered with waxcloth. This desktop can

be used for baby to play on or you can place it onto the table and use it as a gymnastic table for exercising. If you place it on the floor and lift one end so that it has an angle, baby can roll, try to crawl up a slope, and later climb up. Still later you can place the desk top on supports about 8 inches high and the baby can use it to learn to climb up a higher surface and climb down.

Wading Pool: For playing outside on warm sunny days a wading pool is ideal. Fill it with warm water and a 4-month-old baby will learn to lie on his tummy, keep his head high and play with toys. Such a pool can make children happy throughout their preschool age.

I realize that it has become fashionable to teach infants how to swim, but my own research does not indicate that this is a good idea for a baby's health or development, especially not for his breathing. Besides, it's much easier and less risky to teach a child to swim between the age of 2 and 3. Which is why you won't find anything about swimming in this manual for children up to 12 months old.

8

Exercises for the Seventh to Ninth Months

In his third quarter-year baby will free himself from absolute dependence on adults; he will no longer have to wait until you come to him, because he can get to you by crawling. At the beginning of the seventh month your baby will begin to understand some of your words and their meaning. Toward the end of the ninth month he not only understands words, but some babies even say their first intelligible word.

Your baby acquires not only motor skills for individual parts of his body, but also skills which use his entire body. Thus, in crawling not one muscle is unused.

During his sixth or seventh months baby will start kneeling on all fours. At first he remains stationary in this position, later he will lean forward and sometimes fall onto his face. Then he will learn to sway backward and forward on all fours (sway on his knees). Later he will swing forward, draw his legs up, move forward a bit and back to kneeling. Soon he will do this wormlike movement quicker. At the same time he learns to alternate forward movements with his right hand and left knee, and then left hand and right knee. This coordinated movement of rear and front limbs soon becomes automatic, so in his seventh to eighth months the baby will crawl like an ant and is also able to crawl up an inclined or even a vertical ladder. Parents usually try to stop him, but if you give him the opportunity he soon learns to climb up a ladder. During his eighth to ninth months the baby learns to negotiate spaces under tables and chairs, climb up low steps, and thereby exercise his entire body.

Crawling is exceptionally important for the development of the spine, and the back and neck muscles; it is excellent preparation for correct body posture later on. Therefore it is better to try and teach baby to crawl before sitting.

During the sixth month a baby pulls himself up into the sitting position if you hand him your fingers. In the seventh month he sits up alone but rather unsteadily; he leans far forward and leans on his hands. Only during his eighth month will he sit up straight without support and with his spine straight. During the eighth to ninth months he should be sitting up so firmly that he can lean forward and backward and turn around, without losing balance.

A baby who does a lot of crawling will learn to stand on his own legs comparatively early. During the fifth month he stands up by himself if you give him your fingers to hold, but still uncertainly. During the sixth month he stands firmly. During the seventh month, he will crawl up to his playpen and by grasping the bars pull himself up to a kneeling position. Soon afterward he stands up on one leg and moves up to an upright kneeling position on one knee. He will often stand up at once on both legs and pull himself upright. He usually manages that around the eighth to ninth months. At first he stands motionless and holds onto something. Then he will start transferring his weight from one leg to the other and slightly lift the unloaded leg; for a fraction of a second he will stand on one leg.

At the same time he starts moving his arms; at first he bends and stretches them, pulling his head toward and away from the walls of the pen he is holding on to. Later he loosens his grip and stands holding on with one hand for some time. After that he will start to play with his free arm while standing up. During his ninth month he should learn to lift up something from the ground if he can hold onto something with one hand; in other words, he can do a knee-bend and straighten up. At the same time he may sometimes play with both hands while in the standing position and keep his balance by leaning against a support.

Walking develops after the baby has learned to stand up against some furniture and transfer his weight from one leg to the other. He lifts his free leg and places it further away from the loaded one, then places his weight on this leg and draws the other up. At first he makes small steps sideways to the right and left, a sort of marking time. Between the ninth and tenth months he repeats the side step with one leg and draws the other up. At the same time he moves his hands in the same direction along the support he is holding. Soon he starts taking deliberate side steps to approach something interesting; generally, deliberate sidestepping appears in the fourth quarter of the first year.

The development of delicate hand movements is closely connected with the development of play and, as I have repeatedly stressed, strongly influences the development of cognition: experience, thinking, and such traits as concentration and precision. During his fourth to fifth months your baby reached out and deliberately grasped a toy. In the fifth month he placed his thumb opposite his other fingers. During the sixth month he no longer grasped an object with the palm but with the fingers. By the seventh he usually stops grasping small objects with all his fingers. First, the little fingers cease to participate in the grasping. By the eighth to ninth months a baby will hold small objects just with thumb and forefinger. At first these fingers are stretched out and the small object is held in the middle of both. By the ninth to tenth months both fingers are bent and the object is held only with the fingertips.

In the fifth month baby grasped an object with only one hand; when you offered him a second object for the other hand he grasped it but dropped the first at the same time. In his sixth month he held the object with both hands. By the end of the sixth month he passed it from hand to hand, and this skill is further perfected in the seventh month. Gradually he learns to turn the object over in his hand. At the same time he will have developed the ability to hold two objects in both hands.

During the fourth and fifth months your baby held an object in one hand and could, to a limited degree, manipulate it and turn it to inspect it. In the sixth month, when he holds an object in both hands, he has greater scope for manipulation, because he can squeeze, bend, or twist it. Passing it from hand to hand gives him greater scope for manipulation. And even greater manipulation is achieved when he can hold one object in each hand.

First he performs symmetrical movements with the objects, knocking them both on the table or against each other. His first attempts to bang two cubes against each other are not very successful because the movements are not entirely symmetrical, so the baby will often miss. At the same age he will also learn to clap his hands. Only during his ninth month will he learn to perform deliberately asymmetrical movements (one hand holds an object while the other bangs into it).

During the sixth month a baby bangs his empty hand or bangs an object on the table without aim. During the seventh month he begins to knock on another object on the table which calls for more precise movements. Soon he also learns to bang against objects both hard and softly, and gentle banging is the basis of the ability to carefully bring one object close to another. Only after that will a baby be able to place an object gently onto the table (during the ninth month), place objects into a box, insert things into a hole, or show similar muscle control.

Before that he must master one more seemingly simple skill: to let go of objects at the right time. Actually this is very difficult and he will only master this between his eleventh and twelfth months. During the second and third quarter-years an object will just happen to fall out of his hand. He trains for greater skill while shifting an object from one hand to the other. Even during his ninth month baby will hand you an object but will not let go of it; it's not that he does not want to give it to you or is trying to tease you; even in their eleventh month some babies will hold a cube above an open container but will not drop it although the mother has demonstrated it and tries to persuade them to imitate her.

You'll be able to observe how your baby develops experience and knowledge with manipulative games. During the fifth, sixth, and seventh months he did not respect the characteristics of the objects he was manipulating; he used them to train motor skills by banging, passing them from hand to hand, and so on. Around the eighth month he will start doing one thing with a cube, something else with a rubber toy, and something else again with a diaper because all three objects differ considerably in their properties and manipulative scope: the cube can be used to bang and make a noise, the rubber doll can be squeezed and bent, the diaper can be squashed.

After nine months a baby starts using one object to acquire others; he draws a toy toward him with the aid of the tablecloth. This use of tools is an expression of thinking; it proves that he understands the relationship between two objects and deliberately uses one to achieve a result with the other. At nine months you will also find that baby is capable of solving simple problems of bypassing. If you place a barrier between him and a toy, he will first try to grasp the toy through the barrier, but will very soon go around the barrier and grab it. The achievement of an aim by indirect means (bypassing) and the inclusion of intermediate activities (baby went around the obstacle) also is an expression of the thinking process.

During the seventh to ninth months a baby learns to react to words and appeals and you can teach him to clap his hands when you say "Clap, clap, clap your hands . . ."; to wave his hand when you tell him "Do bye-bye"; to spread his hands when asked "Show how big you are." During the ninth month he will start pointing his finger at an object when you ask "Where is . . . ?" By the end of the ninth month he will react to words which identify people close to him, some animals, things, and everyday activities. The richness of his passive vocabulary, the store of words which he "understands," is very hard to determine, because his reaction to many words is often not very expressive.

Active speech develops much more slowly. During the sixth month a baby can pronounce such two-letter syllables as "ba," "ma," "ta." At around the seventh month he begins to repeat these syllables and mumble them in duplicate: "ma-ma," "ba-ba-ba." Once he makes it obvious that he is saying "ma-ma" deliberately in relationship to you, these vocal expressions become words. A baby usually says his first word during the fourth quarter, but during the ninth month some babies already pronounce certain syllables in connection with a certain situation or object, so that these syllables or sounds assume the character of words.

Now he becomes active in his social relationships with

people. During the seventh and eighth months he draws attention to himself vocally, by stretching out his hands and approaching people by crawling up to them. He begins to understand hide-and-seek and to differentiate in his relationships. He will be used to being fed by mother, but may prefer to play with father. Many children at this age start to become frightened of unknown persons, but after a while will look out curiously at another person, and will soon lose their shyness and establish contact with this unknown person.

In general, your baby's development does not need to be stimulated as directly or intensively as during the first 6 months. Now it will be sufficient to ensure enough opportunities and scope for self-development and to channel, support, and motivate these activities. The direct stimulation during his first 6 months has given him a certain momentum which is more or less maintained throughout his entire development.

Training Your Baby to Crawl

Objective: By his eighth month your baby will usually be crawling energetically around the whole house and I have repeatedly stressed how important this skill is.

The following exercises strengthen the arms to enable your baby to carry at least half his weight on them. They also strengthen his tummy muscles to enable him to draw his knees up to his tummy. Either father or mother acts as a live but safe obstacle. You place your baby onto your own body and then encourage him to move in order to grasp a toy. The baby will try to crawl up your body, push with his arms and legs, and perform other exerting movements. The soft, warm human body stimulates more intensive movements than a hard table.

EXERCISE 118

Exercise 118: Crawling over father. Lie down on the floor and place your baby by your side so he kneels on the floor and leans on your stomach. Place some toy on your other side. In his attempt to grasp the toy he will lie across you and push off with his legs. You can help him push off by supporting his legs with your hand. You can also lay baby across your stomach so his head and shoulders are above the floor, forcing him to support himself with his hands about 6 inches away from your side. Place the toy on your other side and baby will then have to push himself backward to get to it.

EXERCISE 119

Exercise 119: Pushing to the left and right. Father, again lying on the floor, places baby onto his chest with both arms resting on his chest and his legs embracing his waist; in other words, astride you. Place one toy on either side of yourself about 12 to 18 inches away. Baby will push himself to both sides with his arms in order to try and grab the toys.

Exercise 120: Climbing over father who is lying on his side. Lie down on your left side with the baby kneeling behind your back, his arms resting against your right side; or lay him over your right side with his arms on the floor in front of you. Place a toy about 12 inches away from him and make him grab for it. You can make the obstacle higher by lifting your right arm. If you draw your left arm in you can make it easier for him, because baby will be able to gain more support with his legs.

Exercise 121: Climbing down from the position astride father's side. Again lie on your left side with baby lying astride your right side and holding onto your bent arm. Place a toy either in front or behind your chest so he can reach it by letting go of your arm, leaning his arms on the floor, drawing one leg to the other and climbing off you.

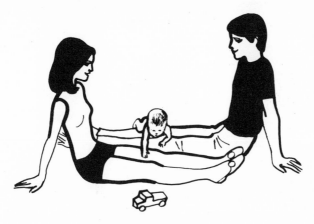

EXERCISE 122

Exercise 122: Climbing over the thighs of both parents. Sit opposite each other on the floor so that father's left shin is by mother's left hip and mother's left shin is by father's left side. Slightly part your legs to form a sort of crawling ladder. Place baby across the legs of one of you and coax him to try to crawl over your thighs toward a toy lying next to the thigh of your partner. Baby will learn to crawl over your thighs as if they're a safe soft ladder. You can make the exercise more difficult by slightly bending your knees. Or you can grasp each other's left elbows so that your arms form a slightly elevated obstacle for baby to overcome.

Exercise 123: Crawling into and out of nest. Father lies on his left side and mother opposite him on her right side. They join hands, slightly bend their legs so they touch. Your bodies will thus form a circle—"a nest." Encourage baby to crawl into this nest and out again. Depending on the baby's maturity you can let him crawl either over your arms, legs, or the highest part of the wall: your hips or shoulders.

EXERCISE 124

Exercise 124: Crawling in a sling. Fold a diaper to form a wide sling and wrap it around baby's chest with both ends over his back. Grasp both ends and with the aid of the sling lift baby's chest, about 4 to 6 inches above the ground. This makes it easier for him to draw his legs up to his tummy. Baby will kneel on all fours and begin to push off with his hands and feet and crawl toward a toy which you have placed in front of him.

Exercise 125: Crawling down a slope. Lift up one narrow end of a couch with a chair so it forms an inclined surface of about 15 degrees. Place baby (who should be able to kneel on all fours) on the couch so he can crawl downward. Crawling down a slope is easier than on a flat surface.

Note: If your baby is to learn to crawl his legs should be bare. Otherwise crawling over smooth surfaces is much harder.

Here now are exercises by which baby, in his eighth to tenth months, perfects his crawling over obstacles.

Exercise 126: Crawling over a flat surface under various conditions. After baby has learned to crawl over a flat surface a bit, give him the opportunity to crawl around in pants, over a carpet, parquet floor, sand, grass, or shallow water, for example. Be very careful that he does not hurt himself on splinters, holes, or rough edges, and that the surfaces he crawls over are as clean as possible. Also make sure he does not put his fingers into his mouth before you have washed his hands.

EXERCISE 127

Exercise 127: Chase on all fours. By his tenth month baby should have learned to crawl forward and backward quickly, move sideways and turn left and right. Train him with the game of "chase on all fours." Mother or father crawl after baby and call, "I'll catch you!" Baby will laugh and try and get away by crawling away on all fours as quickly as he can, forward and to the side. This game requires a certain degree of motor and social maturity.

Exercise 128: Playing "dog." If your baby has the opportunity to observe dogs, father can imitate how dogs run and bark and persuade him also to play "dog." This imitation is usually successful during the fourth quarter, but many babies can learn it in the third.

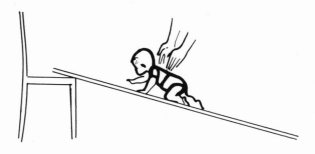

EXERCISE 129

Exercise 129: Climbing up and down a slope. Use the open ground and allow baby to climb up and down a slight slope in a field or in the garden. At home you can use a wide plank or desk propped up to an angle of 15 to 20 degrees, covered with a blanket, and allow baby to crawl around on it, taking care he does not fall off.

EXERCISE 130

Exercise 130: Crawling among obstacles. Place some large cartons, chairs, and other objects around the floor so that if the baby wants to get to a toy he will have to crawl among these obstacles and move to the left and right. This exercise produces a healthy and vigorous bending of the spine to both sides.

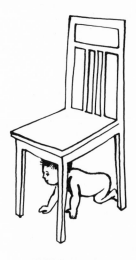

EXERCISE 131

Exercise 131: Crawling under and through objects. Various objects can be used for this exercise: chairs, benches, or cardboard boxes without bottoms. First, persuade baby to crawl through (or under) larger spaces, and gradually through smaller ones, to get him used to protecting his head against knocks. With practice he will learn to keep his head down until he has crawled through (or under) a space. Crawling through low openings is especially good exercise for the back muscles.

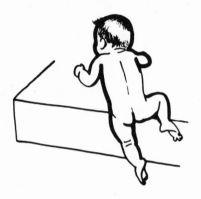

EXERCISE 132

Exercise 132: Crawling onto a step. Urge the baby to approach a step, a low bench, a suitcase, or box and persuade him to climb on top of it. He will first lean on it with his arms and must then find out that he will have to lift his leg up high until he can get his knee onto it. Then he must transfer the weight of his body onto the object and draw up his second knee. You should help him at first; place one knee onto the obstacle and hold the heel of the lifted leg to enable him to bring the other leg up more easily.

Lifting the knee demonstrates the technique he'll need for climbing.

EXERCISE 133

Exercise 133: Crawling along a raised surface. Use either a low bench or place an ironing board on two stools to make a bridge. Place baby onto his tummy at one end of the bridge and try to persuade him to crawl toward the other. For safety, you must accompany him and be prepared to catch him if his hand slips from the board and he is in danger of falling off.

Exercise 134: Climbing down. Babies start to climb down from steps or benches head first and there is danger of falling onto their head. They will often crawl along a couch and not stop at its edge. Teach baby how to stop at the edge, turn around and climb down backward, feet first, by placing him onto the couch with his feet over the edge. Press his shoulders and gradually push him down off the couch until he lands on his legs. This of course assumes that he can stand on his legs (around the end of the ninth month). Repeat this several times and help him less in climbing down, but be careful that he does not fall. After some time baby will grasp the principle and will learn to turn around himself, move his legs back over the edge of the couch and land safely on the floor— usually during the fourth quarter-year.

EXERCISE 135

Exercise 135: Climbing over obstacles. You can make an obstacle out of a rolled carpet, a low bench, or a mattress. Outdoors you can use a tree trunk (watch for splinters or twigs). The safest obstacle is you, lying down. As soon as baby has learned to climb up and down he quickly learns to climb over obstacles.

EXERCISE 136

Exercise 136: Climbing a ladder. If you give your 9-month-old baby the right kind of ladder, perhaps the side wall of his crib, and place it against a wall, he will crawl toward it, pull himself upright, step onto the first bar and then soon climb up the rest. As I've said, 9-month-old babies do not climb a ladder—not because they don't know how, but because parents prevent them from doing so for fear of baby falling and injuring himself. Of course you must supervise him. Allow him first to climb up steps, then a slightly inclined ladder which you can gradually make steeper. Constantly watch that he does not let go. Grant him the pleasure of this skill and don't rely on the mistaken notion that even slight missteps are impossible because you have removed every opportunity.

Note: All exercises to train crawling entail a degree of risk of skin scraping or other minor hurt. But much more serious dangers can be avoided through these slight, calculated risks: babies who early acquire good motor abilities and many positive and negative experiences are better protected against serious accidents than children who lack experience and exercise.

How to Train for Sitting Up and Sitting

Objective: I want to stress again that when you exercise your baby you should give preference to the dynamic aspect over the static. Teaching baby how to sit up should precede the act of sitting. I'm even tempted to exaggerate slightly and say that the later baby learns to sit the better for his overall development. And he should definitely first learn to crawl before he learns to sit.

Exercise 137: Sitting up with the aid of a ring. This exercise, already described among the exercises for children in the second quarter-year, should be done in the seventh month so that the rings are held stationary. The baby should be given a minimum assistance and pull himself up to the sitting position almost by himself.

EXERCISE 138

Exercise 138: Sitting up on an inclined surface. Baby should lie with his bottom and legs on an horizontal surface but should have a desk under his back with an angle of 20 to 30 degrees. Hang or hold a diaper in front of him. Baby will grasp it and easily pull himself up into the sitting position. You can also sit on the floor or couch, leaning back on your elbows with baby half sitting on your thighs and half lying with his back on your stomach. If he grasps a diaper hanging above him he will sit up easily.

EXERCISE 139

Exercise 139: Sitting up by the bars of his crib. Place baby right next to the bars of his crib and hold a toy above him. He will grasp the bars and sit up.

EXERCISE 140

Exercise 140: Sitting up by pushing up from a support. Demonstrate to baby how to sit up when you have nothing to hold on to. Baby is lying on his back. Lift his legs up into the air (the trunk and legs form a right angle) and roll him over to the right side. Then place the palms of both his bent arms to his right shoulder and hold a toy above him. Baby will push up with his arms, lift up his trunk, and sit on the right half of his bottom, leaning toward the right. Later he'll learn to brace up with more strength and sit on his entire bottom. He will assist himself by lifting his left (almost stretched-out) leg. It acts as a counterbalance to make sitting up easier. This teaches him how to sit up when he has nothing to hold on to.

When you help baby to sit up, do not let him sit; lay him down again at once. Once he has learned to sit up by himself, allow him to sit for a little while and play in this position. But do not permit him to loosen his body tension by sitting up too long, or he will sit crouched up and bent. Lay him on his tummy and allow him to play in this position. When baby does sitting up, do the following exercise to prevent him from sitting motionlessly.

Exercise 141: Rewarding sitting. Once baby sits up, hand him a toy from the right, left and back so he'll turn around, bend forward, backward, and sideways without losing his balance (ninth month).

Note: Between his fourth and eighth months you can let baby sit in your lap several times a day, feed him in this position and play with him. But he must lean against your arms and stomach and lie against you, rather than sit. Usually you should also hold him under the arms so he sits straight and his spine gets only normal strain.

When children aged 4 to 7 months are allowed to sit in the corner of their crib and prevented from falling by being surrounded with pillows, this is totally inappropriate for teaching good posture. A baby who lacks strength to hold his spine correctly will usually collapse or sit with a bent spine and he can easily get used to this unhealthy bending of the spine.

How to Train for Standing Up and Standing

Objective: Again, to teach baby how to stand up and only then to stand! Be sure to consult an orthopedist first to make sure that baby's hip joints are OK.

Exercise 142: Moving on from the seated to the standing position with the aid of a hand. Sit baby down on a box about 6 inches high so that his shins are perpendicular to the ground. Offer him your fingers. He'll grasp them and usually jerk himself with his legs from the sitting to the standing position. Sit him down again at once and repeat several times. You can also sit down on the ground, sit baby onto the thighs of your bent legs, grasp his hands and baby will bear his legs against your stomach and stand up. Repeat several times.

Exercise 143: Standing up from the lying down position with the aid of an offered hand. With baby lying on his back offer your fingers, a ring, rod, or other suitable tool. When he grasps it, pull. Baby will sit up, and stand up. You can make this exercise more challenging by holding your hand still so that baby gets up onto his feet with increasing independence. You can then make this even more difficult by holding the aid so high that the baby, getting up, has his arms stretched out and upward, then straight out. The most difficult exercise for him is to get up when holding his arms out in front of him but low down.

EXERCISE 144

Exercise 144: Independent rising near a bar from the kneeling position. At 7 to 8 months, after your child can crawl to the bars of his bed or a chair or couch, hold some toy above his head and encourage him to get up and grasp it. Baby will grasp hold of the bars and first pull himself up onto his knees, then straighten one leg and finally both legs, and get up. You should reward achievement of these stages by handing him a toy; first reward him when he has managed to kneel up, then when he manages to kneel on one knee, and so on as he progresses.

EXERCISE 145

Exercise 145: Independent standing up next to a smooth wall. After baby has managed to stand up next to some furniture which he can grasp with his hands, persuade him to stand up next to the wall or some smooth cupboard which he can lean against but has no holds. The come-on can be a doll suspended from the wall or the key of the cupboard.

Exercise 146: Standing with one hand for support or by leaning of the body. Stand your baby next to the couch and place a toy in one hand. He must let go with that hand and support himself with only one hand. He will often solve the problem by taking the toy in both hands and leaning against the couch.

EXERCISE 147

Exercise 147: Picking things up. After baby has learned to stand up and hold himself safely with one hand, place a toy in front on him on the floor. When he tries to pick it up, baby will learn to lean forward in the standing position, lower himself to a crouch position and then get up again, straighten up and hold onto something all the time. You can make this easier for him at first by placing a tall toy in front of him, or placing the toy on a box.

Training for First Steps

Objective: When your baby can hold onto something during his ninth month he will start to mark time when he stands up, and start walking around furniture sideways, but sometimes he will turn around sideways to the furniture and take a step forward. During the fourth quarter-year he will probably learn to take his first independent step without holding on.

Note: Teach him to walk naturally. When you teach walking with the aid of various "runners" and "walkers"

I am convinced that you slow down independent walking. Usually a baby takes no steps in walkers. He just pushes himself up. Also, he will not learn the most important skill: keeping his balance, because he holds onto the edge of the carriage. The way babies move in these walkers has very little in common with actual walking and it's also contrary to our "principle of minimum assistance" because the walker always gives the baby the same amount of assistance and therefore does not stimulate him to perfect his walking.

For baby to learn how to walk he must gradually learn to stand on his feet and carry his whole weight on them (about the fifth to sixth months); take steps (seventh to ninth months); keep balance when walking (ninth to fourteenth months). The walkers aid none of these objectives. It is equally unsuitable for baby to learn to walk by pushing a chair or carriage in front of him; when they push something in front of them, babies are apt to lean far forward and you must get them out of this habit when they take their first independent steps and teach them to walk upright.

Exercise 148: Transferring body weight from one foot to the other. Stand baby in front of the couch and place a toy about 6 inches out of his reach to the right. Baby will lean to the right, transfer the weight of his body onto his right foot and take it off his left. When he has grasped the toy and played with it, place another to his left so he'll transfer his weight to his left foot, and off the right.

EXERCISE 149

Exercise 149: Kicking a ball. Stand baby sideways to the couch and hold a ball on a string in front of him. If the ball is near his foot, the baby will accidentally kick it. Soon he will start kicking the ball deliberately. Give him the opportunity to kick with both legs.

EXERCISE 150

Exercise 150: Sidestepping. Stand baby in front of the couch and place a favorite toy about a yard to his right. Move up behind baby and grasp both his hands. Gently pull his left arm sideways and his right arm up so he'll stand on his left leg and slightly lift his right. Then pull his right arm sideways to his side and lift his left so he'll stand on his right leg and make a step to the right. Repeat until baby reaches the toy. Do this exercise in the seventh month before baby has learned to walk alongside the furniture.

EXERCISE 151

Exercise 151: Steps forward when led by the hand. After baby has learned to walk alongside the furniture you can start leading him by the hands. Stand behind baby, grasp his hands, slightly pull them forward and baby will start taking steps. Gradually decrease the assistance of your guiding hands. At first baby will walk with his arms in the air. When he is more sure of himself, you can make it more challenging for him by letting him hold onto you with his arms outstretched in front or to the sides.

Exercise 152: Steps forward, led by one hand with the other leaning against the furniture. Place baby sideways by the couch. He will hold onto the furniture with one hand and your hand with his other. Move slowly forward and baby will keep hold of your hand but will have to let go with the other and again put it out for support. This exercise trains baby for walking while holding out one hand.

How to Develop Delicate Hand Movements and Play

Objective: During the seventh to ninth months I recommend that you try and teach baby: to adapt the posture and position of the hand before grasping an object; to grasp small objects that lie on a surface; to act on an object with another object; to lower and build up objects; to open drawers and boxes, to empty and fill them; to process various kinds of materials; to develop self-serving movements; to make movements on verbal requests.

When you want to pick up something you adapt the position of your hand and spread your fingers when approaching it so you can pick it up. You spread your fingers differently to pick up a large or small object, and you turn your hand to a different position if the object is horizontal or vertical. A baby must learn to assess the size, shape, and position of an object and adapt his hand accordingly.

Exercise 153: Grasping various-sized and -shaped objects in various positions. Frequently offer baby differently shaped objects with which he has little experience and which he cannot yet grasp. A round cardboard disc (like a small plate) can be grasped only by the edge; a large inflatable ball can be grasped only with the aid of both hands; cubes with 1-inch edges can be picked up in pairs in one hand. The adaption of the hand before grasping can be trained easily by handing baby elongated or flat objects (cooking ladles, lids) in various positions. The baby will have to turn his hand differently when you hand him the cooking ladle in the vertical, horizontal, and tilted position.

Exercise 154: Grasping moving objects. Hand your baby a toy, but in fun move it here and there for baby to try and grasp it while it is still moving. You can gradually make your movement faster and the object larger to make the exercise more difficult.

EXERCISE 155

Exercise 155: Grasping objects inside containers. Place an attractive toy into a container in front of baby and then persuade him to take it out again. Start with containers which have large openings and gradually move on to those with smaller openings (a toy into a pan, then into a pot and finally into a jug). Offer baby the container in various positions—with the opening toward him, away from him, upward, to the right or left, or slightly backward. Baby must not only adapt his hand movements to the position of the container but also his arm and shoulder. The game with the jug is especially good preparation for the solution of detour problems by side-stepping and develops his spatial and shape imagination and thinking.

Picking up small objects is much more difficult than picking up large ones and can be performed only after baby has acquired the so-called tweezer grip with the end of his thumb and forefinger, which is harder than grasping an object when it's handed to him.

EXERCISE 156

Exercise 156: Picking up small toys. Place various small toys in front of baby: buttons (about 1 1/2 inches in diameter), a pencil, marble, chestnut, sugar cube, pebble, thick string. These objects encourage baby to use only his fingers to pick them up because when he places his entire palm over the object and bends his fingers he will not be able to do so. You can make it easier for him to pick up these objects if you place them on a piece of foam rubber, sponge, or cotton wool; it's much harder to pick up a small object from a hard surface.

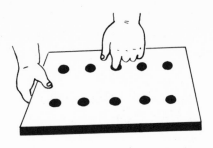

EXERCISE 157

Exercise 157: Playing with a "desk" with holes in it. Give baby a wooden board (about 4 by 4 inches) and bore some small holes in it (about 1/2 inches). Baby will feel the desk, put his fingers into the holes, and learn to grasp objects with stretched fingers. Equally suitable is a cube with holes in it (edges about 1 to 1 1/2 inches long) or a ball (about 2 inches in diameter).

Acting with One Object on Another

For the following exercises you will need some simple toys which you can offer to baby either individually or attached to a desk top (about 1 1/2 by 2 feet) which should be suspended low on the wall so that baby can play with the objects on the desk top.

Exercise 158: Playing with puppet or bell. Give baby the opportunity to activate a puppet or a bell by pulling a string. During his eighth to ninth months baby will enjoy creating new effects by pulling the string.

EXERCISE 159

Exercise 159: Turning a wheel or cylinder. Take out the desk top mentioned in Exercise 157. Attach a round, brightly colored cylinder to it (perhaps a can about 4 to 5 inches long and 2 inches in diameter). You can also use other geometrically shaped bodies (a Ping-Pong ball or a cube) as long as they will begin to rotate when the baby bangs at them. An abacus with large balls will serve the same purpose.

EXERCISE 160

Exercise 160: Turning a handle. Attach a rotating handle to a wooden box or cube with walls about 5 inches long.

Offer it to baby in various positions: with the handle on top, on the sides, in front. Your baby will try to turn the handle and will succeed in turning it by about 180 degrees here and there, but only during his fourth quarter-year will he succeed in turning it around completely. Babies like turning handles of various instruments, such as a pencil sharpener or a coffee mill. You can also buy music boxes or musical toys which emit tones when their handles are turned.

Exercise 161: Turning a key. Place a large key in a desk drawer so that baby can turn it to both sides. Round furniture handles or similar objects will serve the same purpose.

Exercise 162: Pressing a button. Place two or three bell pushbuttons on the desk and attach these to a pocket battery with the same number of small bulbs in the upper end of the desk where baby cannot reach. Connect the bells and the batteries so Pushbutton 1 lights up Bulb 3 and so on. Show baby that you can light up the bulb by pressing the button. Baby will soon begin to push the buttons and later will look up at the bulb which he wants to light up, showing that he has grasped the connection between which pushbutton belongs to which bulb.

Exercise 163: Clapping hands. Grasp baby by the wrists and demonstrate how to clap. Baby will soon begin actively clapping himself. During this period baby will also be able to perform symmetrical movements with both hands—and clapping is the prototype of such movements.

EXERCISE 164

Exercise 164: Banging two objects against each other. After baby has learned to clap, give him a toy or cube to hold in each hand, and baby will begin to knock them against each other.

Exercise 165: Drumming. Give baby a drum and drumstick (a box and a cooking ladle will do) and show him how to beat a drum. When he is learning to drum with one stick, let him hold the stick alternately in one and then the other hand. Then give him a stick for each hand. He will again perform symmetrical movements: he will bang and lift both sticks at once. He will not learn to beat first with one hand and then the other until his fourth quarter-year.

EXERCISE 166

Exercise 166: Drawing a toy closer with the aid of a string. Place a carriage or a doll on the table, out of baby's reach. Tie a piece of string with a small ball on one end of the toy. Place the string directly in front of baby. The ball on the end of the string is important because baby is more likely to notice it than the string itself, and will pick it up better. He will first play with the ball on the string and will later notice that by pulling the string he can bring the toy closer to him.

EXERCISE 167

Exercise 167: Pushing a cube with a ladle. Place a cube in front of baby, put a ladle into his hand, and show him how he can push the cube here and there.

Note: When baby has learned to deliberately pull a toy toward himself with the aid of a string, or how to push a cube around with a cooking ladle, he has acquired not only a manual skill, but has also begun to think, because he is using primitive tools and with their aid is achieving certain effects in an expression of awakening intellectual abilities. In both exercises baby is proving that he is really beginning to think with his hands.

Teaching Baby to Place Objects on Top of Each Other and Build

For an adult, placing a thing down, e.g., a cube, is so simple and natural an activity that there seems no need to teach it to baby. In actual fact it is a very complicated activity and demands such complex neuromuscular coordination that baby will only learn to do this between the third and fourth quarter-year, and he will require a year to place one cube on top of the other. But first he must learn (a) to guide his hand holding the cube to his target with precision, i.e., to the other cube lying down; (b) turn the hand holding the cube so that it covers the surface of the stationary cube; (c) stop the hand holding the cube just above the target; (d) open his hand at the right time; (e) withdraw his hand and at the same time no longer touch the cubes. Each individual act is extremely difficult and baby will master only part of them by his ninth month.

Exercise 168: Handing over an object. Place various small objects in front of baby and ask him to hand them to you. Put out your hand and wait until he places it in your palm. This teaches him to guide his hand to the target (your palm), which should meet his hand halfway. You will usually have to grasp the object yourself and take it away because deliberate release is still difficult for him. Praise and stroke baby for each object he hands over to you.

Exercise 169: Slow laying down of objects. At 6 months your baby is not capable of stopping his hand when it holds something above the table. His movement is stopped by the table itself and baby bangs the cube onto the table. During his seventh to eighth months give baby some flat object (a small bowl or box) and demonstrate how to lay it down slowly. Lead baby to lay it down slowly, quietly, gently with its wide base downward. Do the same with other objects such as a lid.

EXERCISE 170

Exercise 170: Standing objects up. When baby has been taught to lay down flat, low objects, you can start teaching him to set down higher objects. Give him a plastic cup and ask him to place it onto the table. Play at standing up cylinders and cubes.

Opening, Emptying, and Filling Drawers and Boxes

During his third quarter-year your baby will express increasing interest in hollow objects and will like to play with various containers, boxes, and drawers. He will feel their inside with his hands, empty their contents, and fill them up with objects.

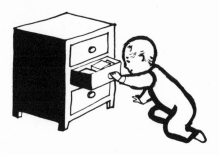

EXERCISE 171

Exercise 171: Opening drawers. Allow baby to play with a small, light drawer (in a child's chest or table) with a handle in front. The front wall of the drawer should be about 1 inch smaller than the opening into which it is placed. This will prevent baby from getting his fingers pinched when he shuts the drawer. Baby will open and close the drawer with great interest, and his interest will be all the greater when the contents of the drawer are interesting.

Exercise 172: Emptying containers. Give baby a container to play with: a box, cup, basket, drawer. Fill it with small objects: cubes, nuts, fir cones. At this age baby will be able to empty the drawer not only by extracting individual objects, but also by tipping the vessel bottom up.

Exercise 173: Filling a container. If your baby can empty containers that doesn't mean he can fill them; this skill is usually acquired a bit later. Use the same containers and objects as in Exercise 172. Baby will learn to fill the containers in various ways: picking up individual objects with one hand, picking one up in each hand, scooping up several with both hands. At first baby will hold a cube above the box but not let go of it. Be patient. Parents often think he does not want to let go, when in fact he still does not know how to and must learn.

Exercise 174: Transferring objects from container to container. Give baby two containers such as a box and a basket. At this age baby will transfer the objects from one to the other without any system, but will most often drop them outside the container.

The following group of exercises teaches your baby to fill containers with small objects and to place objects into small holes.

EXERCISE 175

Exercise 175: Sticking the rod into a hole. Give baby a cube with a hole in each side, and also offer him a cooking ladle. If baby does not start doing so himself, show him how to stick the handle of the ladle through the hole. Most babies master this task only after their ninth month. The difficulty is that baby must hold the ladle further away from its end, aim the end straight into the hole and hold the ladle vertically above the wall of the cube; all of this calls for new manual and practical experiences.

How Baby Learns to Process Materials

Give baby the opportunity to see that he can alter the shape and size of objects by manipulating them, which is the basis for creative activities.

Exercise 176: Kneading dough. When you're making something out of dough give a piece to baby and show him that he can press it, pull it out, twist and tear it. This play with dough exercises not only his fingers but his imagination, too.

Exercise 177: Playing with string and rags. During his third quarter-year you will find baby likes to play with rags which can be compressed, twisted, and drawn out in various ways.

Exercise 178: Playing with aluminum foil or tinfoil. These wraps are different from paper or textiles, because they are easy to bend, twist, and compress and yet maintain the shape that the baby gave them. (Always watch baby carefully to see that he does not stick little bits into his mouth.)

EXERCISE 179

Exercise 179: Breaking up spaghetti. Give baby a few dry, raw noodles and show him how he can break them. Baby who devotes himself to this activity with great pleasure will learn to use the tips of his fingers. Again, be sure he does not put bits into his mouth.

Exercise 180: Tearing off leaves. Give baby a wild plant and show him he can tear leaves off the stems and tear larger leaves into small pieces.

Self-Serving Motions

At the beginning of his second 6 months your baby can perform a few simple manipulative movements which help him to gratify his needs or help him prepare for this gratification.

Exercise 181: Grasping the bottle and bringing it to his mouth. Starting with the fourth to sixth months, place baby's hand around the bottle. During the seventh to ninth months baby will grasp the proffered bottle himself, place it to his mouth, grasp the nipple with his mouth and hold it himself while he drinks.

EXERCISE 182

Exercise 182: Taking a cup up to his lips. Give baby the opportunity to grasp a cup, hold it up to his mouth and tilt it correctly. At first, train this skill in the bathroom or in the yard in summer and pour only a little water into the cup. By his eighth to ninth months baby will be able to drink from the cup without spilling too much.

EXERCISE 183

Exercise 183: Putting a spoon to his mouth. In his seventh to eighth months give baby a spoon and he will guide it to his mouth. Before giving baby his bath you can hand him a spoon with some pasty food which sticks to it: baby will place the spoon into his mouth himself and lick it. After the first attempts you will probably have to bathe him for all too obvious reasons.

Exercise 184: Munching a crust, roll, apple. During his seventh to eighth months baby will learn independently to eat a piece of roll or apple.

Exercise 185: Stirring with a spoon. Give baby a cup and a spoon and he will soon place the spoon into the cup. You can then teach him to use the spoon for stirring.

Exercise 186: Using a towel. During his eighth to ninth months when bathing baby you can give him the towel and tell him to dry himself as well. Baby will move the towel, e.g., over his face, and imitate toweling.

Movements or Verbal Request

During his seventh to ninth months you can start to train baby in various games and movements at verbal request.

EXERCISE 187

Exercise 187: "Clap your hands," "Do bye-bye," "Show how big you are." When baby begins to understand words (which he shows, for example, by turning his eyes to the clock when asked "Where's the tick-tock?") you can start to train the above motions. Take baby's hands into your own, clap them together and say "Clap, clap, clap your hands . . ." After you have repeated this game with him several times, he will actively clap his hands himself when you tell him to. Train other movements the same way.

I have mostly described activities that your baby performs with you and under your instruction. But you should also give him maximum opportunity for playing by himself. You will soon see that he will spontaneously perform many movements which he has not been taught; most of them are extremely useful for his further development. During this unsupervised play, I'm sure you'll see to it that his toys aren't sharp, brittle, have poisonous coatings, or are so small that he might swallow them. Protect him against sharp corners, uncovered electric sockets, hot stoves, and radiators, all of which will be of increasing interest to him. It is better to avoid undesired activities rather than to forbid them, because upbringing should consist mainly of stimulation, encouragement, praise; bans, threats, or punishments which disrupt the relationship between parent and child should be used only in exceptional cases.

How to Develop Thinking

Objective: At the beginning of his seventh month your baby should be able to deliberately act on an object to create a given effect. By his ninth month he should act in various ways on different objects with the obvious expectation of various effects. By the end of his ninth month he should be capable of using at least one primitive tool and to solve a simple task in a roundabout way.

At the start of his third quarter-year, give baby the opportunity of training his understanding of the relationship between cause and effect.

Exercise 188: The deliberate creation of an expected effect. Use all reasonable means at your disposal to allow baby to create various effects or some change, perhaps by banging on a bell or drum to make a sound, or by making a doll move by pulling a string, make a whistling noise by pressing a rubber doll and so on.

From his behavior it should be obvious that baby is performing the movement not for the movement alone but for the effect which this movement can create. It should be apparent that he expects this effect; that the

effect is the main motive for his action; and that he is
surprised and disappointed if the effect does not take
place.

Exercise 189: The creation of various effects on the same
object. Try and create situations where one motion creates one effect while a different motion creates a different
one. Give baby a piece of paper. One movement will
crumple it; another can smooth it out; completely different movements can tear it. Or give baby a rubber hose.
When he grasps it and spreads out his arms the hose
stretches; when his hands come close to each other the
hose forms a ring; with other movements he can wrap it
around his hand. If you give him a plastic bag containing
various small objects he will soon begin to experiment.
He sees that certain motions make the objects fall to the
right or to the left; other motions produce rattles; with
still others the bag can be made larger or smaller.

Exercise 190: Creating graded effects. Thinking is best
developed with jobs and objects which enable the attain-
ment of graded effects depending on the degree of intensity of motions which cause them. The slow shaking of
a rattle creates quiet rattling. Faster movements make for
louder rattling. The careful slapping of a ball makes it
move only a small distance. A sharper slap will make it
move here and there. A soft slap on the water will create
only a ripple, a big slap will make the water splash on all
sides. If a vessel is tilted only slightly only a little water
will spill out, if it is tilted more all the water will run out.
You can tell whether baby is aware of this relationship by
the way he deliberately alternates fine movements and
watches their effects and then very rough movements
and then observes the difference in their effects.

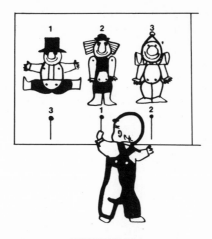

EXERCISE 191

Exercise 191: Deliberately creating one effect from several possible ones. An example of this is Exercise 162. Baby has three pushbuttons in front of him. Further away are three bulbs. These are connected so that Pushbutton 1 lights up Bulb 2, pushbutton 2 Bulb 3, and Pushbutton 3 Bulb 1. You'll know that baby has understood the relationship between the pushbutton and the appropriate bulb when, before pressing the button, he watches for a certain bulb to light up. You can make a similar toy out of a box. Make three entry and three exit holes arranged so that a marble dropped into the first hole will come out of the second hole, and so forth. Or another game is to have three marionettes with three strings coming out of a hole in a board in a different order to which they hang. By the end of the ninth month baby should understand these relationships and when, e.g., he throws a marble into one hole he will beforehand watch the hole out of which the marble should come.

EXERCISE 192

Exercise 192: Acquiring objects with the aid of an interposed action. Up to his seventh month baby will approach a target directly and only when he sees it. During
his eighth month he is capable of interposing an intermediate action which will enable him to achieve his aim: if
you place a toy in front of him and cover it with a diaper

the baby will first pull the diaper aside and then grasp the toy. The removal of the diaper is an interposed action only if baby pushes it aside and does not play with it and when it becomes quite obvious that the aim was the toy, not the diaper. Another example: place a toy in a box in front of baby and then hand it to him. The baby will pull the box toward him, take out the toy and then ignore the box. You can think up many similar situations. You can also make this more challenging by asking him, in effect, to perform more interposed actions before grasping the toy itself, e.g., to place the toy into a box and cover it with a diaper.

EXERCISE 193

Exercise 193: Acquiring objects with the aid of tools. I've basically described this in Exercises 166 and 167. After baby has discovered that he can get hold of a toy tied to a string when he can grab one end of the string, and when he has mastered this problem manually, you can develop his thinking further by altering the situation, and enabling him to acquire several toys with the same string or one toy with various strings. Use strings of various lengths, thicknesses, and colors. Then try other tools: ribbons, belts, strips, diapers. Finally, combine objects and tools: let baby get hold of an apple with the aid of the tablecloth on which the apple lies, or pull a newspaper toward him on which you've previously placed a toy. Let him do all these exercises in various surroundings: on the table, the floor, the crib, in the yard. This way he learns to generalize, and from generalization he passes on to abstraction. He will begin to realize what is common to all these situations. You'll recognize that this is not only an exercise in dexterity because the hand must be guided by a thinking brain.

Exercise 194: Acquiring an object by overcoming an obstacle. After baby has learned to crawl, show him a toy which he can reach only by climbing over or under an obstacle, or when he removes it, perhaps by climbing over a low bench or a step or opening a door.

EXERCISE 195

Exercise 195: Acquiring an object by indirect means. By the end of his ninth month your baby will learn to approach an object indirectly—by a roundabout route. To let him solve problems in that way, place him next to the long side of the couch and show him a toy which you have placed in the middle of the other side. At first baby will stretch out his hands and try to reach for the toy directly across the couch. It will probably take him some time to find a different solution—to go around the couch. It's not just that he can still only move from place to place with difficulty but mainly that he must first move away from the toy to approach it from the other side. Perhaps you'll have to lead him around the couch several times to the toy before he realizes that this is the only way to achieve his aim. This exercise is extremely demanding, because at this stage your baby still cannot walk around furniture and when he gets down on the floor to crawl he loses sight of the toy and his sense of direction in relation to it. The task is easier if you prepare him for it with a transparent barrier. Place baby onto one side of the obstacle and the toy on the other, out of reach on the floor. Baby can then crawl around the obstacle without losing sight of the toy.

EXERCISE 196

Exercise 196: Acquiring an object by indirect means while losing sight of it for some time. Place your baby next to a small table. Place obstacles so he cannot climb over the table or move around it. Place a toy at the other end. Baby can get to the toy only by climbing under the table. If he is unable to find this solution himself, seat him a bit further away from the table and show him the toy both above and below the table so he can discover both approaches and decide on the easier one: to crawl under the table even at the price of losing the toy from sight for a little while.

Exercise 197: Seeking the shortest indirect route. Arrange a situation similar to that in Exercise 194, but don't place baby in the center of one of the long sides of the couch, but between the center and end of that side. Place the toy opposite him. Baby can already solve the task of Exercise 194 in which he could select the bypass to the right or left; both were equally long. Now one of the bypasses is longer and he should learn to select the shorter one. You should alternate so the bypass to the right and then to the left is shorter. This teaches baby to solve situations by assessing, deciding, and acting.

No doubt you can think up lots more games to develop your baby's mental faculties during his seventh to ninth months. It all depends on the opportunities you have at home or in the yard or park. Don't show him right away how to solve a problem. It's best for him to find out himself. But simplify it; if, for instance, an obstacle is too high, then try to make it easier to overcome.

How to Develop Speech

Objective: By the ninth month your baby should enrich his vocabulary of words that he understands and to which he responds in some way (the passive vocabulary). His babbling should have proceeded from the pronunciation of simple syllables to their repetition ("ba-ba-ba") and duplication ("ba-ba"). Some babies begin to pronounce a certain syllable or groups of syllables in connection with a certain object, person, or activity, and this can be considered to be the first active word. Baby will usually pronounce his first active word between the age of 9 to 15 months.

Developing Passive Speech

Exercises 114, 115, and 116 are good for the development of baby's passive vocabulary during the seventh to ninth months, too. But here are some more advanced tasks.

EXERCISE 198

Exercise 198: Training more complicated movement responses to objects identified by words. After baby responds to such an object by turning his head toward it, you can help him develop a more complicated movement reaction: have him point to it with his finger. When you ask him "Where is the tick-tock?" and he turns his head toward the clock, point to it, take his hand, let him perform the same movement passively, and say "There's the

tick-tock.'' After you repeat this several times the baby
will point to the clock himself. If he learns to point to
several named objects, he will start to point out others
toward which he previously just turned his head.

Exercise 199: Complex movement responses to a request. Now you can teach your baby to clap his hands to
the rhyme "Clap, clap, clap, your hands . . ."; to lift his
arm when he's asked "Show how big you are," or wave
when he is told "Wave bye-bye."

These early responses cannot always be stimulated
and not in every situation. If you have taught baby to
"Wave bye-bye," he may react to this every time. But for
several days afterward he may not react at all. Then he
might wave in all kinds of situations without being told
to. This comparatively slow stabilization of reactions to
verbal stimuli is normal at this age.

Exercise 200: Complex movement reactions to verbal appeals concerning everyday tasks. Use all everyday situations (dressing, feeding, bathing) to increase baby's passive vocabulary. During these situations baby is in close
contact with you and his attention is focused on what you
are doing with him at the moment. They're good occasions for various associations to be brought about quite
easily. Here are three rules to help you increase his passive vocabulary during everyday care:

1. Always name whatever has attracted your baby's
attention.

2. Always use the same word or expression for whatever you are doing.

3. Select a limited number of words and repeat
them frequently and appropriately so as not to overload him with too many new tasks. When you feed

your baby, don't talk to him about going to bed. Tell
him to open his mouth or what a nice plate he has.
And don't tell him to "nap" one day and "go sleepy-
bye" the next. Furthermore, all members of the family
should agree on one name for each activity. Select
words that baby is most likely to understand and
which are most important during your contacts with
him. At first you should teach him to respond to very
simple requests such as "Sit down!," "Open your
mouth!," "Give me your hand."

EXERCISE 201

Exercise 201: Gymnastics at verbal request. One of the
best opportunities for the development of passive vocabulary are the everyday exercises you perform with your
baby. When he lies on his back and you offer him your
forefingers to help him sit up, say "Sit up!" and "Lie
down!" After a while he will do the exercise only at
verbal request.

EXERCISE 202

Exercise 202: Development of the passive vocabulary while looking at pictures. By the ninth month, give baby colored pictures with simple objects he knows. I would recommend the use of cardboard pictures with two or three such objects as people and animals. Point them out with your finger and say "This is a doggie!" Then ask, "Where is the doggie?" and baby should point it out at age 9 to 10 months.

Active Speech

Babbling

The method for the development of babbling is the same as for the preceding 3 months. During the sixth month baby begins to pronounce individual syllables. In the seventh month encourage him to repeat syllables several times; if he says "ma," repeat "ma-ma-ma-ma." Praise him and show how pleased you are when he has repeated the syllable several times. In the eighth month reward him the same way when he starts to repeat a syllable twice ("ma-ma," "ba-ba") or when he links two different syllables ("ba-ma").

Active Words

Although your baby will probably not learn his first active word in his first 9 months, you can lay the foundations for active speech. By the end of the ninth month, teach baby to pronounce syllables he knows well and to repeat them after you in connection with a particular action, as in the following exercises. You will be most successful if the baby achieves some interesting effect when he pronounces certain syllables.

EXERCISE 203

Exercise 203: Calling dad. Seat baby on your lap, let dad sit opposite you and hold a diaper in front of his face. Mother should tell baby to "Say daddy." When baby pronounces the word "daddy," father should uncover his face and call "Here's daddy!," and the baby will almost certainly laugh. Cover up your face again and play this game 3 or 4 times. You can vary the game by hiding under the table, in the cupboard, behind the curtain or door. The reward will be even greater if you appear with a new toy each time.

Exercise 204: Calling animals. Sit at a table with baby in your lap. Put three boxes with their bottoms up onto the table. Under each box place some toy animals: an inflatable dog, cat, or chicken. Then say "Call doggie bow-wow!" When baby says "bow" uncover the box with the dog and say "Here's doggie bow." Then tell him to call kitty "meeow" and chicken "cluck." Repeat this several times. By the end of the ninth month baby may start calling the animals himself. At first always have the same animals under the same box and in the same order; when baby has frequently named the animals correctly you can replace them with other toys.

Exercise 205: Naming pictures. Use the picture from Exercise 202. In this exercise do not ask "Where is doggie-bow?," but point to the picture of a dog and ask "What's this?" and add "Say bow." During the ninth month baby will usually repeat what you tell him to, but during the tenth to twelfth months he may start to answer correctly if you just ask, "What's this?"

Exercise 206: Naming activities. After baby has learned to wave his hand correctly when he is told, "Do bye-bye," then tell him to say "Bye-bye." Always combine this response with the same situation (for example, when father leaves the room). During the tenth month some babies say "bye-bye," when they see the father standing in the door. After baby has learned to wave to his father and to call this "bye-bye" you can gradually teach him to apply this to other people. Soon he will learn to wave and say "bye-bye" to everybody who leaves the room. You can also teach him to say "boom" if he falls and to imitate animals. Eventually, if you ask, "What does a cow do?," he'll reply, "moo-moo."

Note: Here are four rules to remember when you develop the baby's active speech during this period:

1. Active words are best learned from words which a baby already knows passively (understands). For instance, teach him that a cow does "moo" only after he knows what a "cow" is and can point to it on a picture.

2. Create active words from syllables baby can already pronounce. If baby gabbles "na-na-na-na," try to create the word meaning grandmother from these senseless syllables. Only after he has learned to use a few words actively can you begin to teach him words which are more difficult to pronounce.

3. The first active words naturally deal with things and people to which baby has an active relationship, that are vital to him and most attract his attention. These are usually the persons nearest to him (mother, father, granny), interesting objects and animals (car, dog) or important activities (feeding, sleep).

4. The best way for senseless gabbling to become a word is for the babbled syllables to acquire significance as "starters"—to create some reaction. So if baby says "na-na" for granny to appear, pick him up and play with him. Baby will thus come to realize that if he speaks certain syllables, something pleasant will happen. The word thus become the tool for achieving something. And as I have said, the use of a tool to achieve something is

an expression of mental activity. Speech also develops in close connection with thought. Baby will usually pronounce his first word during the tenth to twelfth months but to do so he had best be trained with the preceding exercises from the seventh to ninth months. Incidentally, some babies do say their first word during the ninth month.

How to Develop Emotional and Social Relations

Objective: To create and maintain a baby's good mood. Strengthen baby's emotional ties with the persons closest to him, mainly the mother and father, and at the same time teach him not to be shy with other people. Enable him to establish active contacts with other adults. Teach him to understand more subtle gestures and mimicry and to respond to words in social contacts. Play some simple social games with him.

During this phase it is again the rule that positive emotions result from the good, satisfied, and happy mood of the infant. Do all you can to keep your baby in a good mood. Again: he must be healthy, fed, and rested. Adequate heat, suitable clothing, enough space, and adequate toys are indispensable. So is the absence of negative stimuli which cause unpleasantness: noise, smell, pain, fright, and fear; and the closeness of a known person who is in active contact with him and stimulates him to interesting activities.

The emotional ties between a baby and his parents do not become stronger only because you cuddle, hug, and kiss him. Baby often revolts against these strong (and easy) expressions of love and loves those who not only feed, bathe, change diapers, and give him presents, but mainly the persons who play interesting games with him. It's the fastest, easiest way to gain baby's affection. A baby behaves as if he knew that the person who loves him most is the one willing to devote time to him, although I need to say again that it's just as important for him to have opportunity to play by himself, too.

When you shop, ask a clerk to place some of the things you have bought into your baby's hand. When you ride a train, put the ticket into his hand. Ask your neighbors to look after him sometimes so he can get used to being without you occasionally. The emotional ties between you and baby will be strengthened as a result. Mother and baby should not be together all the time; occasionally they need a rest from each other, to welcome each other happily and get used to the fact that they cannot be together all the time. Of course the baby needs to feel that he is always in good hands and that it is natural for mother and father to return. Otherwise a baby will have difficult times in nursery school or kindergarten.

EXERCISE 207

Exercise 207: Active establishment of contacts. Mother and father sit down away from baby, pretend not to notice him and start to do something interesting by themselves. Perhaps they'll crowd objects into a container and then empty it again. The baby on the floor can crawl up to them. He will observe you and may join in your activities. Later, you'll want to encourage contacts with others.

Exercise 208: Asking for help. Place an object in a visible place just out of baby's reach. Stand nearby but with your back to him. After several efforts to reach the object the baby will try to attract your attention in some way and ask you to hand him the toy. Baby thus learns to use another person as an instrument to achieve an objective, and to make his wishes known.

At this age baby will be able to respond to gestures and mimicry, but this faculty, too, needs to be consciously trained.

Exercise 209: "Yes-no." Take baby on your lap, sit down at the table and put two objects within his reach—a toy and a less suitable object such as a pair of scissors. Baby will observe both objects and reach out for one of them. If he reaches out for the toy, nod your head in agreement and say: "Yes, pick up kitty." But if he reaches out for the scissors, shake your head and say: "No, no, not the scissors," and move them away. The affirmative nodding and the word "yes" should be accompanied with a smile; the negative shaking of the head and "no" should be accompanied with a frown. The objective of this exercise is to teach baby to differentiate between your agreement and disagreement as expressed with a gesture. At the same time you can teach him to express his own agreement and disagreement with head movements; tell him to do "yes-yes, no-no" with his head.

EXERCISE 210

Exercise 210: "Give"-"Here." Give baby a familiar toy (he would not like to give up a new one). Say, "Here you are." After a moment put your hand out and ask him in a pleading voice, "Give me." If he does not hand you the toy, take the hand holding the toy to your open palm and take the toy back. Often baby will pass you the toy but not let go of it; take it away from him gently and remember that it's not that baby does not want to let go of it; he still doesn't know how. He'll soon begin to under-

stand that handing over a toy is a game, and it will teach
him to understand the gestures and words of "Give" and
"Here."

Exercise 211: Responses to frowns: in fun and for real.
When baby does something he shouldn't (touches a hot
radiator, pulls the tablecloth), frown at him, shake your
finger at him and say "No-no-no," or "You mustn't" and
at the same time prevent him from doing it. He will
gradually understand that he must stop doing whatever
his parents react to in this manner. If you prevent him
in this gentle, calm way, baby will learn to calmly obey
you when you say "No-no-no." If you use less gentle
means that cause him to cry, he will learn to react to your
threat by crying. But do remember that babies are different; some don't cry even when you stop them roughly,
others cry even when stopped gently. You need to find
your own approach to your baby and act accordingly.

By the ninth month he should also learn to respond
according to whether a warning is meant seriously or in
fun. You can teach this with a game. Seat baby in front
of you, put on an exaggerated frown and say in a stern
voice "I'll do boo-boo-boo." The frown and the stern
words should contain elements of fun. Bring your head
close to baby's and this will make him laugh. Immediately after making a threat in fun, laugh and do something funny. He will react with laughter and will gradually understand that this "frown" is not meant seriously.
Another way of doing it is to lift your finger at him, frown
and say "I'll poke you in the tummy." Then carry out
your threat gently and with a smile and he will also react
with laughter.

Mother and father can think up other games to teach
baby to learn gestures and facial expressions. Here now
are some other games suitable for this age.

Exercise 212: Hiding behind a diaper. Sit at the table and place baby in front of you and facing you. Hide your face in the diaper and ask: "Where's mamma?" After 2 or 3 seconds uncover your face and say "Here's mamma!" Baby will in time start pulling the diaper off your face himself. Then place the diaper over his head and ask, "Where's Tommy?" Then pull it off and say, "Ah, here he is!" Baby will gradually learn not only to cover up his face but also to show himself.

EXERCISE 213

Exercise 213: Hiding toys. Place baby in your lap at the table and place three or four medium-size plastic boxes on the table with their bottoms up. Place a marble under one of them and then move them around so the baby won't know where the toy is. Then ask him, "Where's the marble?," lift up a box and say, "It's not here." When you find the marble, say, "Here's the marble!" and laugh together with baby. He will soon start to uncover the boxes himself and will look at you in triumph when he has found the one hiding the toy. Then hide the toy again and when he looks for it, keep pace with his efforts by saying "It's not here," "Or here," "Ah, there it is." The common joy at finding the toy is the main reward factor in this game.

Another fun game is chasing baby on all fours (see Exercise 127).

Exercises to Encourage Good Habits

Objective: At night your baby should now sleep 10 to 11 hours and only three times during the day for periods of 1 1/2 to 2 hours. He should be awake during the day for four periods of 2 to 2 1/2 hours. He should be fed five times a day in intervals of 3 to 3 1/2 hours. By the eighth month he should be able to hold a roll or a piece of apple in his hand, place it into his mouth and chew it; he should start to learn to drink from a cup which he holds himself with minimum assistance from you; and he should begin to learn to use the pottie when he is placed on it in time.

Training baby for regular periods of sleep and wakefulness is no different from what I described for babies between 4 to 6 months except that the period of wakefulness becomes longer and the number of sleeping periods during the daytime drops from four to three.

Up to the seventh month, feed your baby as in the preceding 3 months: in a comfortable half-seated position in your arms or lap. During the seventh to eighth months the baby should be able to sit in your lap. During the eighth to ninth months you probably can seat baby (once he can sit) into a baby stool and feed him at the table. Remember: don't distract baby with toys when you feed him; let him learn to concentrate on his food. During the seventh to eighth months start putting a roll (or similar food) into his hand to teach him to put it to his mouth and bite it.

Start teaching him to drink from a cup by first allowing him to grasp the cup with both hands. Tilt the cup so its contents flows slowly into his mouth; he will soon find out that when he tilts the cup the amount of liquid flowing out of it increases. Gradually he'll learn to maintain the correct angle. Your assistance should decrease—just make sure he does not spill too much over himself.

During the ninth month you can also give him a spoon dipped in, say, mashed potatoes and teach him to take it up to his mouth. Let him try this himself for 1 or 2 minutes, then continue feeding him yourself. In the ninth month this is preparatory to learning to eat himself and you have to expect that the baby will soil not only his face, but also head and clothes. Still, don't wait until baby "learns to eat by himself"; he cannot learn without exercise and training.

You can begin toilet training early; some mothers manage to do this by baby's sixth month, but it's a better idea to start after he has learned to sit up himself (eighth to ninth months).

Start by putting your baby on the pot when his need is acute. You have to know his excretion cycle and this is different in every baby. Some babies urinate a few minutes after waking up, some after feeding. So begin by seating him after waking and feeding.

During the baby's first attempts you can artificially stimulate the urge to relieve himself by turning him with his back toward you; put your forearm under his arms, grasp his bent legs under the knees, gently press his knees against his tummy and hold him above the pot in this position. The gentle pressure of the thighs and knees against the tummy will increase the urge to urinate.

Baby should see and hear his urine flowing. Also, encourage him to make "eh-eh" sounds. When baby experiences physical feelings caused by the physiological process of relieving himself and engaging the "stomach press," and simultaneously sees the result of this process and hears the words "Do eh-eh," he gets the associations that are required for the conditioned relays which are expressed by his gradually learning to empty himself when seated or held above the pottie and when he hears the verbal request to "Do eh-eh." If you then gradually seat him on the potty, even when his need is not so urgent, the chances of success will increase.

Successful evacuation on the pottie must be rewarded. Praise baby a lot, and everyone else around him should express admiration of his efforts.

The first attempts should last no longer than 2 to 3 minutes. If nothing happens, stop, even if he soils his diaper a few minutes later. Repeat the training when his need again reaches the critical stage.

During training, and especially during the first attempts, baby should experience no unpleasant feelings. He should not be afraid of falling off the pot if he has not yet learned to sit in an elevated place. The pot should not be cold. He should not sit on it too long. Naturally, you should not punish him for not doing anything, or for soiling his diaper because he cannot understand that not emptying his bowels in the pot is a "no-no." At first he does not even realize that he is doing anything on the pot at all.

For baby to become aware of this physiological act he should not be interrupted or distracted. He should not be seated on the pottie for too long. He must see the result. And you should not keep him amused with toys, talk, or other stimuli which distract his attention.

To set up toilet training, find out first when baby usually empties his bowels or bladder. Hold him above the pot at that time with his knees pressed gently against his tummy and say "Do eh-eh." In this position baby will usually evacuate his bowels or bladder or both. Make sure baby can see the urine flowing out. Show him the content of the pottie. Praise him for his efforts. If you have been successful with this method several times, your success will usually be permanent; baby will learn to empty himself on the pottie if he is placed on it in time. The moment you forget to put him on the pot in time, he will soil his diaper again.

By the ninth month you should be able to achieve a change from an unconditioned emptying of the bladder and bowels to a conditioned reflex. The conditioning signal is being seated on the pot and the words "eh-eh."

Here are some of the most frequent mistakes parents make during toilet training:

Seating baby on the pot regardless of whether or not he needs to empty his bowels or bladder.

Letting baby sit on the pot until he relieves himself. Baby becomes restless on the pot, runs away, distracts himself and does not devote sufficient attention to the act of relieving himself. It's difficult or impossible to train a conditioned response if a baby sits on the pot and doesn't know why.

Creating unpleasant sensations when seating baby on the pot: putting him on a cold pot, scolding him for not sitting still, punishing him for not doing what he should, or other negative actions.

Distracting baby by telling him something, showing or giving him things to make him sit still and forgetting that this distraction prevents the desired condition reflex.

Doing nothing to make baby realize what is wanted of him and failing to reward success with praise.

How to Use Furniture and Toys

Playpen: You should use this mainly when there are serious reasons why you want to prevent your baby from crawling around the entire room for a period of time. If there is no such reason, allow baby to move around freely but be sure to adapt the room to prevent him from hurting himself or breaking something. A playpen with one side that can be opened is a good idea because it lets the baby move in and out at will. If possible, it should be easily unassembled so parts can be used as a fence in his seventh to twelfth months when he learns to walk alone, and as an inclined ladder for teaching him to climb at 8 months.

Foam Rubber and Gymnastic Board: Place a foam rubber or padded gymnastic board wherever your baby likes to play most often. It can become an inclined surface by lifting one end by 6 to 8 inches so that baby can roll down it; or be lifted from the ground by 4 to 6 inches to form an elevated horizontal surface onto which he can climb, crawl over or down.

Baby Seat: Dismantled, it can become a low stool for a desk or a high seat to permit baby to sit at a higher table. It's a good idea for a baby of 7 to 8 months who can sit straight and steadily. At first, don't allow him to sit in the chair longer than 5 to 10 minutes (after his twelfth month 10 to 15 minutes). If you want to "get him out of the way" for longer, place him into his playpen.

Manipulating Board: A clever father, uncle, or grandfather can make a board measuring about 3 by 2 feet and attach the objects mentioned in the above exercises. They should mainly be those which can be turned, twisted, pulled, opened and closed, pushed in and out, pressed, or switched on. They should afford baby the opportunity to train hand movements which should yield interesting effects: something appears or disappears, changes, makes a sound, or moves. Of course these objects need not all be on a single board; they can be distributed throughout the home. The furniture can become a training ground, too. The baby can open and close drawers, turn a dial of the vacuum cleaner, pull the key out of a keyhole, press a lamp switch, and so on.

Baby's toys must be more varied than in his earlier months. They should now include balls, full and hollow cubes, a small mallet, a drum and sticks, various rubber toys (dog, cat, cow, horse), toys on wheels, a doll. Also give him other things to play with: metal pots, jars, cups, boxes, a basket, bell, hose, as well as simple pictures and picture books.

9

Exercises for the Tenth to Twelfth Months

By the end of his first year your baby becomes increasingly independent. He will start to walk by himself, be more able to manipulate objects and furnishings, understand sentences concerning everyday things, start talking and show that he is beginning to think.

Overall Movements: During the tenth to twelfth months he will crawl around the entire home and will usually be able to climb up and down from a low couch. He can also climb up and down a ladder. When supporting himself against furniture, he will be able to stand on his toes or on one leg. During the ninth month he will be able to lean against furniture; in the tenth he will walk around it while keeping hold of it; in the eleventh his hold will be looser and sometimes unnecessary; by the twelfth he will take his first independent step.

As soon as he learns to walk by himself, he will also learn to sit down from the standing position without holding on; and get up again. If you exercise him regularly he may learn to walk between his tenth and eleventh months and, by the twelfth, will walk around the yard, climb over low barriers and, if he can hold on to something, he'll also climb steps. He will sit firmly on an elevated surface such as a bench, and perhaps sit down on a small chair without "missing." His grasp becomes firmer, and he can hang suspended not only when holding your fingers, but also from a bar.

You can achieve considerable progress in developing the baby's delicate hand movements which are the best indicators of intellectual activity and increasing experience. By the end of the twelfth month the hand steadily reaches out for an observed object and, before grasping, adapts itself to its size, shape, and position. Beginning with his tenth to eleventh months you will find that baby likes to pick up small objects and threads with precise tweezer movements of thumb and forefinger. At the same age he may be able to loosen his grasp deliberately and drop an object, e.g., a cube into a vessel.

Guiding the hand with a toy toward a goal also requires steadiness and precision. Baby inserts a key into the lock. By the end of the year the adaptive movement of the hand with a toy guided to a certain goal is sure; baby will guide the key straight to the keyhole or will turn the hand holding a coin to insert it vertically into the slot of a cashbox (during the ninth and tenth months he placed the coin on top of the box and pushed it around until it chanced to fall into the slot).

When he has mastered these techniques he will also be able to place one cube on top of another. And you'll note further progress when, by the eleventh to twelfth months, one hand will perform auxiliary tasks (hold a bottle) while the other does the main job (throws a marble into it). A baby who acquires such manipulative abilities is collecting valuable experience which stimulates him to more intensive thinking.

Experience: When your baby manipulates objects he gains not only physical experiences: that objects are light and heavy, that they fall to the ground, that cubes must be placed on top of each other with precision so that the column does not collapse. He also gets geometrical experience: that a smaller cube can be inserted into a larger one (but not vice versa), that the smaller must be placed into the larger vertically and not at an angle, and that the two cubes cannot be put together if their walls are crossed and not parallel.

Of course the baby does not know the meaning of such words as size, perpendicular, and parallel, but he knows these phenomena from practical experience and respects them in his activities. It will not be until baby is at school that his teacher will recall and identify these characteristics which he has experienced as an infant. The fact that girls used to do worse at geometry than boys had nothing to do with their intelligence; they just couldn't acquire the necessary early experience because games with cubes were considered unsuitable for little girls and they got dolls and kitchens.

By the end of his first year your baby will also widen his range of social experiences. He will express increasing interest in the activities of adults. He'll seek active contact with them and will try to gain more experience with people and their world. He will become interested in adult things, especially in what adults do with them.

By the end of his twelfth month your baby will quite obviously begin to react to the third dimension of objects, start to draw conclusions about their relationships and how they act with one another. He will become interested in hollow objects (containers, boxes), which he will feel from outside and inside. He will also start to penetrate one object with another, will love opening and closing drawers and place pegs into holes. He will find out that you can place objects on top of each other, next to each other, into each other and against each other; that they can be taken apart and put together; that one can be used to act against the other, and so on.

By the end of the first year you'll also notice that your baby has adopted a new attitude toward objects: he'll begin to treat them much as do the adults who are around him by wiping the cupboard with a duster, using a ladle for stirring, and the like. He is adapting his manipulation with objects to his environment.

His experience with people and their work will lead to a further stage in his development toward the end of the first year—the emerging socialization of movement and behavior (twelfth month and onward) which typically appears in the beginning of imitative play; he begins to imitate his surroundings.

At first the baby will imitate only certain isolated movements which are interesting to him (he won't imitate overall human behavior until his third year). How much he imitates at the end of his first year and during his second depends on how much stimulation he gets from his environment. If he has much opportunity to observe humans, animals, and machines, he will acquire a rich repertoire of imitative movements—and these are not mere amusement. He prefers to make something out of real dough and put it into a real oven rather than imitate. But if he is unable to perform an act, he can become fully absorbed in a game (symbol) and will treat a toy as he would a real object. A doll or teddy bear are not mere toys to bend in various ways; they become things which act, feel, live, and need care. So he starts feeding his teddy, cuddles, rocks, and sleeps with it.

All this gives your baby opportunity to collect experience, to develop his thinking and, indirectly, speech. By the twelfth month babies clearly understand the relationship between action and reaction and can apply this knowledge: switch on the light, switch the radio on and off.

He now uses tools to achieve his aims (he will use a

ruler to get his ball from under the cupboard). He will also be able to solve more complicated tasks: to pull a chair to the table, bring a ruler, climb onto the chair, and use the ruler for drawing a toy toward him. He will also discover the principle of analysis and synthesis: he builds something from parts and then dismantles the whole into parts.

The development of speech is significant at this stage. By the end of his twelfth month his passive understanding of speech will have reached the stage when, if properly guided, he will understand nearly everything that is said about everyday situations concerning him. On average, at around the tenth to eleventh months baby will pronounce his first active word; by the end of the twelfth he will use about 5 active words. But if you develop his speech as I've described throughout this book he will probably say his first word in the ninth month; and by the end of his first year he will actively use 10 to 30 words. The active vocabulary of a 12-month-old consists mainly of baby talk, but he will also become interested in nursery rhymes and will express heightened interest in pictures; a 12-month-old can point out a dog on a picture, and say what it is and how it barks.

In the last 3 months of his first year your baby develops higher standards of emotions. He will express his attachment to you by keeping a firm hold on you, press himself against you, seek your protection, stroke you when asked, or give you a kiss. He begins to understand that other people experience pain and will cry to show his sympathy when you pretend to cry. He becomes gentle with his toys, animals, and other children. His social relationships become stronger because his scope of cooperation is greater: he understands speech, can express his wishes with gestures and some words and can actively participate in some activities. His main interest will be in contact with adults or older children who understand him and can adapt to him; he will not yet be able to play with small children who, like himself, expect another person to adopt to them.

Habits also develop significantly during the fourth quarter-year. He will get used to being awake longer: during the day he will be awake for three periods of 2 1/2 to 4 hours. His night sleep will probably remain unaltered (10 hours). So will the number of feeding times (five times in periods of 3 1/2 to 4 hours). The daily food requirements will vary but will be more substantial with three meals plus light snacks, such as fruit, which is digested quickly. Feed him only at table and teach him to take the spoon to his mouth and to drink out of a cup by himself. He should also gradually start announcing his need to use the pot. At this age he will usually just announce that he has soiled diaper. During the second year he'll tell you that he is just in the act. Later he'll learn when a bowel movement is starting and announce his need beforehand. This last stage, so eagerly awaited by all mothers usually appears only during the second half of the second year although some mothers manage to get to this stage during the first half of baby's second year.

How to Train Overall Movements

Objective: During his tenth to twelfth months your baby should perfect his ability to overcome obstacles (crawling through, under, over). He should learn to sit on a chair at the table. He will take his first step and sometimes walk surefootedly through the room or outside. By the end of the year he should be able to stretch himself up when supporting himself against furniture, stand on one leg, and stand up from the kneeling or sitting position in the middle of the room without assistance.

You can perfect his crawling by using the exercises which I've described for 7- to 9-month-old babies: the chase on all fours, climbing up and down an inclined surface, crawling between obstacles, crawling through and under, and climbing a ladder.

Baby will be able to sit up from the lying down and kneeling positions; during the fourth quarter-year you should teach him to sit down on a chair from the standing position. His greatest difficulty will be in controlling his body position in relation to the seat, i.e., the correct positioning of his backside to the seat which he cannot see.

EXERCISE 214

Exercise 214: Seating on a step. Exercise seating from the standing position with a wide object 6 to 8 inches high, preferably a step, low bench or two mattresses placed on top of each other. Tell baby to sit down. At the same time turn him so he faces the step. Then turn him by 180 degrees, take his hand and gently press him to the sitting position. It is important that he first gets a look at where he will sit. In effect, you're teaching him to orient himself in space. You'll want to use a wide surface at first because it'll make no difference whether he places his bottom more to the right or left.

EXERCISE 215

Exercise 215: Seating on a chair at the table. Place a low chair about 4 to 6 inches from a small table. Place baby next to the chair so he can lean on the table with both hands. Tell him to sit down. Baby will take sidesteps and insert himself between the table and the chair and sit down while still leaning against the table with his hands. Space orientation is facilitated because by leaning against the table he is turned toward the chair in the right direction and can also turn around more easily and check his position and distance from the chair.

EXERCISE 216

Exercise 216: Sitting down backward. Start with this exercise only after baby has learned to walk properly and he can take steps backward (which means he is exceptionally gifted during the twelfth month). Place his chair in the middle of the room and tell him to sit down. Stand him about two steps away from the chair. Then turn him around by 180 degrees so he is standing with his back to the chair. Offer him your hand and assist him in his backward approach. When he gets right up to the chair he will lose sight of it and will sense only by touch when he is near or on it. Gradually he will learn to sit down without your assistance. Space orientation is the most important factor in this exercise. When baby nears the chair he will usually turn so he can still see it and will therefore often sit either on the edge or miss it altogether. If he has had an unpleasant experience in connection with sitting down he will turn around several steps away from the chair and back up toward it.

First Steps and Perfecting Walking

If a baby takes first steps in the thirteenth to fourteenth month, this is still normal. Below are exercises for babies who have taken their first independent steps.

EXERCISE 217

Exercise 217: Overcoming greater distances. Place baby next to a piece of furniture he can hold on to and call him toward you. Gradually increase the distance between you and him. One week to one month after his first steps he will cross an entire room and then start to make his way through the whole home. I'm sure that during this period you'll take careful safety measures and remove everything he could hurt himself on, damage, or destroy.

Note: After baby has learned to walk through the home this doesn't mean that the development of walking has ended. The child perfects walking until adulthood and even during it. But even at an early age it's imperative that your baby learns to walk in all kinds of places and all kinds of conditions. It is not enough for him to be able to do something only in certain conditions. Every ability must be generalized. Let me give you a few examples of how you can generalize your baby's ability to walk.

Exercise 218: Walking along an uneven surface. After baby has learned to walk with confidence over the flat floor at home, let him move around over less ideal ground: a path in the park or yard, and on pavement. Gradually make the conditions more difficult by letting him walk in the grass, snow, sand, hay, or a path in the woods.

EXERCISE 219

Exercise 219: Walking over pebbles. Allow baby to walk barefoot on the banks of a stream or wherever there are pebbles. Or you can also collect pebbles and scatter them thickly in a section of the yard. Or use a piece of floor covering and stick small rubber hemispheres (about 1/2 inch in diameter) on it. This exercise is especially important for babies with an insufficiently developed arch; if baby has an inclination toward flat feet do this exercise with him daily up to the age of 2 to 3 years.

EXERCISE 220

Exercise 220: Kicking a ball. Place a ball on the floor and show baby how to kick it. Baby will toddle up to it; just in front of the ball he'll take a bigger step and kick it. During this movement it'll be harder for him to keep his balance and the rhythm of his walk is interrupted. Thus baby learns to take irregular, nonrhythmic steps which is more difficult than regular, uniform, rhythmic steps.

EXERCISE 221

Exercise 221: Overcoming low obstacles. Persuade baby to step over the threshold in the room, a plank on the floor, or your slipper. In the yard this obstacle can be the hose or the root of a tree. Help him at first by offering him your hand; later let him try by himself.

EXERCISE 222

Exercise 222: Getting on and off the sidewalk. Teach him to get on and off a low sidewalk, first with your assistance, later without it.

EXERCISE 223

Exercise 223: Walking up and down a slope. Lead baby to a slight slope, either in the yard or in the park and persuade him to walk up and down it. Walking down is more difficult than walking up. Gradually find steeper slopes, but the maximum incline should be 20 to 25 degrees.

EXERCISE 224

Exercise 224: Walking along a narrow surface. Place a plank, about 6 to 8 inches wide, on the floor. Babies who have not yet learned to walk properly walk with their legs spread wide apart and only later bring them closer to the axis or almost to it. When baby has learned to walk with confidence, persuade him to walk along the plank which makes him place his feet closer to the axis of the movement. A strip of paper or a folded blanket is just as good.

Exercise 225: Walking along an elevated surface. You can make the preceding exercise more difficult by persuading him to walk along a wide beam or a bench. Allow baby to do this only when you are right next to him so you can prevent accidents.

EXERCISE 226

Exercise 226: Walking on bricks. Place 8 to 10 bricks into an uneven row in the backyard and persuade baby to walk over them. For safety's sake hold his hand. The objective of this exercise is to teach baby to deliberately place his feet and to take irregular steps; since the bricks are placed at irregular intervals baby has to take longer and shorter steps and place his feet more to the right or left.

Exercise 227: Walking along bricks placed at uneven angles. Place some bricks into a row—almost next to each other but so that they tilt either backward or forward and toward the right as well as the left. Persuade baby to walk the row but hold his hand. This teaches him to adapt his foot to various angles of the terrain.

EXERCISE 228

Exercise 228: Carrying things. Ask baby to bring over his chair, bucket, or large teddy bear. When he lifts up a larger object he raises and tilts his center of gravity and must assume a different body position than when walking without a load. This exercise will perfect his ability to keep his balance.

Exercise 229: Pushing toys in front of him. Give baby a wooden toy on wheels with a long wooden handle. Figures which move or ring are best. Baby pushes the toy in front of him, watches its movements, listens to it, and devotes less attention to his walking. The purpose is for the walking movement to become automatic and for him to learn to orient himself even when his attention is distracted by something else.

EXERCISE 230

Exercise 230: Pulling a toy behind him. Use the same toy
as in the previous exercise but tie it onto a piece of string
so that baby can only pull it behind him. Baby will often
walk with it and look around at it and so you should walk
with him to prevent him from hurting himself. Gradually
he will become more independent. This exercise is important because when the baby looks backward he has
trouble getting oriented because he is used to looking
where he is going, or going where he is looking. Now he
looks in the opposite direction and learns to orient himself in space even when not looking in the direction
where he is going.

EXERCISE 231

Exercise 231: Walking up steps. Give baby the opportunity to walk up and down low, wide steps. At first he will climb them on all fours. Then, if he can hold onto something with both hands, he will walk upright. Later he'll hold on with only one hand. Finally he'll walk up the steps without holding at all. At first he will always put the same foot up onto the next step and draw the other to him in a shuffle. Later he'll learn to alternate his steps. It's easier to walk up steps than down. If baby is gifted he will be able to climb up steps when holding onto something by the end of his first year, but usually he will still climb the steps on all fours.

EXERCISE 232

Exercise 232: Walking sideways, backward, and crouching. Give baby a toy car, train, or carriage to play with and he usually starts side-stepping, walking backward, or crouching. You can create a similar situation when you play chasing games. With both of you on all fours, get him to dodge you sideways or backward.

Exercise 233: Faster walking. Take baby by the hand and chase father together. The objective of this chase is to teach your child to walk faster.

Learning to Stand Up Without Help

EXERCISE 234

Exercise 234: Standing up next to low objects. Call baby to a low bench or box (about 8 inches high) and hold a toy above him so he can reach it only by standing up. When he has crawled up to the box he will learn against it on all fours and draw himself up with its aid to the kneeling position; then lean against it and stand up; and finally push off with his hands to the upright position.

EXERCISE 235

Exercise 235: Standing up without help. After baby has mastered Exercise 234, repeat it but make the aids lower and lower so he'll get up from a deeper forward bend. Then try to get him up without assistance, straight from all fours. Offer him a toy in the middle of the room where he has nothing to catch hold of. He will change his position from all fours to the crouch, then push off the floor with his hands and straighten up.

Practice Exercises 234 and 235 from the sitting position as well. Baby will move to the kneeling position and will then continue as I've just described.

EXERCISE 236

Exercise 236: Lifting a toy from the floor. Place a toy in front of baby when he is standing in the middle of the room. Baby will lean slightly forward, bend his knees, pick up the toy and straighten up. Help with your finger at first.

Exercising the Delicate Hand Movements

Objective: By his twelfth month your baby should learn to:

Lay things down and to build
Empty hollow containers, pour, fill, insert, and close
Perfect his skill in the processing of materials
Use tools for more complex tasks
Master simple working and self-service motions and start to imitate
Play with sand and water
Move at verbal request and master some manipulative movements in social contact

Learning How to Lay Things Down and to Build

EXERCISE 237

Exercise 237: Placing a cup on a tray and saucer. Once baby has learned to place a cup on the table, teach him to place it on a particular part of the table: first on a tray, later on a saucer. This is difficult because baby cannot put the cup down except on an ever-smaller surface, so his movements are increasingly influenced by external conditions. Practice this exercise with other similar objects; he can try placing a spool on a box or a cube on a piece of paper.

EXERCISE 238

Exercise 238: Placing flat objects on top of each other. Give baby a few flat wooden discs or low flat boxes and show him how to put one on top of the other. Baby can use other objects, such as notebooks, books, or plates. It's important for the construction not to tumble down if baby puts the objects a bit too far to the right or left. He will gradually acquire the ability to place objects on top of each other with precision, so by 11 or 12 months he will build towers with toy bricks.

Exercise 239: Building upward. Give baby elongated objects which can be stood up: spools, cones, small bottles, plastic cups, oblong boxes, and show him how to stand these up.

Exercise 240: Placing smaller objects on larger ones. Give baby various objects of different sizes (two boxes or bricks of different sizes), and persuade him to place the smaller on top of the larger. The smaller the difference in size, the more difficult the game.

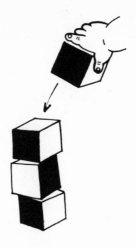

EXERCISE 241

Exercise 241: Placing objects of the same size on top of each other. Give baby similar-size cubes and tell him to stand them on top of each other. If he can do it, praise him loudly and make a fuss over him. A dexterous baby will be able to build a tower of more than two cubes at 12 months. First let baby use larger cubes (2 to 4 inches), later smaller ones (1 to 1 1/2 inches).

Emptying, Pouring, Filling, Inserting, Closing

EXERCISE 242

Exercise 242: Taking an object out of a pocket or bag. Place some small toys into a canvas bag and tell baby to take them out. He will learn to hold the bag by the edge with one hand and pull the objects out with the other. Use different types of bags: canvas, plastic, and paper.

Exercise 243: Pouring out. First give baby the opportunity to pour things out of boxes and baskets, cups and jugs and finally from bags. Baby should discover the principle that the container must be turned upside down for the contents to fall out.

EXERCISE 244

Exercise 244: Opening and closing boxes. Start with cylindrical, tall and small (flat) cardboard boxes, or boxes made of wood, plastic, or tin with lids which are sunk (easier) or overlapping (harder). Do not use lids with sharp edges. It's harder to place a lid on a square container.

EXERCISE 245

Exercise 245: Inserting a rod into a hole. Make a "throw box" out of a small wooden, plastic, or cardboard box. Make a hole about 1 inch in diameter in the upper wall (lid) and cut a rod about 1 inch in diameter into lengths of 3 to 4 inches. Show baby how to insert these rods into the hole and box.

EXERCISE 246

Exercise 246: Inserting and pulling out a cork. Give baby a bottle and show him how to insert and pull out a rubber cork. The cork should be shaped like a truncated cone so it can easily be inserted into the bottle neck but not fall through. In Exercises 245 and 246 you will have to hold the box or bottle at first so that baby can concentrate on his hand and not have to hold the object at the same time.

EXERCISE 247

Exercise 247: Inserting hollow dishes into each other. Give baby a set of same-size plastic dishes, the kind you use for cereal. They are narrower at the bottom than at the top; any dish can be placed into any other. Baby will soon learn to put one inside the other because he does not have to worry about their size or shape.

EXERCISE 248

Exercise 248: Placing cylindrical dishes of unequal size onto each other. Give baby a set of unequally sized dishes. The objective of this exercise is for baby to assemble the dishes according to size (smaller into larger), to learn to assess sizes of objects in relation to each other, and also to realize that objects are large and small. In the kitchen baby can learn this skill with various-size pots and pans.

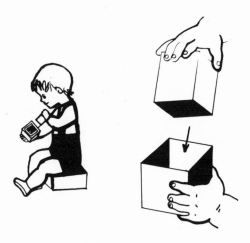

EXERCISE 249

Exercise 249: Inserting unequally sized hollow cubes. Buy a set of 6 to 10 hollow cubes of gradually increasing size which can all be inserted into the largest. The insertion of cubes is much harder than that of hollow cylindrical bowls.

Exercise 250: Placing a key into a lock. Call baby to a low cupboard with a key. Baby will turn the key, pull it out and try to insert it again which is more difficult to do than the game with a rod, because the key must be correctly positioned in the lock.

Exercise 251: Inserting rods into holes. Make several holes (about 1/2 inch in diameter) in a board and make several small rods of the same diameter and about 3 to 4 inches long. Show baby how to insert the rods into the holes. The diameter of the holes and rods must match so the rods can be easily inserted and taken out. Make the rods round at one end and square at the other. The baby will soon start to differentiate between the two ends and stick the round ends into holes. This exercise is different from Exercise 245 because the holes are smaller and the insertion of the rod more difficult.

EXERCISE 252

Exercise 252: Inserting a marble into a bottle. Buy some small marbles or hard candies and persuade baby to insert them into a bottleneck, which should be wide at first and narrower later.

EXERCISE 253

Exercise 253: Putting coins into a bank. Give baby a bank and show him how to insert coins into the slot. It's difficult for him because baby must turn his hand so that the edge of the coil is in line with the slot. Boil and cool the coins to clean them before giving them to baby to play with.

EXERCISE 254

Exercise 254: Threading rings onto a rod. Use the board from Exercise 251 and insert it in three rods. Show baby how to thread curtain rings (1 to 1 1/2 inches in diameter) onto these rods.

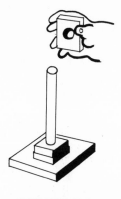

EXERCISE 255

Exercise 255: Threading discs and cubes on a rod. Make Exercise 254 more challenging by replacing the large rings with various items that have holes but are harder to thread: discs or (harder) cubes. The most difficult is the threading of a sphere with a hole. Few babies can manage this at this age because it calls for practical geometrical experience. Much also depends on the thickness of the rod and the diameter of the hole; the larger the hole and the thinner the rod, the easier it is.

EXERCISE 256

Exercise 256: Placing geometrical pictures. Cut a circle, square, or triangle (about 1 1/2 inches) in a piece of cardboard or plywood (4 by 4 inches), paint the geometrical shapes in various colors, and ask baby to place them into the right openings. He will be able to place the circle easiest; the most difficult is to place the triangle. You can make several such games using a variety of pictures (fruit, leaves, animals).

By his twelfth month the baby should work with both hands and perform a different movement with each. Here are a few exercises that require the cooperation of both hands.

EXERCISE 257

Exercise 257: Inserting a rod into a cylinder. Give baby a plastic cylinder, about 6 to 8 inches long and with a diameter of about 1 inch; also a wooden rod about 8 to 10 inches long and about 1/2 inch in diameter. Show baby how to insert the rod into the cylinder so that it falls out the other end. Hand it to baby so he grasps both toys by the ends; this will make the exercise much easier for him. Baby will gradually learn to grasp objects and control them better, and when he inserts them he will learn to hold them both perpendicular.

EXERCISE 258

Exercise 258: Buttoning. Give baby a large button and a coat with the appropriate-size buttonholes. Baby will grasp the edge of the coat in one hand and push the button through the hole with the other like a coin in the cashbox. When he has learned to push a loose button through the hole, try the same with a sewn button. At first let him button a coat when it's lying in front of him; then the coat while you wear it; and finally his own while he wears it.

Exercise 259: Threading bored discs onto a rod. Use the discs from Exercise 255. Place the discs in one hand and the rod in the other. Baby will try to thread the discs onto the rod, but this exercise is different from the earlier one because baby now works with both hands and performs a different movement with each. When he has mastered this he can start threading other objects.

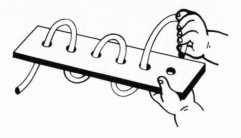

EXERCISE 260

Exercise 260: Threading insulated wire through a bored disc. This differs from Exercise 259 because a wire has different characteristics from a rod.

EXERCISE 261

Exercise 261: Threading a shoelace. Give baby a normal shoelace with covered ends and a clean shoe with sufficiently large laceholes. Ask baby to thread the shoelace. This is a very difficult task at 12 months because it requires very complex cooperation between both hands.

Learning to Process Materials

Exercise 262: Bending, breaking, and tearing cardboard. Give baby a light cardboard box and he will soon find out that the cardboard can be bent, broken, and torn.

By the end of his first year your baby will discover that

manipulation can alter the shape of things. The ideal material for gaining this experience is ordinary dough. Never forget to give him a bit to play with when you're baking.

Exercise 263: Sticking in. Make a few dough balls and show baby how to stick matches or small twigs into them.

Exercise 264: Tearing up dough. Show your baby that a piece of dough can be torn apart and that the pieces can be simply joined together again. During his tenth month, baby may begin to realize the principle of dismantling and assembly—analysis and synthesis—when playing this game.

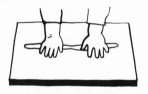

EXERCISE 265

Exercise 265: Forming dough. Show baby how he can flatten dough by slapping it with his hand. Some gifted babies can roll the dough into a snake or make a ball with both hands by the end of their first year.

Exercise 266: Cutting dough. Give baby a piece of dough shaped like a roll and a blunt plastic knife. Persuade him to cut the roll up.

Exercise 267: Play with soft rubber toys. Give baby some soft, flexible rubber toy, perhaps a monkey. Baby will bend the monkey's legs which will straighten out again; this will probably be his first experience with flexibility.

Exercise 268: Folding paper. Till now baby has merely squeezed paper, but by the end of the first year it is possible to teach him to fold paper and make a sharp edge by running his hand over it.

Exercise 269: Spreading a squashed diaper. Teach him to spread out a squashed diaper or dishcloth on the table and flatten it out by running his hand over it.

Exercise 270: Snapping matches. Show baby a burnt-out match or a twig. Show how to snap it and ask him to do the same.

Exercise 271: Rolling up a strip. Give baby an old roll of film with the spool and let him play with it. You can also use a soft strip of leather attached to a rod and let baby roll the leather on the rod.

Using Tools for Complex Tasks

(A tool in this context is any object which baby uses to attain a particular end).

Exercise 272: Pulling with the aid of a string. Place a toy out of baby's reach and tie a piece of string to it, leaving one end near him. He usually realizes that he can pull the toy toward him with the string. Also give him the opportunity to get toys with the aid of strings of various colors, thicknesses, and shapes. He should also learn that this is the way to get hold of a toy which is placed on a diaper, paper, or plank.

After baby has learned to use a string and other aids which are firmly attached to a toy, start teaching him to use aids which are not joined to it.

EXERCISE 273

Exercise 273: Pulling toys with a hook. Get an object shaped like a hook (a poker). Place a toy out of baby's reach and try to teach baby to get hold of it with the aid of the hook.

EXERCISE 274

Exercise 274: Hunting with a net. Get a butterfly net. Stand him next to the bathtub containing various toys. Baby will try to get at them with the net.

Exercise 275: Pulling toys with the aid of a ruler. Tell baby to use some elongated object to get hold of a toy lying under a cupboard. Using a ruler is much harder than a hook.

Exercise 276: Pushing a cube into a hole with a ruler. Dig a small hollow in the yard and give baby a cube and a rod (a pebble and a dry twig will do) and show him how he can shove the cube into the hollow with the aid of the stick.

EXERCISE 277

Exercise 277: Pushing things out of a tube with the aid of a stick. Wrap a toy into paper in front of baby and place it into a tube about 8 inches long. Give baby the tube and a rod with which he can shove the toy out of the tube.

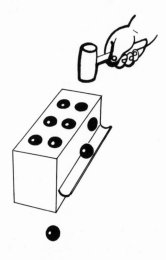

EXERCISE 278

Exercise 278: Nailing board. Make a letter H out of three planks, each about 4 to 6 inches long. Into the crosswise piece bore three holes 1/2 inch in diameter and insert cylindrical pins which fit almost exactly. Give baby a mallet to knock in the pins. When baby has knocked the pins in, turn the toy over and let him knock them out from the other side. Baby will gradually learn to hit the pins on the head with the hammer.

Exercise 279: Opening a drawer with a key. Place a toy into a drawer which can be opened by pulling the key, but without a handle, take the key out and hand it to baby. By the end of the twelfth month many babies can insert the key and open the drawer. Some babies can even turn the key to unlock the drawer.

EXERCISE 280

Exercise 280: Opening the door with the handle. Place baby onto a low stool by the door and protect him from falling down when the door opens. Baby will soon find that it is easy to open the door if he grasps the handle at the end, not near its pivot; this gives him experience with the principle of the lever.

How to Learn Simple Working and Self-Service Motions and Imitation

Exercise 281: Unwrapping paper. Wrap a toy in paper in front of baby. He will try to unwrap it. Wrap objects not only into a variety of paper (thin, thick, small, large, plain, patterned) but also into tin foil, canvas, or plastic.

Exercise 282: Opening and closing a zipper bag. Hide something in a zipper bag in front of the baby. He will try to open and close the zipper.

EXERCISE 283

Exercise 283: Turning pages. First teach baby to turn the pages of cardboard picture books. Later give him some old books and teach him to turn their pages.

EXERCISE 284

Exercise 284: Scribbling on paper. Give baby some old wrapping paper on the floor and a slightly blunt colored pencil. Show him how to scribble and try to get him to scribble as well. He can also do this at the table sitting in your lap.

Exercise 285: Wiping his mouth with a diaper. After you feed the baby, hand him a diaper for wiping his mouth. Baby will try but is more likely to smear the remnants of the food over his face, at least to start with.

Exercise 286: Spearing food onto a fork. When you feed him, sometimes give baby a fork to spear some food with, perhaps a potato. Then feed him the potato yourself.

Exercise 287: Dusting. When you dust furniture, hand baby a diaper and ask him to "help" you. Baby will imitate you.

Exercise 288: Opening and closing a matchbox. Give baby an empty matchbox or similar box and show him how to open and close it. This manipulative activity gives you a chance to teach him to work with both hands, each doing something else.

EXERCISE 289

Exercise 289: Screwing a top onto a bottle or jar. Show baby how to open and close a bottle with a screwtop or a jar with a similar lid. This teaches baby how to do screw-like movements. A toothpaste tube top is also useful.

Exercise 290: Turning a handle. Baby can learn to turn a handle on domestic appliances such as a manual coffee grinder or a pencil sharpener. At first he will use swinging motions to the right and the left, but then he will learn to turn the handle around smoothly. With some appliances you must be careful to prevent him from hurting himself.

Exercise 291: Attaching pegs to a string. Tie a string, about 3 feet long, between two chairs. Give him some pegs and teach him how to attach them to the string by opening and closing them.

Exercise 292: Other working movements. In various domestic chores you perform simple movements which baby observes and would like to imitate. Use every opportunity to enable him to do so. He can perform the movements of a whisk, a rolling pin, mixing with a ladle, and so on.

Playing with Sand and Water

At 11 to 12 months your baby can gain experience with sand and you should allow him sometimes to play in a sandpit under your supervision.

EXERCISE 293

Exercise 293: Shoveling sand, filling a container. Baby learns to use a shovel correctly, to pour the sand from the shovel into a bucket or truck and not to pour the sand next to the container.

Exercise 294: Patting and smoothing a surface. Show baby how to smooth the sand in the bucket by flattening and patting.

Exercise 295: Pouring sand. Give baby several containers to teach him to pour the sand from one to the other. This seemingly simple task is extremely difficult for a baby toward the end of the first year, because it calls for considerable imagination concerning space, some experience, and good coordination of both hands.

You can teach baby all about water when you bathe him. But richer opportunities are afforded by water outdoors, in the swimming pool, lake, or ocean.

Exercise 296: Pushing toys floating on the water. Show him how to push toys with the hand across water to make them float in a particular direction.

Exercise 297: Bubbles. If baby squeezes a punctured ball or rubber toy under water, bubbles come out. Baby will find out that he must first take the toy out of the water and loosen his grip in order for the toy to suck in air and not water. This is the only way he can continue making bubbles. And it's how he learns to realize the existence of air.

EXERCISE 298

Exercise 298: Squirting. If baby loosens his grip on a toy under the water, it sucks in water; when he presses it, it squirts. Baby will learn to distinguish the conditions under which they squirt or emit bubbles. Both Exercises 297 and 298 will give him rich experience in physics and teach him to think.

Exercise 299: Pouring water from one container into another. Give baby several containers so he can pour water from one to the other while he is taking a bath. He will learn to pour the water slowly and fast, from a low and a high point. At the same time he exercises the ability to alter the tilt of the containers slightly, place them into a space relationship with each other so that water pours from one to the other and not into the tub. This gives him valuable experience in physics and geometry.

EXERCISE 300

Exercise 300: Squeezing a sponge. Show baby that when he squeezes a sponge water will run out.

Learning from Manipulative Movements During Social Contact

During his tenth to twelfth months your baby will learn movements in response to verbal requests that are part of social contacts.

Exercise 301: "Make nice to Daddy!" "Show how you love Mummy!" At these words baby can be taught to stroke father, or embrace mother around the neck. Teach him other movements at verbal requests. You need not stay with the traditional ones. Think up new ones that fit simple movements: Let him offer his hand to his uncle, wave good-bye, clap for something, ask for something, say "No-no," not only by shaking his head but also with his hands.

Making the Best Use of Play

Objective: Manipulative and imitative games which I described earlier can be further developed in the last three months of the first year by giving your baby the opportunity to watch people at work and elsewhere and to observe movements of animals and machines. But let him imitate what fascinates him and try to enable him to participate directly in adult activities.

If your baby is to imitate, he must obviously experience and see what he is to imitate; the more scope he has for observation the richer his imitation. Initially, babies imitate only a few typical isolated movements, not an entire sequence of adult activities. At the end of his first year it's still not a baby's aim to achieve some end by imitation. But here are some typical situations which spark baby's interest and stimulate him most to imitate toward the end of his first year.

Baby most often imitates movements you make when performing some act involving his care: feeding, bathing, washing, dressing, laying down to sleep, sitting on the pot, playing. By his twelfth month baby may feed his teddy with a spoon or bottle, cuddle him, seat him on a pot and lay him down to sleep.

Household chores also stimulate him to imitation: cooking, cleaning, washing, ironing, washing the dishes. When you cook, you can give baby a small bowl and ladle and let him imitate you stirring. If you grind coffee in a hand grinder, give baby a similar handle to turn. When you sweep the floor, give him a small dustpan and brush or a small duster and let baby imitate your movements. If you have no small iron, give him a block and a diaper and he can play at ironing.

Father's chores around the home also excite baby's interest and stimulate him to imitation. He is interested in things like sawing, banging nails, turning screws. He will watch the activities of workmen in the home with the same interest. By his twelfth month baby will imitate banging a hammer, sawing, and the like. Don't chase him away! Think of how you can let him see as much of what is going on as possible.

Baby can find many opportunities for imitation outside the home, too. Take him shopping then at home he'll imitate a salesclerk wrapping purchases, workmen digging a ditch, and other activities. He will imitate what he saw in the streets: the honking of taxis or a policeman directing traffic.

In the sandbox, baby will imitate some movements his father makes in the yard: digging, loading, carting. And the observation of animals stimulates him to imitate a dog's bark, a bird's song, and a chicken waving its wing.

A city child has other opportunities from a country child. But both have enough to enable them to develop fully at an early age if parents keep an eye out for opportunities. It depends on you how many stimuli baby acquires. Acquaintance with life around him is the main condition for the development of imitative play and richly developed imitative play is proof that baby has gained much valuable experience.

How to Teach Imitation

It's not enough to give baby plenty of opportunities to observe life around him. You are needed to help him learn to imitate, to actively express what he saw. You need to activate him to imitation.

When you feed baby with a spoon at 11 to 12 months, take his teddy and play at feeding it as well. Then give the teddy to baby and tell him to feed it. When you move smoothly from feeding baby to feeding teddy and then tell him to continue the feeding, you enable him to understand the act of feeding. If you do this with baby two or three times, it will be enough for you to place a bowl and spoon next to the teddy. The baby will understand the connection and start feeding teddy himself.

When you bathe your baby, take a doll and bathe the doll together with him. Wash his hands and then wash the doll's. Then wash his back and then the doll's. Next time ask baby to wash the doll himself. Baby will soon understand this game and will then take his doll before going to the bath so he can wash it.

If you teach baby several imitative movements in this way he will soon grasp the principle of imitation and will start imitating whatever has excited him without your stimulating him. The repertoire of baby's imitative movements will increase and this is the best preparation for so-called "task games" in his third year when he no longer imitates individual movements but performs continuous sensible acts to express that he has assumed somebody's role (playing at mother, salesclerk, doctor). Some older authors say that babies reach this stage without outside influence and that there is no need to bother with these games. But experience from educationally badly managed children's homes has shown that imitative games develop very slowly without stimulation by adults and sometimes not at all. Baby needs some initial stimuli, even from older children, and only after he has mastered the fundamentals of imitative play, can he develop by himself with less help from adults.

Teaching your baby imitative games should not be too formal. Suppose mother observes birds in the park with baby. At home she reminds baby of what they saw and asks him to show her how the birds flapped their wings. Baby understands and waves his hands. Then she asks him to show how the birds ate the seed. Baby does not react, so mother taps her fingers on the floor and says "This is how they did it—how you do it!" Baby looks at her without comprehension but imitates. He obviously did not understand what mother meant when she tapped her fingers on the floor. He did perform this movement, but it expressed nothing because it did not express his experience. Such games are formalistic and have no educational value.

How to Develop Speech and Thinking

In my discussion of delicate hand movements and games I showed how your baby gains experience and knowledge by contact with objects. Here I'd like to show how acquired experience and knowledge is reflected in the development of speech and thinking and how you can contribute to the development of these two closely related functions.

How Thinking Develops in the Tenth to Twelfth Months

Objective: By the twelfth month baby can probably acquire an object with the aid of another which is related to it and this ability should be "generalized" to a certain extent. Baby should be capable of using an object or tool in other situations as well, and should solve problems involving intermediate actions. He'll solve simple tasks with confidence by indirect means (bypassing) and will begin to synthesize.

Acquiring One Object with the Aid of Another

Some of the exercises in this connection have already been mentioned above, 272, 273, 274, and 275. When baby has learned to use similar tools make things more difficult for him by teaching him to find the suitable tool himself.

EXERCISE 302

Exercise 302: Seeking a tool. Repeat Exercises 272, 273, 274, and 275 and offer the same attraction but not the tool; place this nearby where he can see it. Attract baby's attention to the toy and tell him to get it. He will often try to get hold of it with his bare hands, but when he sees his actions are of no avail he will start looking around for some tool.

Exercise 303: Recognition of an object as a possible tool. After baby has mastered the preceding exercise and is able to find a tool that's known to him, make the situation more challenging by removing "familiar tools" from sight and replace them with others that are similar. If baby has been accustomed to using a ruler to push a toy from under the cupboard, remove it and replace it with a handbroom, which baby has never used but is just as suitable. He should solve the problem of whether he can use the handbroom as he did the ruler.

Exercise 304: Using a means to approach his goal. Place a toy on the table out of baby's reach. Nearby put a stool that he is used to climbing on when he wants to get at something on the table. Baby will look around, see the stool, pull it to the table, climb onto it, approach the toy, and take it. You can later make the exercise more difficult by hiding the stool and making him find it first.

By the end of their first year some babies can solve complex problems which demand that they combine several operations.

Exercise 305: Getting a toy with the aid of a tool which is not directly available. Draw his attention to a toy under the cupboard. The ruler which he normally uses to get it is visible on the table but not readily reachable. Baby must first survey the situation, see the stool nearby, pull it up to the table, use it as a tool for getting the ruler and then use it to get the toy.

You can create many similar situations to use the scope of your home. Complex situations requiring two to three operations will usually be too difficult before baby is in his second year, but some intelligent infants who know how to use tools for simple tasks will solve them by the end of the first year. These intellectual gymnastics help to develop his orientation in space and his technical and practical thinking.

Let me show you some other problems which babies like to solve while they exercise their ability to think practically.

EXERCISE 306

Exercise 306: Opening and closing doors with various locks. Baby loves to open doors and look to see what they hide. His interest is even greater when the door has a closing mechanism and he can learn how it works. Allow him to get to know these mechanisms. A clever father can make a board and fasten several small doors on it, each with a different closing mechanism: a padlock, a lock and key, a one- or two-armed lever, a socket. Baby will spend a long time trying them out, opening and closing the doors, and training his intellect.

Exercise 307: Opening and closing various boxes and containers. Baby has learned how to open boxes and containers with lids. Now give him boxes and containers of all shapes and sizes so that he can learn what's different when a lid is pressed on, pushed in, screwed on, or whatever. Next, give him several containers and the same number of lids. His problem is to find which belongs to which. At first give him containers and lids which obviously belong to each other. Later, make the differences smaller so he'll have to *test* which belongs to which.

Exercise 308: Servicing instruments and equipment. By the end of his first year baby will try to imitate with domestic instruments just what his parents do. He will be greatly attracted to switching the TV and the lights on and off. Let him do whatever you don't consider dangerous and prevent his access to dangerous or delicate items.

One of the most complicated problems that baby can solve by the end of his first year is the bypass or indirect approach: having to move away from an object before being able to grasp it because it is not directly available. In some of the above exercises baby already solved this problem (trying to get a toy under the cupboard and moving away from it to get the poker). And he solved it not only by means of a tool but indirectly, too.

Exercise 309: Longer bypasses. In discussing thinking for babies age 7 to 9 months, I described several exercises for baby to learn to get at a toy by a simple bypass. Your 12-month-old baby can get to the toy by means of a longer one. Show him through the window of the kitchen door that granny has come and is in the next room. Baby cannot enter the room directly because the door is closed, so he runs through the next door into the corridor and then into the room. This arrangement of the exercise assumes that baby is well oriented in the home. It is easier when he can take the situation in at once. For instance, baby is in the yard and sees his granny by the fence and wants to get to her; yet he moves away from her along the fence to the gate, passes through the gate, and then moves to her on the other side of the fence. Use other opportunities in the home or outside and use people and objects as the goal to get baby to solve a problem. In summer, father can jump over a stream and call baby to him—if baby can reach him and keep dry by crossing a nearby bridge.

EXERCISE 310

Exercise 310: Getting an object by pushing it away. Stand baby on a stool by the table and place an ironing board or other obstacle on the table and a toy at the other end. Give baby a ladle. Since he cannot pull the toy toward him because the obstacle is in the way, he can push it to make it fall off the table. Then he gets off the stool, runs around the table and picks the toy up from the floor. He also deserves a reward if he gets off the stool, carries it to the other side of the table, gets on it and takes the toy this way.

Another problem that baby is able to solve by the end of the year is to recognize an entity as a whole when he sees one of its parts.

Exercise 311: Seeking a hidden toy. Hide a toy so that one part is visible and tell baby to bring it. At first he may have trouble finding it, especially if only a small part is visible but he soon understands that the toy is beyond the visible part. The toy can also be hidden under a diaper so its contours are obvious. Outside, father can hide behind a tree so his shoulder is visible or he casts an obvious shadow.

I'd like to reiterate still again that it's not enough for your baby to be born bright. To develop his intelligence, he must actively solve problems which require intelligence. I have described such problems, but baby also needs to be surrounded by intelligent people who can think up similar problems and use all the opportunities afforded by their surroundings.

An intelligent baby soon recognizes that the most important instrument for solving situations is the human being. He will recognize that a human being can think and is also very willing to think for baby. He will discover ways to try to force the people who surround him to think and act for him. If the baby is allowed to exploit this discovery, it can be tragic for him. He will then do a minimum to think and act; his surroundings act and think for him.

I therefore need to stress a most important principle: think a lot *about* baby, but not *for* him; do a lot for him, but not instead of him; think and do a lot to gently get baby to like to think and do things himself.

Exercising Speech in the Tenth to Twelfth Months

Objective: To increase baby's passive vocabulary by the end of the first year so he understands simple sentences about situations in which he finds himself every day: feeding, washing, bathing, games, walks, sleep, people, and objects that are close to him. Baby should be able to use at least 5 words. He likes nursery rhymes and can name a person or a picture.

Most of the exercises for the development of passive speech between the seventh and ninth months (198 to 202) are also useful in this next period. Again, be sure to speak slowly and distinctly, limit your vocabulary to words he can understand, speak about a concrete situation in which he finds himself and always use the same words for the same things.

Exercise 312: Naming activities and persons while playing. If you want baby to distinguish between, say, a cube, box, and cup, sit him on your lap at the table. Accompany the following sentences with pointing and activity: "Here's the cube; that's a box. Put the cube into the box. Where's the cube? Here's the cube. This is a cup. Put the cube into the cup. Now put the cup into the box. . . ." Here you perform simple activities with several objects and describe your actions in very simple words. After baby has heard a certain word 5 to 10 times during the game and his attention is attracted to the activity (object) he will most probably form an association and will know the meaning of "cube," "box," "cup."

Exercise 313: Naming common activities while playing. In the preceding exercise baby was passive and only watched and listened to what you were doing and saying, but associations are easier to form when baby is active. Select activities which baby can perform with you; Exercise 312 can be made more challenging if you persuade him to perform some of these activities himself. Or you can play with a doll. Take one, give baby another and say these words while you perform the appropriate activities: "Let's cuddle baby. Cuddle baby. Let's stroke baby. Stroke her, too!" When baby sees what you are doing with the doll and is told to imitate you, he learns the appropriate movements and also learns to understand the words.

When your baby responds to your requests he shows that he has understood them. Here is how to make this process more challenging.

Exercise 314: Request a certain activity with various objects. It is easier for baby to understand the meaning of words which define objects rather than activities. This is why he will first learn more words defining objects and persons. Here's how to get baby to understand the meaning of "Give me . . ." Place a row of toys in front of baby and say, "Give me the car!" Guide baby's hand to the toy with one hand and when he grasps it guide his hand to your open hand; then gently take the car and praise him. Gradually ask him to hand you the ball or a doll. Assist him into a gradually decreasing degree and reward every correct response with thanks. Praise, a pat, a kiss. This exercise is OK at 10 to 11 months. Repeat it daily with other objects: "Cuddle teddy (baby, doggie) . . . ," or "Hide your ball (car, pussy) in the basket. . . ."

Exercise 315: Ask him to do various things with the same object. Give baby a doll and tell him to "Cuddle baby, stroke baby. Feed baby. Give me baby. Take baby. Put baby to bed." Tell him daily to do these things with other objects.

Exercise 316: Do various things with various objects. When baby has mastered Exercise 315 you can tell him to do different things with various objects. This can be done with well-trained babies by the end of the first or beginning of the second year. Now you can use more complicated verbal instructions and more complex games. For instance, persuade baby to play more complex games with his doll: "Bring baby from his bed. Put baby to bed. Where's your blanket? Cover baby with the blanket. Bring the milk bottle. . . ." If baby does not know how to respond, demonstrate the activity. By the beginning of his second year baby will not only imitate but also understand what is wanted of him.

Exercise 317: Development of the passive vocabulary in everyday tasks. Make full use of your daily chores with baby: feeding, bathing, dressing. Name and clearly demonstrate the objects and activities which have a close relationship to him and he will form an association between the word and the action or object very easily. ("This is a roll. This is a cup of milk. Stir your milk with the spoon. Open your mouth. . . .")

Exercise 318: Development of passive words with the aid of pictures. Show him pictures of things he knows from real life. A picture should remind him of something, not replace something. By comparing the picture with reality baby learns to understand the picture, but he cannot understand reality just from a picture; that is, he cannot imagine the size of an elephant from a photo. A baby who has never seen or heard a dog bark cannot tell from a picture that a dog barks. This does not mean that baby should look exclusively at realistic pictures. An artist may depict the typical characteristics that distinguish a dog from a puppy, which teaches baby how to tell a small adult dog from an equally large puppy.

In the tenth to twelfth months, don't just show him pictures of individual people, animals, or things. Draw his attention to activities plus relationships: "This is a doggie, he barks bow-wow, jumps hop-hop, doggie is in his dog house, barking at kitty." After baby has understood, get him to be active by asking him questions. Baby will point at the picture when you ask, "Where is the doggie? Which doggie barks bow-wow? Which doggie jumps hop-hop? Where is doggie's kennel?"

Training Active Speech

The method for developing active speech which I described for the seventh to ninth months can be used for ages 10 to 12 months. It is even more suitable then. It had to be introduced earlier because many babies already say their first active word by the ninth month. Here now are exercises to develop active speech for babies who know a few active words.

Speak
to Daddy.

EXERCISE 319

Exercise 319: Sending messages. To train baby in the active use of words in appropriate situations, send him to somebody with a message. Tell him to "Call daddy and tell him to come and eat; tell daddy to eat." Or: "Give grandpa the book and say: 'Here you are.' " The person who got the message should, of course, not act on the message and praise baby and thank him.

Exercise 320: Discussing observed things. Use interesting situations to "talk" to baby. When you are out with baby in the street talk to him about what is going on around you: "Look, what's that coming?" Baby will answer, "A car." Reward the answer, praise him, and say,

"Car! It's a car. And what does a car do?" Stimulate baby to activity with other words, and always reward them by repeating them, praising him, and smiling at him. In the tenth to twelfth months and later, a baby gets great pleasure out of close social contact and will often try to keep the "conversation" going and draw your attention to something by himself. He may point to a dog and identify him with a word. The spontaneous use of words by baby is the main educational objective during this period.

Exercise 321: Acting out scenes with toys for baby's comments. Let father sit at the table with baby on his lap and act out simple scenes, perhaps with a teddy: show baby how teddy jumps, falls over, waves his paw, lies down in bed, hides behind a box, and calls to baby. Always ask what teddy is doing, and baby will tell you he's doing "hop-hop," "bye-bye."

Exercise 322: Discussing a picture. This is similar to Exercise 318, but when you talk about the picture persuade baby to define some of the activities with words. If he begins to do so by himself, he deserves special praise and admiration.

Exercise 323: Completing nursery rhymes. Look at a picture book with rhymes with him and recite the rhymes. If you do this often, some 12-month-old will be able to say the last one or two words of some of the rhymes you recite.

Note: The vocabulary of the smallest baby consists of two types of words: those that sound similar to words in his mother tongue, and those words he has formed himself, "baby talk," which only the people closest to him understand. In the first year of developing active speech try to increase baby's vocabulary regardless of whether the words are from the adult vocabulary or not. The objective is for baby to realize the function of words in his contacts with the people around him. Once you have awakened interest in verbal contact, start to see that he replaces baby words with real ones. Baby will usually stop using baby words after 18 months.

Training Emotions and Social Relationships

Objective: In the tenth to twelfth months, try to help your baby develop emotional relationships with his objective and human environment. Make sure he does not experience accidental and unnecessary fear of harmless phenomena, but let him learn to recognize dangerous situations and objects which could harm him.

Even with the best of love, care, and training, negative emotional attitudes can form. Let's assume that your baby for some reason is afraid of a black furry coat. Whenever he sees one he begins to cry and hold on to you with fright. The sooner you rid him of this senseless fear the better it is for him. Let me show how to go about it.

Exercise 324: How to rid baby of fear of an object. Place the black fur coat of which baby is afraid in one corner of the room. Your baby, who needs to be in a good mood, should sit with you and feel safe in a distant corner; the further you are away from the object of fear the safer he will feel in your arms. Father should pull a new toy dog out of the sleeve of the fur coat and hand it to baby. Mother should play with baby and the dog and then return it to the coat. Repeat this scene several times a day and baby will play ever nearer to the coat until you can incorporate the coat itself into the game: the dog will hide in the coat and peep out of it, and finally baby will pull it out of the coat himself. Incorporate the coat into the game until it becomes an object of the game and loses the character of an object of fear. After a while baby will sit on it or hide in it. The reprocessing of an emotional attitude is possible because you create a pleasant situation (new toy) into which the object of fear is incorporated from a distance. The object of fear gradually becomes a more important part of a pleasant situation, which causes it to lose its negative emotional character and gain an increasingly stronger positive emotional relationship. Proceed slowly and with extreme caution. Otherwise your child could wind up being afraid of the new toy as well as the fur coat.

Other emotional attitudes can be changed in much the same way. You can encourage your baby's fondness of wallowing in dirt or create antipathy for dirt and dirty things. The rule is very simple: all things toward which you'd like your baby to have a positive attitude need to be combined with pleasant stimuli. Those toward which you'd like him to have a negative attitude should be connected with unpleasant stimuli and situations.

In the seventh to ninth months baby learned to tell a smile from a frown; he learned whether a frown was meant seriously or a look was encouraging or discouraging. By the tenth to twelfth months, a kind smile and praising tone of voice should itself become a reward, and a frown or stern and scolding tone of voice should be inhibiting.

Exercise 325: Turning a mimical expression, gesture, tone, and the like into a reward or inhibition. If baby does something constructive, smile at him, stroke him, praise him. Immediately afterward do something that is especially pleasing to him: hand him a toy, do something funny with him—whatever he enjoys. At first his reward is either the toy or what you do afterward. But gradually the smile should suffice as reward or praise. If you stick to these recommendations systematically and uniformly to the twelfth month, the baby himself will start seeking these rewards or even reward himself; he may start stroking his head and say, "Good boy!" if you forget to praise him. The same method works in the opposite direction. Whenever your baby does something he shouldn't, frown and say "bad" and immediately after that do something unpleasant: stop playing with him, take away his toy, walk away from him. After this negative reward baby will venture into these unwanted activities less often and hopefully stop altogether. Gradually it will be enough to adopt a strict tone and a frown for baby to stop doing what he shouldn't. A smile and praise become a reward, a frown and scolding a punishment.

By his tenth month your baby should begin to get acquainted with the practicalities of life. To realize that something exists he must experience a moment when it does not. You want baby to remain happy and satisfied, and to have a good time, so you surround him with love and comfort. But to experience these things fully, the baby should not bask in an ideal situation all the time. To realize that mother loves him he must also experience the opposite: that mother can get very annoyed at him; then, when mother makes up with him again, it is one of the most pleasant experiences he can have. For baby to realize that he is well off, it is necessary that he occasionally experience being worse off; he may lack something, or something hurts. Only by experiencing these contrasts can he realize what he has and how well off he is —and learn to sympathize with others who lack something.

Love, comfort, and relative plenty should not become everyday things. Baby should experience their opposites, but let him realize that these changes depend on his behavior; if he misbehaves many pleasant aspects of life will disappear. Unhealthy absolute security is created by parents who are excessively kind and suffer and forgive and cannot refuse their baby anything. Baby then takes their love and gifts for granted, demands ever more and returns ever less. This relationship often ends with the child becoming ungrateful to the parents. Relative emotional security is created by parents who reward baby's desirable behavior with love and kindness, but respond to his undesirable behavior so baby understands their action as a punishment; they are less kind and do not give him the pleasant stimuli which usually follow constructive behavior.

This is how your baby can gradually incorporate himself into human society and learn to adapt his behavior not only to his own needs but also to the needs of other people. The process of socialization begins with infancy because the relationship between a baby and his parents is the basis of his relations to people in general.

Baby should learn early in life to share with others or to give up something in favor of another person. The sooner you start teaching him an altruistic attitude toward others, the more likely you'll avoid the egoistic behavior which usually appears in the second year.

Exercise 326: Creating the habit of sharing with others, or giving up something in favor of another person. Occasionally ask baby to give his favorite toy to father. Father should take the toy from baby and play with it for a moment and then give it back to him. At other times father should tell baby to give his toy to mother or his brother or sister. You might tell baby to lend his toy briefly to another baby in the park. Whenever baby gets his favorite dish, tell him to give a bit of it to somebody else. The other person should accept the delicacy and eat it in front of him—not just to thank him for it and return it to him. Baby should not get used to giving things up only formally and expect the other to accept it and then give it back. Sometimes he should give up a delicacy altogether in favor of another. Some parents think that this is being too hard on baby, an unnecessary torture. They should realize that at an early age your baby overcomes egoism easily and can avoid many unpleasant and troublesome moments at a later age. Also, there are many ways of inconspicuously returning something to baby that he gave up in favor of another person.

Elsewhere I have said that the best way to incorporate baby into the family group is through common activity. By the end of the first year, give him the opportunity of joining you at dusting, and when you wash the dishes allow baby to wipe the spoons and "help" with other work he can do.

Playing together is equally important, and here are some games.

EXERCISE 327

Exercise 327: Butting. Sit down with baby in your lap and play the age-old game of gently butting your heads. By the ninth to tenth months baby will be moving his head toward yours.

Exercise 328: Seeking and catching a toy. Sit on the floor on a low stool, take a small toy and hide it behind your back. Baby, standing in front of you, will try to grab it. You should move it from hand to hand, lift your arms to the side and upward, but after a while let him catch it.

Exercise 329: Hide-and-seek. Hide behind a cupboard or door and call baby. When he approaches and sees you, call "boo," lift him up into the air, and then hide somewhere else. Baby will usually soon understand the principle of the game and go and hide himself. Usually he will be unable to wait for you to find him and will call out as soon as he is hidden.

EXERCISE 330

Exercise 330: Passing a ball. Sit down on the floor oppo-site baby with your legs spread apart. Roll a ball toward him and ask him to roll it back. By his eleventh or twelfth months baby will have grasped the principle of the game and will hand or throw the ball back and laugh happily.

Exercise 331: Chase. Stand facing baby, put out your hands and call him to you. He will try to grasp your hands, but when he reaches you you should laugh, re-treat a few steps and then let him catch you. Your hands should also be stretched out in case he falls. The chase can be made more interesting if you have a toy in your hand.

EXERCISE 332

Exercise 332: Mirror. Place baby in front of a mirror, and let him look at himself. He will soon start laughing at himself, touching his image, butting. He will alternately look at himself and at your image and will learn to distin-guish between image and reality.

Exercise 333: The social element in imitative play. Baby already knows how to cuddle, feed, and otherwise handle his doll. Gradually teach him to play with his doll or teddy as if it were a real person who has the same needs, joys, and pains as he does himself. Teach him to handle the toys gently, kindly, and lovingly. Thus training for parenthood begins at the earliest age.

Learning to Acquire Habits

Objective: Starting with the tenth month your baby will probably sleep 10 to 11 hours at night and twice in the day for 1 1/2 to 2 1/2 hours, in the morning around noon and later in the afternoon. Teach baby to eat by himself with a spoon and to drink from a cup. After the twelfth month baby should soil his diapers only rarely during the day.

Baby can sit up by himself, so feed him from a baby chair at a normal table. Teach him to use the spoon alone. Let him first experiment with mashed food: give him a large bib and a spoon and allow him to spoon up the mash and take it to his mouth by himself. At first stand right behind him so you start immediately to prevent him from forming bad habits. Baby will soon learn to eat mash reasonably well, so by the beginning of the second year he will be able to take a few spoonfuls of soup. At first he will take two to three spoonfuls himself, with the rest fed by you. Gradually, get him to eat more by himself, but only during the second year will he learn to eat an entire portion alone.

Teach him to drink out of a cup alone. During the first attempts pour only a bit a liquid into the bottom of the cup and only after he has learned to tilt it properly should you gradually give him fuller ones.

Now baby should remain dry and clean during his period of wakefulness (if you put him on the pot in time) and he will not soil his diaper when awake. But he still needs it at night. Train him to announce that he needs the pot. This only happens after he has become aware of internal signals that tell him his bladder or bowels are full. He usually reaches this stage during his second year, but toward the end of the first you can take measures for this awareness to develop.

Baby becomes aware of the evacuation process in three stages. First he realizes the *end* of the process, then the act itself, and finally he learns to tell when the process of evacuation is preparing itself. This is why he first learns to announce that evacuation has finished and that he has soiled his diaper. In the next phase he will announce that the evacuation is taking place, which does nothing to help you. Only in the third phase will he announce that evacuation is about to begin and give you time to sit him on the pot and save you from changing his diaper. Phases 1 and 2 usually do not last very long and you can speed them along.

Earlier I explained how to create a simple conditioned reflex so baby will evacuate when he is placed on the pot in time. I stressed not to seat baby on the pot for long periods. If baby sits on the pot for a short time and does what he has to to, he is far more likely to become aware of the feelings connected with defecation and is also more likely to recognize the feelings which precede it. If he sits on the pot for too long, starts playing on it, or is distracted in other ways, he will not notice these physical sensations and cannot learn to control them. Do not, therefore, distract him. Get him to concentrate on what he is to do; draw his attention to it verbally: when you hear the urine flowing out or see him pressing and getting red in the face praise him and say he's doing "eh-eh."

After he has finished ask him to say what he had done and try to motivate him to say he had been doing "eh-eh." When you take him off the pot, show him the contents, repeat the words, praise him, and tell him to name his activity once more. If baby soils his diaper he should be scolded not for soiling the diaper but for not saying what happened. If he announces the soiling, first praise him for announcing it. But praise is relevant only for a while. If he announced too long after the fact that he has soiled himself, show your displeasure that he announced it too late.

The first timely announcement should be praised with exaggeration. If you devote sufficient attention to this act it's possible that by the middle of his second year (or even earlier) he will announce his need himself and save you a lot of work with diapers as well as the nervous energy you need to put him on the pot in time. If you neglect toilet training, he may still have to wear diapers during this second and third year.

Toys and Furniture You Need

After his ninth month your baby should occasionally sit and play at a table. He needs a small table and chair or armchair. He sits better in an armchair because he can lean back, but it's harder for him to sit on it in the beginning. He will soon learn to grasp the arm rests and sit down. I therefore advise you to buy an armchair, and buy him a higher chair only when he is older and physically more mature.

A bench, about 3 by 3 feet long and about 6 by 8 inches high is good for sitting and excellent as gymnastic equipment.

Toys for babies of 7 to 12 months are much different from those for young infants. I shall only list them because I've described in the exercises how to use them.

Toys on a string (animals, cars, trains)
Doll, teddybear, and other toys for imitative games (spoon, bowl, pillow)

Wooden cubes (1 to 4 inches)

Board or cube with holes which can be used for threading with round and square pegs

A board with hollows into which round, square, triangular, or other-shaped pieces can be placed (around 1 inch in diameter)

A stand with vertical rods for threading rings and discs with a hole in them

A board with keyholes and keys

A cashbox

Hammering board with hammer

Board or instrument with a turning handle (coffee grinder)

Tube and rod which can be inserted into it

A set of conical bowls which can be stacked

A set of unequally large cylindrical bowls which can be stacked

A set of hollow cubes

Various boxes and containers with lids that can be inserted or screwed on

A board with doors and various locks (handles, padlocks, keyholes)

Plasticine

Drilled objects for threading a wire

Pictures and picture books

Isn't it good to know how many of these important aids to bringing up your baby are already in your home, waiting to be used by your child?

10

What Is "Normal"?

How can you tell whether a baby is developing as he should? Obviously, psychological development can't be measured the way a yard measures length, a pound measures weight, or an hour measures time. The psychological development of a baby can be assessed only in relative terms: a particular showing is better, the same, or worse than the average performance of a large group of babies of the same age. "Average" means all the babies with the exception of the 10 percent who do best and the 10 percent who do least well. For instance, in Czechoslovakia about 50 percent of all babies take their first step by the end of the first year, but 10 percent make it before the tenth month and 10 percent do not even make it by the end of the fifteenth. Therefore we say that, on average, babies take their first step by the end of the twelfth month, but consider as average all babies who take it between 10 to 15 months. Incidentally, these standards vary only very minimally between all civilized countries, so they apply to American children, too.

At the beginning of each section containing exercises I have outlined "objectives." These are comparatively high and hard to reach. They set a goal, not necessarily what you should achieve.

This is why I include here a "Table for the Assessment of an Infant's Psychological Development." Please do not use these findings as precise yardsticks for your baby. The tables merely indicate development of "average" unexercised children. If a certain skill is mentioned in the table as reached in the sixth month, this means that it appears in about half of all babies in the sixth month, but is not yet developed in the remaining half. If the skill appears at the end of the fifth or seventh months this is also considered average. The rule is: if a certain skill or ability appears one month sooner or later in the second quarter-year than given in the tables; or 2 months in the third quarter; or 3 months in the fourth quarter; it is not a sign of genius nor is it a tragedy.

The tables could harm babies considerably if parents abuse them and try to make a baby "come up to the standard" at all costs, or even exceed it. Such arbitrary acceleration could do great psychological harm with grave consequences for further development. It is better to do nothing at all with him rather than to try and force development because overloading is worse than insufficient stimulation. So use the tables sensibly. Be very cautious in trying to forecast your baby's future on the basis of his development compared with the tables. Even after a child goes to school it is impossible to forecast with certainty and often a child who does not do too well in school succeeds later in life, while a star pupil may become a failure.

In no way do I wish to make light either of the tables or school grades; as a rule, most children develop at school as they develop later in life. But I would especially like you to believe that development is a process that can be influenced to a considerable degree, mainly at an early age.

There will of course be people who will consider my advice to be "acceleration of development." But after you read this book I trust you will see that my purpose is only to ensure that the development of your baby is not slowed down by traditional habits based on old-fashioned, incorrect theoretical assumptions. I stressed again that a baby should not be forced into any activity, but persuaded to be active.

I have tried to show you the importance of bringing up your baby at his earliest age for the rest of his entire life and development. It would be hard to do later whatever good you have done him at this age. If you devote yourself to baby during his first year you will get used to this joyful vocation and will continue your efforts later because he is your child forever and the results of your endeavors will be obvious and encouraging.

If I have said that mother should do one thing, father the other, I could just as easily have said "mother" instead of "father," and also "grandpa," "grandma," "uncle," "aunt," or "older brother or sister." Everybody who lives with baby or comes into contact with him can and should participate in his upbringing but all should be united in their efforts and agree on the same principles and methods. This does not mean that everybody should do the same thing. Everybody has different interests, abilities, and knowledge and can concentrate more on this or that aspect of upbringing: the father can concentrate on the development of physical movements while mother stresses the development of speech; grandpa may be more interested in developing his dexterity, or what have you.

By now I am sure you understand my motive for writing this book. I had no intention of writing either a strictly theoretical treatise or a "handbook." The aim is to combine theory with practice. It wants to tell you

ASSESSMENT OF AN INFANT'S PSYCHOLOGICAL DEVELOPMENT

Month	Development of Overall Movements	Development of Hand Movements and Manipulative Play	Development of Speech and Social Behavior	Development of Habits
1.	Lifts his head for a moment on his tummy, mostly has it on one side. Occasionally sticks out his backside and performs crawling movements with the lower limbs.	Reflexively grasps a toy when it touches his open hand. Looks at a toy placed in his range of vision.	Occasionally emits throaty sounds such as: "ah," "eh." Fixes onto a human face which appears in his range of vision for a short moment.	Must be fed once a night.
2.	Lifts his head about 4 inches and keeps it lifted for at least 5 seconds. When held in the vertical position under the arms he holds his head straight.	Holds a toy longer than 10 seconds. Visually follows a toy which moves.	Reacts to a smile with a smile. Observes people closest to him.	Must be fed once a night.
3.	When lying on his tummy he holds his	Holds a toy longer and waves it about. Inspects	Begins to mumble when talked to. When talked	Demands no feeding at night.

	head up longer, arches his back, leans on his elbows.	his hands. Visually seeks the source of a sound.	to and smiled at, moves vigorously.	Stays awake calmly longer.
4.	Pushes himself up with the arms when on the tummy and sometimes passively falls over on his back. When pulled up to the sitting position the head does not drop. When held under the arms lightly touches the ground with his legs.	Inspects toys in his hand. Brings his hand unsteadily to an offered toy.	Mumbles spontaneously. Begins to laugh aloud when teased.	Regular rhythm of wakefulness and sleep.
5.	Turns over onto his tummy by himself. On the tummy, rests only on his palms. When pulled up to the sitting position, draws his head up, bends his arms and pushes his legs forward. When held under the arms strongly pushes with his legs.	Guides his hand steadily to a toy. Transfers the toy from hand to hand and puts it in his mouth.	Mumbles and shouts. Discerns a kind and strict tone of voice and mimicry.	Plays with toys for a longer period of time.

6.	When lying on his tummy he lifts one arm. Actively turns from tummy to his back. Holds offered fingers and pulls himself up to the sitting position. When held under the arms in an upright position he can support his entire weight on his legs for a moment and dances (does knee bends).	Holds a toy in each hand.	Mumbles and pronounces vowels and consonants. Begins to combine them into syllables. Behaves differently toward known and unknown persons. Establishes contact by mumbling.	Can take food from a spoon. Holds the cup from which he is given liquid.
7.	Turns onto his tummy to the left and right. Pulls himself up to the sitting and standing position when offered a finger.	Grasps a cube in each hand by himself.	Babbles syllables ("ba," "ma," "ta," "va"). Visually seeks at least one named object. Understands the game of "hide and seek" with a diaper.	Eats unmashed food.
8.	Crawls on his tummy and sways on his knees.	Begins to grasp smaller objects with the thumb	Repeats syllables "ba-ba-ba," etc., and	Chews a roll he holds himself.

	Sits by himself but unsteadily. Stands steadily if he can hold onto something.	and forefinger. Sticks cube into cube.	begins to duplicate. Visually seeks more objects (about 5) which are marked only with words. Understands the game of "butting."	
9.	Crawls. Sits steadily and sits up without assistance. Stands up by his playpen and walks on the spot.	Touches details on the toy. Bangs toys against each other.	Claps his hands when told.	Evacuates his bowels when seated on the pot in time.
10.	Begins to walk sideways around the furniture.	Pulls cubes out of container, opens drawers and boxes and empties them. Pulls out keys.	Understands the words "Give," "Do bye-bye." Understands the game of "chase on all fours."	Can drink a small amount of liquid from a cup by himself.
11.	Walks forward around the furniture and walks when guided with both hands.	Throws objects into boxes, holes, fills containers, inserts keys. Pulls up a distant toy with the aid of a string.	Can show you where he has his hand, foot, verbally "marked" people, and objects. Understands praise and repeats activities in order to be praised again.	If placed on the pot in time, needs only few diapers during the day.

| 12. | Walks when held by one hand. Will make one step (from chair to couch). | Will grasp 2 cubes in one hand, drop a small object (pill) into a bottleneck. Switches a table lamp on and off. | Pronounces 1 to 5 intelligible words. Reacts correctly to simple orders ("Bring your spoon"); understands and reacts to the negative "Mustn't"; imitates (dusting). | Tries to eat with the spoon by himself. |

about the latest discoveries in child psychology; to draw from them the most important conclusions and tasks for bringing up your baby; to show concretely how to fulfill these tasks; and draw your attention to other opportunities.

Parents would be well advised to read the whole book and, if possible, do all the exercises at the appropriate time. Please don't select a single exercise and try it without knowing what it is for. It might amuse baby for a while, but the educational effect would probably be negligible.

Much cannot be dealt with in "exercises." Emotional upbringing and the achievement of good social behavior call for systematic and constant influence of both parents and society on the baby.

It is very important for you to understand the term "exercise" as I use it. By now I'm sure it's clear that it includes tasks, games, and amusements—any activity through which your baby can learn something useful. It corresponds to his level of development, has an educational objective, is of interest to baby, and offers happy, spontaneous amusement. The transition from one "exercise" to another is much like the transition from one activity to another during a spontaneous game. If you look at it this way, it's likely that your baby will return to an activity himself even when he's not stimulated or persuaded by an adult.

Finally I would like to recommend that you not only record the baby's first year on film or tape, but also in a diary because it brings more of your own mind to bear on developments. When you make notes in your diary—you'll think about your baby and about yourself, and analyze what went right or wrong—not why. When you think about the good results of your upbringing efforts it will make you happy, give you strength to carry on, and help you to improve whatever you're not satisfied with. In a few years you'll read this diary again and you will treasure it because it captures some of the best moments of your life. Don't deprive yourself of this joy!

Appendix: Results of Experimental Testing

Parents who use the methods offered in this book have the right to ask to what extent they can accept their usefulness and reliability.

I have received many letters from enthusiastic parents who thank me and describe how their children, brought up by this method, are developing. But letters of thanks are no scientific proof that a method is beneficial. Neither is the claim that over the past 25 years I and my colleagues in the Institute for the Care of Mother and Child in Prague have been concerned with the problem of the psychology and upbringing of babies.

Here, then, are some results of our research in which we experimentally examined how the development of children was influenced when they were systematically stimulated during their first year of life. First let me describe a project in which we examined the influence of stimulating babies systematically toward activities that require intensive motion.

What led us to this project? New facts published in various scientific papers and many checks and rechecks of our preceding experiments, including two chance discoveries.

To give the babies in our nurseries more space for movement they were placed into higher than normal playpens: 6 feet by 4 feet, 2 feet above the floor, with its sides 18 inches high and made of crosswise bars. In such playpens the babies learned, among other things, to crawl in the eighth month and to stand up by the wall of the pen in the ninth month.

As soon as they had stood up they started to climb up the wall of their pens, so there was danger of their falling out. They were therefore placed onto a clean floor at the age of 8 months. Taking advantage of this situation, we gave the babies a small ladder; babies who were unable to walk easily climbed up a vertical ladder. So it is obviously easier for a baby to climb up a ladder than to walk without holding on.

"Normal" 8-month-old babies do not climb ladders— not because they do not know how, but because they are systematically prevented from doing so. So since we wanted to rear babies naturally and make use of their inborn scope for development, we placed at their disposal (at 8 months) a wall with rungs. The babies first learned to crawl across the floor and then up the ladder. In the end they walked on the floor without support.

This made us realize that what we called "normal" was not always natural and that "normality" is the result of certain cultural concepts. If we leave a baby's feet bare he often learns to grasp objects not only with his hands but with his feet; he plays with an inflated ball hanging above him with hands and feet, then with one hand, one foot, and so on. But if he spends all his time with his feet wrapped, he neither touches or feels with his feet.

These observations led us to the conclusion that not only the development of movements, but development in general was strongly influenced by the stimuli the baby received at an early age and that a change in the method of stimulation could alter his entire development.

We were then confronted with the ethical question of whether intensive stimulation of movements would overload the baby and damage his development. We consulted physiologists and they supported our views. They, too, were of the opinion that babies today are more prevented from moving rather than stimulated and that more intensive stimulation would only do them good.

We next calmed our consciences with the so-called "transport hypothesis"—so-called because we can assume that prehistoric mothers often transported their babies, grasped them in various ways, carried them, laid them down, shifted them from hand to hand, and bent over with them when working. A baby cannot be entirely passive during these movements. He had to adapt himself to these movements and positions by holding his head up, moving trunk and limbs, and holding on with his hands and feet. The baby was therefore stimulated and activated for long periods to energetic movements. He was equipped with many neuromuscular mechanisms which enabled him to perform these movements from the very beginning.

Today's babies are still equipped with these mechanisms. They include the so-called postural reflexes (baby holds his head in the extension of his trunk when you lean him forward or to the side) and the grasping reflex (baby holds our hands so firmly that he can be lifted up). Carrying a baby around was a very intensive and natural exercise for him.

When we felt certain that we would not harm our babies with our experiments, but would do them good, we began our experimental work. We worked with three groups of babies. The first (I) group consisted of babies who lived in the Institute for the Care of Mother and Child from birth up to age 6 to 7 months. One specialist devoted himself to each baby every day for one period of wakefulness (about two hours), played with him to stimulate him to movement activities described in Chapter 7 and recorded his development from the fourth week after birth to the end of the sixth month.

The second (II) group consisted of babies who lived at home with their parents and during their first year visited us regularly once or twice a week, in all about 20 times. We showed the parents how to stimulate their babies' movements; at the same time we examined them. The parents then worked with their babies at home. After the first year we no longer instructed the parents, but the progress of these babies was followed up through their third year. We showed these parents the exercises described in Chapters 7, 8, and 9.

The third (control) group (III) consisted of babies who came to one of Prague's children's centers for periodic routine pediatric checkups. They lived in normal family conditions without any special stimulation. Every child was examined once, either in the third, sixth, ninth, or twelfth month of his first year. The parents came from every walk of life. They were not informed about our work and regarded it as part of the medical checkups.

There were boys and girls in each group. To present as homogenous material as possible we mention only our results with boys. However, I wish to stress emphatically that we accumulated very adequate experience with little girls and that the differences between the sexes were almost invariably without statistical significance (which again shows that if boys tend, for example, to be more proficient than girls in such fields as geometry and physics, this difference is the result of different toys and other environmental differences to which the sexes have traditionally been exposed by parents).

In Group I (babies stimulated in the Institute) we had 10 boys. In the Group II (stimulated at home) there were

20 boys. In the Group III (control babies from families without stimulation) there were 10 boys three months old; 13 six months old; 11 nine months old; and 15 twelve months old. For all the children we recorded the development of head movements, upper limbs, lower limbs, complex locomotion, play, speech. We statistically processed about 200 development traits, about 15 traits for each month. Each of the six tables mentions seven to eight typical developmental milestones for each group. The tables give the average age in months at which the 20 boys stimulated at home by their parents (Group II) achieved each milestone. Instead of presenting average ages for Groups I and III we report the statistical significance of the difference in the achievement of each milestone. Thus we compared differences in development between Groups I and II, II and III, and I and III.

The statistical significance of the differences in the development of the three groups was determined as follows. For example, no child could transfer a toy from one hand to the other in his third month. But in the ninth month, all the children in all the groups could perform this task. So we determined how many children in the first, second, and third group could perform this task in their sixth month. These figures enabled us to calculate whether the differences between the groups were significant or not.

A difference is statistically significant when $p < 0.05$, and statistically highly significant when $p < 0.01$. We could compare the development of the babies in Group I only up to the sixth month, because after that the children left the Institute to live with their real or adoptive parents, mostly outside Prague, so that we lost contact with them.

The tables show that the two groups of stimulated babies (Groups I and II) showed similar development while the unstimulated group (III) lagged behind the

DEVELOPMENT OF HEAD MOVEMENTS

Developmental Milestone	Age of Appearance in Group II	Difference between Groups		
	X	I:II	II:III	I:III
Lifts his head higher than 45° when lying on the tummy	2.00	-/3	p<0.05/3	-/3
When pulled to the sitting position by the hands the head is straight	2.30	-/3	p<0.01/3	p<0.05/3
Holds his head up when lying on his tummy	2.60	-/3	-/3	p<0.05/3
When leaning forwards lifts his head by more than 45°	2.65	-/3	p<0.01/3	p<0.01/3
When leaning backwards pulls his chin to his chest	3.50	-/3	-/3	p<0.01/3

Pulls his chin to his chest when lying on the back	4.25	$p < 0.01/3$	$-/3$	$p < 0.05/3$
Tilts the head when lying on the tummy	4.35	$p < 0.05/3$	$p < 0.05/3$	$p < 0.05/3$

Significant = $p < 0.05$
Very significant = $p < 0.01$

Development of Upper Limb Movements

Developmental Milestone	Age of Appearance in Group II	Difference between Groups		
	X	I:II	II:III	I:III
Grasps proffered fingers and holds on when pulled to the sitting position	2.60	$-/3$	$p < 0.01/3$	$p < 0.01/3$
Leans on both hands when lying on the tummy, arms straight	3.35	$-/3$	$p < 0.01/3$	$p < 0.01/3$
Grasps rings and holds on in mixed suspension	3.70	$-/6$	$p < 0.01/6$	$p < 0.01/6$
Steadily guides hand to objective	4.20	$-/3$	$-/3$	$p < 0.05/3$
Transfers toy from hand to hand	4.80	$p < 0.05/3$	$-/3$	$p < 0.05/3$

Holds cube in each hand and knocks them together	6.80	p<0.01/6	-/6	p<0.01/6
Inserts cubes into each other	8.00	not tested	p<0.01/12	not tested

DEVELOPMENT OF LOWER LIMB MOVEMENTS

Developmental Milestone	Age of Appearance in Group II	Difference between Groups		
	X	I:II	II:III	I:III
Grasps proffered hand and stands on his legs	4.20	-/6	p<0.01/6	p<0.01/6
When lying on the back lifts legs and catches them with his hands	4.75	-/6	p<0.01/6	p<0.01/6
When lying on the back draws his knees to his body	4.95	-/6	p<0.01/6	p<0.01/6
Stands up by himself next to the furniture	7.95	not tested	p<0.01/9	not tested
Stands and holds lightly with one hand	8.05	not tested	p<0.05/9	not tested

Stands without holding for 5 seconds	9.45	not tested	p < 0.01/12	not tested
Gets up without holding	11.35	not tested	p < 0.01/12	not tested

DEVELOPMENT OF PLAY

Developmental Milestone	Age of Appearance in Group II	Difference between Groups		
	X	I:II	II:III	I:III
Grasps object in his fist with thumb opposite	3.65	p < 0.01/3	not significant	p < 0.01/3
Turns toy in hands and inspects	4.50	—	not significant	p < 0.05/3
Bangs toy on table	5.20	—	not significant	p < 0.05/6
Grasps toy with tip of thumb and forefinger	7.90	p < 0.01/6	not significant	p < 0.01/6
Inserts key into lock	10.55	not tested	p < 0.01/12	not tested
Places 2 cubes into each other	11.60	not tested	p < 0.01/12	not tested
Feeds teddy, doll	11.65	not tested	p < 0.01/12	not tested
Turns handle	11.75	not tested	p < 0.01/12	not tested

DEVELOPMENT OF COMPLEX LOCOMOTIVE MOVEMENTS

Developmental Milestone	Age of Appearance in Group II	Difference Between Groups		
	X	I:II	II:III	I:III
Crawls clumsily	8.10	not tested	$p < 0.01/9$	not tested
Holds onto furniture and takes sidesteps	8.40	not tested	$p < 0.05/9$	not tested
Crawls around furniture with ease	9.25	not tested	$p < 0.05/9$	not tested
Takes first 2–3 independent steps	10.65	not tested	$p < 0.01/12$	not tested
Climbs onto the couch (18 to 20 inches high)	10.65	not tested	$p < 0.01/12$	not tested
Walks around the room	11.50	not tested	$p < 0.01/12$	not tested
Walks in the yard, garden	12.30	not tested	$p < 0.01/12$	not tested

DEVELOPMENT OF SPEECH

Developmental Milestone	Age of Appearance in Group II	Difference between Groups		
	X	I:II	II:III	I:III
Gabbles (pronounces syllables)	5.20	-/6	$p < 0.01/6$	$p < 0.01/6$
Repeats syllables ("ma-ma-ma")	6.50	-/6	$p < 0.05/6$	-/6
Performs movement when told (do "bye-bye")	7.25	not tested	$p < 0.05/9$	not tested
Looks at a named object	8.40	not tested	$p < 0.05/9$	not tested
Identifies a known person verbally ("papa," "mama")	9.25	not tested	$p < 0.05/12$	not tested
Understands everyday sentences	11.20	not tested	$p < 0.01/12$	not tested
Names activities (sleep)	11.55	not tested	$p < 0.01/12$	not tested

other two in the acquisition of many developmental milestones. The tables also show that the more complex the activities, the more significant the statistical difference between the babies stimulated and not stimulated at home; the difference increased with age and the complexity of the activity. The babies were stimulated mainly to motional activities but the difference also appeared in the development of play and speech. The difference between Groups I and II—babies stimulated in the Institute and at home—on the contrary decreased with age. What do these dry statistics mean?

As you can see, the difference between the development of babies stimulated in the Institute and at home is comparatively small. The statistically significant differences are mostly the result of better development in the Institute. This does not allow us to draw the general conclusion that the rearing of infants in the Institute was better than at home. In fact, the opposite is true. The cause of these results is the fact that we devoted special care to these experimental babies and created conditions which cannot possibly be attained in normal nurseries. The babies were under the care of experts with specialized experience. The babies in the families were in the care of their parents, who lacked this experience in the beginning and only acquired it gradually from workers in the Institute.

The tables show that the differences in the development between both groups gradually decreased with age. During the second half year the Institute workers could hardly compete with the parents. By that time the parents had gained practice and also had certain advantages over the Institute workers: more intensive contact with the baby, more opportunities to demonstrate real life and adult tasks, and so on.

Our data shows that the differences in the development of babies who were systematically stimulated at home and those who were not stimulated and lived under traditional conditions is great and gradually increases. This documents that intensive early stimulation is soundly based and contributes to better baby development.

We also showed that the difference was not only in the development of movements, but in the overall development of systematically stimulated babies—and for two reasons. First, pure locomotive stimulation is not in fact possible: when a baby is stimulated to move we are in close social contact with him, speak to him, or give him toys and other materials, so that this is in fact complex stimulation in which the locomotive stimulation is stressed because it influences not only the development of movements but also the development of speech and thinking. The second fact is that parents who succeed in a complex child-rearing method work tend to develop their baby in all aspects and therefore deliberately develop play, speech, thinking, and other functions.

Some additional technical details may be of interest.

The children in Group II, who were stimulated under the supervision of the parents, visited us twice a month during their first six months and once a month during their second six months for a total of 20 times. Since we followed the development of these children longitudinally, we were able to determine in what month the children reached a particular criterion and this enabled us to calculate the mean ages.

The children in Group III (control group) were examined only once: in the third, sixth, ninth, or twelfth month. We could not observe these children longitudinally because it is not ethical or feasible to ask a mother to bring in her child 20 times within one year only to examine the child and not to counsel her. So with the children in the control group we could determine *which* stages of development were reached by the time of a particular examination, but not precisely *when.*

Also, frequent examinations of a child would obviously influence the parent, so that the group would not retain the character of a control group living in a traditional environment.

I should like to stress again that the rate of development of abilities in a baby was only one possible yardstick for recording the development of a baby. It is *not* our purpose to accelerate development; such attempts could only lead to overloading the baby. Our aim is the overall development of the baby's personality.

It remains an open question whether the higher quality development of a baby who has been systematically stimulated in his first year of life is permanent or temporary. We would like to resolve this question by observing the development of the babies in Group II up to age of 4 to 6 years. The material collected to date seems to indicate that the lead in development is permanent, expecially when the child is deliberately and systematically further stimulated. Since we have shown that during the first year of a baby's life his psychological development can be given impetus and direction, this possibility should be exploited more intensively.

We are continuing our experiments. We have a new group of 20 babies who are being raised by their parents at home. They visit us once a month with their babies. During the visit we give them instructions on how to influence the development of delicate hand movements; at the same time we observe the development of these movements. The parents are greatly interested in our work: half of the children do not come with their mothers but with their fathers, who are willing to leave work and make up for the lost time to be informed about how their baby is progressing and how to continue rearing him in this sphere. Fathers are finding out that work with a small baby is perhaps even more interesting than repairing a car or radio or other activities, because here the most precious thing is achieved—a good, fully developed human being.

Index

Active speech, *see* Speech
Activity/activities
  creative, 20
  goal-oriented, 6
  imitation of, 20
  individual traits and abilities
    and, 14
  restriction of, 18–19
  self-development, 70, 112
  stimulation of, 17–20
  see also Exercises and games;
    Stimuli
Aksarina, N. M., 41
Animals, experimental experience with, 11

Bathing, 57, 58, 75, 102
Biorhythms, 34–36ff., 43, 104

Clothing, body movement and,
  58–59
Communication, early infancy
  and, 21–22ff.
Crawling, 110, 119, 140, 179–80,
  185, 254

Development
  activity and: stimulation of,
    17–20; success in, 20

experimental testing in, data
  on results of, 329–45
grasping and manipulation,
  play and, 109–10, 112–15
hands, infant's discovery of,
  68–69
heredity *vs.* environment
  question and, 12–13ff.
individual traits and abilities
  and, 13–14
level of, ways to establish, 44–
  48; feedback, mother's behavior and infant's reactions, 45–48; normal
  development, variations
  in, 44–45
of movements, fourth to sixth
  month, 109–14
objects, reaching out for,
  14–16
physical, exercise and (general
  discussion), 3–8 *passim*
psychological, 16–20; assessment of, table on, 318–27;
  exercise and, general discussion, 5–8 *passim*, 10;
  fourth to sixth month,
  112–17, 162–76; new-
  born, communication
  with and, 21–23 *passim;*

rate of, factors affecting, 15; second to third month, 67–70, 100–3; seventh to ninth month, 183–85, 212, 221–36; tenth to twelfth month, 295–307
rearing, main principles for and, 48–50
scope, stimulation of, 14
signals, use of, 17
social contacts and, 20
see also Exercises and games; Stimuli

Early experience, 9–11
Early infancy, 10, 11, 14
communication during, 21–22ff.
see also Exercise and games
Early learning, 9–11
conditions involved in, need to vary, 33–34
spontaneous, 26–27 objects, use of to influence, 27–29
see also Exercises and games
Environment, 12–13ff., 16–17, 19, 32, 100, 116, 172
activities, guidance of and, 37
Excitation/excitation process, 31–32, 78, 104–5
Exercises and games
badly performed, 48
father's involvement in, 6, 40, 72–73, 125, 132
first month, 51–52; body movements, 58–66; hand movements, 66–67; sensory perception, development of, 52–58; sight and hearing, 54–57
fourth to sixth month, 109–17; "airplane" game, 110, 111, 125, 127, 128; arm movements, 119–25; back

muscles, 127–30; back roll, 131–32; cradle, 135; emotions, development of, 164, 172–73; furniture and toys, 176–78; habits, cultivation of, 173–76; hand movements, grasping and manipulation of objects, 112–13, 148–62; head movements, 117–19; jumper, use of, 111–12; leg movements, 111–12, 134–38, 140–42; manipulation games, thinking and, 115; materials, processing of, 161–62; rhythmical jumping, 138–40; seesaw, 130–31; sensory perception, development of, 112, 142–48; side muscles, 132–33; sitting, 111; social relationships, development of, 164–65, 167–69, 171–72; speech, development of, 164–71; stomach muscles, 130–32; thinking, development of, 162–64; trunk movements, 125–27
mini-program for busy families, 8
passive, 21–22
second to third month: arms and hands movements, 77–85; body movements, 85–91; emotions, development of, 100–3; furniture and toys, 106–8; graze horses position, 85; habits, cultivation of, 103–6; head movements, 70–77; leg movements, 91–95; play, development of, 99–100; sensory per-

ception, development of, 96–99

seventh to ninth month: clapping, 210; climbing a ladder, 180, 194–95; crawling, 179–80, 185–95; emotions, development of, 236–42; furniture and toys, 246–47; habits, cultivation of, 242–46; hand movements, refinement of, 181–83, 184, 205–18; materials, processing of, 217–18; movements at verbal request, 220; picking things up, 181, 201; self-serving motions, 218–19; sitting up and sitting, 180, 195–98; social relationships, development of, 184–85, 236–42; speech, development of, 184–85, 228–36; standing up and standing, 180–81, 198–201; thinking, development of, 183–84, 212, 221–28; unsupervised play, 220–21; walking, 181, 201–5

tenth to twelfth month: building, laying things down, 268–70; emotions, development of, 252–53, 307–14; furniture and toys, 316–17; emptying, filling, inserting, closing, 271–80; experience, manipulation of objects and, 249–50; habits, cultivation of, 253, 314–16; hand movements, refinement of, 249, 268–91; imitation/imitative play, 251, 286–88, 292–95; materials, processing of, 280–82; movement, socialization of, 251; overall movements, 248–49, 253–56; sand and water, playing with, 288–91; social relationships, development of, 250, 251, 252–53, 307–14; speech, development of, 251, 252, 295, 301–7; standing up, 266–67; thinking, development of, 295–301; tools, use of for complex tasks, 251–52, 282–86; verbal requests, movements in response to, 291; walking, 256–66; working and self-service motions, 286–88, 292–93

unsuitable, 48

see also Development; Stimuli

Experience, *see* Early experience

Feeding, 37, 38, 40–42, 43
first month, 51, 57
second to third month, 102, 103–6
fourth to sixth month, 115, 116, 117, 175–76
seventh to ninth month, 242–43
tenth to twelfth month, 253, 314
see also Development

Furniture
fourth to sixth month, 176–78
second to third month, 106–7
seventh to ninth month, 246–47
tenth to twelfth month, 316–17

Grazing horses position, 85, 110
Growth: heredity, environment and, 12

Half-wakefulness, 4–5
Heredity, 12–13, 100, 172
Humming, 99–100, 165

Imitation, 29–31
    see also Exercises and games
Inhibition, 31–32
    active, 32–33
    delayed, 32
    differential, 32
Institute for the Care of Mother
    and Child, 3, 330–31
Intelligence, 6, 114, 301
    see also Development, psycho-
        logical

Jumper, 111–12, 134, 138–40,
    177

Language ability/development,
    5, 146
    imitation and, 30
    see also Speech
Learning, *see* Early learning

Manipulation, 6
Motor development/coordina-
    tion, 5, 6, 16–17
    see also Exercises and games
Mumbling, 165–66

Normality, see Development
Nursing, 71–72

Objects
    cause and effect, discovering
        relationship between
        through, 221–28
    grasping and manipulation of:
        fourth to sixth month,
        113–14, 148–64; second
        to third month, 78–82;
        seventh to ninth month,

181–84, 205–19; tenth to
    twelfth month, 249–51,
    268–91
reaching out for, 14–16, 27–
    29, 68–69
Orientation-investigatory beha-
    vor, 17
Orientation reflex, 17

Passivity, 6, 21–22
Perception, passive, 17, 21
Play, development of, 99–100,
    109
    see also Exercises and games
Psychological development, *see*
    Development, psychologi-
    cal
Punishment, 25–26, 221

Rearing
    authoritative *vs.* nonauthorita-
        tive, 18
    directive *vs.* nondirective, 18
    main principles for, 48–50
Reflex/reflexes
    defensive, 26
    grasping, 67, 69, 109–10
    inborn, 23–24, 60
    postural, 330

Security, 19
Self-demand system, 104
Sensory organs/perception, 22,
    68
    newborn child and, 16–17
    see also Exercises and games
Shchelovanov, N. M., 41
Signals, 17, 26, 144–45
Sitting, 111, 180, 195–98,
    254–56
Sleeping, 36–39, 41–42, 43
    fourth to sixth month, 116,
    117, 173–75

second to third month, 102,
103–6
seventh to ninth month, 242
tenth to twelfth month, 253,
314
see also Development
Smiling, 67, 68, 103
Speech, 251, 295
active, 169, 184, 228–29, 232–
36, 252, 304–7
passive, 169–71, 184, 228,
229–32, 252, 301–4
see also Development
Standing, 180–81, 253
Stimuli, 47
acquired, 24
biorhythms and, 34–36ff., 43
emotional development in second and third month and,
100–3
excitation, inhibition and,
31–33
imitation, stages of and, 29–
31
internal and external, 23–24
kinesthetic, 99
muscular motion process, active, 22–23
nervous process, cortical and
subcortical brain func-
tions, 22–23
new, learning new responses
to, 26–29
newborn and, 52
nonspecific, inborn reflexes
and, 24
objects, use of to influence
spontaneous learning,
27–29

passive exercise as, 21–22
positive and negative reward
through, 24–26
relationship between, learning
of, 57–58
sensory, during first month,
52–58
specific, inborn reflexes and,
23–24
timetables for training, 36–43;
activities, direct and indirect guidance of, 37, 40–
41; direct activation, three
types of, 39–41; regularity
in, need to adhere to, 43;
sleep and digestion as factors in, 37–43
verbal, influencing responses
through, 31
see also Exercises and games
Swimming, 178

Task games, 294
Toilet training, 253, 314–16
see also Development
Toys
fourth to sixth month, 176–78
second to third month, 107–8
seventh to ninth month,
246–47
tenth to twelfth month,
316–17
Training, early, 242, 243–46
see also Exercises and games;
Stimuli
Transport hypothesis, 330

Walking, 33, 181, 201–5, 253,
256–66